POLITICS OF SHARING POWER

The Punjab Unionist Party

1923-1947

POLITICS OF SHARING POWER

The Punjab Unionist Party 1923-1947

RAGHUVENDRA TANWAR

MANOHAR
1999

First published 1999

ISBN 81-7304-272-1

Published by
Ajay Kumar Jain for
Manohar Publishers & Distributors
2/6 Ansari Road, Daryaganj
New Delhi 110002

Typeset by
A J Software Publishing Co. Pvt. Ltd.
305 Durga Chambers
1333 D.B. Gupta Road
Karol Bagh, New Delhi 110005

Printed at

Replika Press Pvt. Ltd.
Plot No. A-229, DSIDC Narela Indl. Park
Delhi 110040

Contents

	Preface	7
1	Origin	19
2	Growth of the Unionist Party, 1924-1936	60
3	Elections of 1937: Unionists Form Government	88
4	The Unionists and Provincial Autonomy	109
5	Politics and Political Relations	130
6	Eclipse of the Unionist Party	168
	Glossary	199
	Bibliography	203
	Index	211

Preface

THE CIRCUMSTANCES under which the British relented and surrendered their colonial empire on the subcontinent in 1947 contain enough elements to fascinate students of history for a long time to come. The independence of India and the creation of Pakistan are but only a small part of the dramatic events. Partition meant the destruction of a way of life. The barbarity of the violence unleashed was unprecedented in the annals of modern history. The last decade of British rule in India as such was tumultuous, to put it mildly. With all their efficient resource and foresight the British were unable to maintain control.

The Punjab had for long enjoyed a subconsciously favoured status among British officialdom in India. It was a remarkable province in that even while having a Muslim majority it returned only two Muslim League nominees in a House of 175 in the League's first serious attempt at an electoral battle (1937, Punjab Legislative Assembly Elections). Mohammad Ali Jinnah, the unquestioned leader of the Muslims all over India remained a non-entity in Punjab until the Muslim League had put forth the Pakistan Resolution (1940) as its new political agenda. The Punjab Unionist Party was on the centre-stage in the events that unfolded in Punjab in the two decades preceding partition.

The Unionist Party had appeared on the political scene of Punjab only in 1923 and with its demise in 1947, its total life span extended to just about 24 years. In the decade preceding partition (1937-47) it operated as the party in power. With partition of the province the party not only disintegrated but disappeared into anonymity with practically every individual remnant that survived its disintegration joining either the Muslim League or the Indian National Congress;

a few left politics all together. The eventful history of the Unionist Party also shows how a fairly successful political organization became irrelevant under circumstances which were not only alien to it but which it was not equipped to react to.

History is cluttered with reference to political parties, institutions and individuals who profoundly influenced the developments of their times but subsequently got obliterated. In the case of political parties an important reason for such a fate has usually been failure to confront successfully the demand of changing times and circumstances. There is an element of historical irony in the fact that in such a brief period of existence the Unionist Party was able to play an important and successful role in the political life of Punjab during its most crucial phase. The last pre-partition decade was also in many ways the most critical period of modern Indian history. In the context of Punjab as time was to prove the years emerged as an important pointer to what the subcontinent was heading for. Punjab had in fact been converted into a kind of a 'boiling pot' of caste, communal, ethnic, regionalistic and most importantly feudalistic politics. The Unionist Party was not only deeply involved in but actually personified most of these reactionary political trends.

The Unionist Party's politics was essentially collaborative with colonial rule and as a result also somewhat in isolation of the national mainstream. At the same time however there is need to remember that it provided the most significant opposition to the proposal of partitioning Punjab. Pre-partition Punjab was not only a Muslim majority province but the demographic spread of Muslim population was such that the Muslim League projected it as the basis of its theory for partition. Some of the districts in the western regions of the province had up to 95 per cent of Muslim population and likewise some eastern districts had upward of 95 per cent Hindu population. Further when we consider that the Unionist Party was composed mainly of Muslim and that but for a few exceptions all important leaders were Muslim, its opposition to the Muslim League's proposal of partition needs to be fairly underlined and appreciated.

Like the Unionist Party's policy of opposing the Muslim League's plan of partitioning Punjab some of its economic policies too need a more objective reassessment. The various legislative enactments and other measures which were aimed primarily to improve the quality of life in rural Punjab, give relief to the peasantry from the burden of debt and provide to the rural population more avenues of progress significantly add to the need of reviewing the Unionist Party's role. The academic requirement of this work is also rooted in the fact that in the attention that has up to now been given to studies on the Unionist Party, strongly divergent viewpoints particularly with regard to its economic programmes seem to emerge. For reasons of politics coloured by 'collaboration', feudal attitudes and regional chauvinism some of its good work particularly in the economic field has been more commonly brushed aside by scholars with indifferent disdain.

The Unionist Party was among the major and most assertive opponents of the partition of India. Its stalwarts Sikander Hayat, Chhotu Ram and the young Khizr Hayat remained the most vocal critics of the idea of dividing Punjab on the basis of 'faith'. Khizr believed partition would destroy the 'very fabric of Punjabi society and a whole way of life'. The consensual attitude to politics practised by Unionist stalwarts was in fact inherently equipped to deal with problems usually known to arise in regions that are inhabited by people with significant differences based on religion and ethnicity. Political power sharing and an inclination to decentralize power were the essence of Unionist politics. This healthy attitude even though overshadowed by the compulsions of colonial rule provides, I felt, enough basis for a completely focussed work on the Party.

This work is in a way an extension of my Ph.D. thesis (1989). I have kept in mind the new works that have since appeared and also sources of which I was earlier not aware or did not have access to. The study is essentially based on Proceedings and Debates of the Punjab Legislative Council and Assembly most of which were well recorded. Such information has been frequently supplemented from newspaper reports particularly *The Tribune* (Lahore). Government documents mainly Administration Reports and Gazettes too are important sources in the context of the Unionist Party particularly in relation to legislations, policy announcements and development programmes. Correspondences between the governors of Punjab and the viceroys particularly in the last few years of the Unionist Party's life have been very helpful. Diaries, letters, notes and such writings are invaluable sources to study such 'small time party' histories, more so as very little official party documentation is available. Some of these diaries and letters have appeared in published form in good works from Pakistan and are extremely helpful specially in the context of Fazl-i-Husain and his relations with Jinnah and likewise of Jinnah's interaction with Sikander Hayat, Chhotu Ram and Khizr Tiwana. Some very good and important secondary sources include research papers published in journals and books besides of course, the large number of books that relate to partition, communalism and Punjab's political history in general have also made helpful references to the Unionist Party.

Among the more important works in recent years relating to different aspects of the Unionist Party particularly its politics are those of Ian Talbot. His *Punjab and the Raj* (New Delhi, 1989), though covering a long period of almost 100 years contains valuable information on the Unionist Party. Talbot's latest contribution *Khizr Tiwana: The Punjab Unionist Party and the Partition of India* (Richmond, 1996) provides an important insight of the last days of the Unionist Party besides being an extremely valuable source on Khizr Tiwana. From Talbot's long list of research papers and chapters contributed to books, 'Deserted Collaborators: The Political Background to The Rise and Fall of the Unionist Party', *Journal of Imperial and Commonwealth History*, October 1982 and his 'Muslim Political Mobilization in Rural Punjab 1937-46' in *Rural India: Land, Power and Society* (London, 1983), require special mention.

In a recent article in the *International Journal of Punjab Studies* 3:1, 1996, Ian Talbot has shown how the Unionist Party's policy of intercommunal accommodation helped it to achieve and maintain power in the complex and plural society of Punjab. Talbot has discussed Unionist politics and their relevance to contemporary India and Pakistan in view of Arend Lijphart's theories of consociational democracy. Talbot's suggestion that Unionist politics provides a good example of leaders acting autonomously of social forces and communal cleavages even in situations of deep social conflict is interesting and meaningful. Talbot's attempt at understanding Unionist politics in terms of Lijphart's theories of consociational democracy in fact underlines the need of a more incisive look at the Unionist Party and its politics. Indeed there are for the strife-ridden and communalized India and Pakistan of today some important lessons in the operative style of the Unionist Party. Political leaders of today can learn from Sikander Hayat and the manner in which he allocated positions of power and patronage among various communities thereby considerably harmonising relations between communities.

Syed Nur Ahmad's, *Mian Sir Fazl-i-Husain, A Review: His Life and Work* (Lahore, 1936), and Azim Husain's, *Mian Sir Fazl-i-Husain: A Political Biography* (London, 1946), form essential reading for understanding the founder of the Unionist Party. The work of Azim Husain being a biography by a son, frequently appears influenced by emotion but all the same remains indispensable particularly for the years that Fazl-i-Husain managed the party. Two other equally important works in the context of Fazl-i-Husain are by Waheed Ahmad, *Diary and Notes of Mian Fazl-i-Husain* and *Letters of Mian Fazl-i-Husain* (both Lahore, 1976). Important references are also available in two important autobiographies, those of Ahmad Yar Khan Daultana, *Leaves from a Unionist's Diary* (Lahore, 1949) and Firoz Khan Noon, *From Memory* (Lahore, 1966). Both Daultana and Noon were close associates of Fazl-i-Husain and provide a very useful insight into the Unionist Party. The work by Lajpat Rai Nair, *Sikander Hayat Khan: The Soldier Statesman of the Punjab* (Lahore, 1943), as also that of I.H. Malik, *Sikander Hayat Khan: A Political Biography* (Islamabad, 1985) provide considerable assistance in understanding Sikander Hayat.

Likewise Sir Chhotu Ram the other important leader of the party has been covered in published works by Tikka Ram, *Sir Chhotu Ram: An Apostle of Hindu Muslim Unity* (Lahore, 1946). D.C. Verma's *Sir Chhotu Ram: Life and Times* (New Delhi, 1981) too seems shadowed by the author's close association to Chhotu Ram, yet both are helpful in understanding Chhotu Ram particularly in relation to the development policies of the Unionist Party. The work of Madan Gopal, *Sir Chhotu Ram: A Political Biography* (New Delhi, 1977), and the recent work (edited) by Pardaman Singh, *Chhotu Ram: Contemporary Opinions* (New Delhi, 1992) are also helpful in understanding Chhotu Ram. Some very important contributions on Chhotu Ram are by Prem Chaudhary. These include *Punjab Politics and the Role of Sir Chhotu Ram* (Delhi, 1984) as also numerous articles on Sir Chhotu Ram and the Unionist Party mainly in the *Punjab Past and Present* (Patiala). Her contributions are essential reading for any study of the Unionist Party.

Y.P. Bajaj's 'Sir Chhotu Ram and His Work' (unpublished Ph.D. thesis, Kurukshetra, 1972) remains perhaps the most exhaustive study of the development and economic policies of Chhotu Ram and by implication of the Unionist Party. In a number of research papers published mainly in the *Punjab Past and Present*, Bajaj has dealt with various aspects and policies of the Unionist Party, for example, land revenue (October 1976, vol. X-II), Chhotu Ram and Congress (April 1978, vol. XII-I), Bhakra Dam (April 1977, vol. XI-I). The *Punjab Past and Present* has also in various issues reprinted some important viewpoints of important Unionist leaders, for example, 'The 1937 Elections and the Sikander-Jinnah Pact' by Khizr Hayat Tiwana (October 1976); 'Punjab Politics' by Fazl-i-Husain (April 1971); 'Serving the Weak and Raising the Fallen' by Chhotu Ram (April 1974).

The major thrust of the Unionist economic policies was towards easing the burden of debt on the peasantry. While the plight of the debt-ridden peasantry of Punjab stands accepted, the honesty and earnestness of the Unionists in eradicating this problem and fighting its source has been well disputed by many scholars notably, Neeladri Bhattacharya in 'Lenders and Debtors: Punjab Countryside 1888-1940', *Studies in History* (1985). Prem Chaudhary has made extensive contributions in this regard. N.G. Barrier's *The Punjab Alienation of Land Bill 1900* (Duke, 1966), as also Shadi Lal's *Commentaries on The Punjab Alienation of Land Act* (Lahore, 1933), are helpful in understanding the root of Punjab's debt and land hypothecation problem. The contributions of British civil servants like Ibbetson on castes, Calvert on land-holding and economic condition, Darling on debt, Rose on tribal systems, even with their colonial biases would remain perhaps for ever absolutely essential for studies relating to rural Punjab particularly its society, culture and economic conditions. The immense effort that must have been involved in these works particularly the love for detail leaves one amazed. Griffin and Massey's *Chiefs and Families of Note in the Punjab* (two volumes) ed. by G.L. Chopra (Lahore, 1940), is extremely helpful in understanding the feudal and collaborative roots of leading Unionist leaders. The family trees and long histories of loyalty and the deep involvement of leading Unionist families in the British administrative system serve to reveal the intrinsic character of the Unionist Party.

Some other works that require mention are S. Zaheer, *Light on The League Unionist Conflict;* and *A Case for Congress League Unity* (both Bombay, 1944); Chaudhary Khaliquzzaman, *Pathway to Pakistan* (Lahore, 1961); Penderel Moon, *Divide and Quit* (London, 1961); C.H. Philips (ed.), *The Evolution of India and Pakistan, 1858-1947* (London, 1962). Among more relatively recent works having significant references to the Unionist Party are Imran Ali, *Punjab Politics in the Decade Before Partition* (Lahore, 1974); M.A.H. Isphani *Quad-i-Azam: As I Knew Him* (Karachi, 1976); Ayesha Jalal, *The Sole Spokesman Jinnah: The Muslim League and Demand for Pakistan* (Cambridge, 1985); Anita Inder Singh, *The Origins of the Partition of India 1936-47* (Delhi, 1989); S.M. Ikram, *Modern Muslim India and The Birth of Pakistan* (Lahore, 1977). Mushirul Hasan's (ed.) *India's Partition: Process, Strategy and Mobilization* (Delhi, 1994), is extremely valuable for understanding the varying perspectives of partition, as also M.D. Wainwright, *The Partition of India: Policies and Perspectives, 1935-37* (London, 1970) and Wali Khan's, *Facts are Facts: The Untold Story of India's Partition* (Delhi, 1987). David Gilmartin's *Empire and Islam: Punjab and the Making of Pakistan* (New Delhi, 1989) has made a major contribution by explaining how the Muslim League was able to sway the Muslim masses in its favour. The work is essential reading for understanding the Unionist Party and the circumstances of its growth and decline.

It is proposed here to discuss the Unionist Party in its various dimensions—background, origin, leadership, political and economic policies, political actions and affiliations, the attitude towards partition and communal relations, etc. An effort has also been made to explain why the Unionist Party was able to gain in popularity vis-a-vis the Muslim League in 1937, only to be completely routed less than a decade later. Up to about 1940 (Pakistan Resolution) the vast majority of Muslim masses of Punjab appeared to support the more secular Unionists in comparison to the Muslim League. Even after acknowledging the fact that the 1937 election results were not truly representative because of the highly restricted franchise, the Muslim League's winning just 2 of the 175 seats as compared to the Unionists 98 in the Legislative Assembly is a fact of remarkable significance. This aspect has been looked into in some detail.

Considerable space has also been devoted to understanding the ironical events that led to Punjab's partition and how the rural Muslim masses were uprooted by the force of the Muslim League propaganda and prompted to immigrate. While there are practically no recorded sources to prove this but the fact on the basis of reliable oral evidence is that large section of the Muslims who left their ancestral homes for the new state of Pakistan did so unwillingly and half-heartedly. I came across many references to this effect particularly in the Rajput villages of Kurukshetra district where Muslim families were earnestly discouraged from leaving. In some cases when persuasive options were exhausted, Muslim families were escorted to the safety of immigrating convoys.

The first chapter deals with factors that led to the origin of the Unionist Party, like the problem of debt, the widespread influence of religious leaders, the hold of feudal lords on the economy and the unequal distribution of land. The chapter discusses why and how the British worked to ensure stability in the province by creating a loyal and influential intermediary chain of influence. This chapter also deals with the role of Fazl-i-Husain and Chhotu Ram in bringing together a group of predominantly rural legislative council members to form the nucleus of the Unionist Party, essentially being born without the 'pains of labour', a creation of the elite with practically no ground-level or mass support.

The second chapter discusses the early years of the Unionist Party (1924-36), the hypocrisy inherent in 'dyarchy' or the supposed sharing of 'power', the complexity of the interaction between elected members and ministers of the Punjab Legislative Council on one hand and the 'official block' on the other. The chapter also relates the efforts of Unionist leaders to project themselves as wielders of 'real power' and how they were curtly 'cut to size' by the British administrators whenever the occasion so required. The formation of a political and economic programme aimed principally towards rural development and providing relief to the peasantry from debt are issues also dealt with in the third chapter. Such measures gave to the party a fair amount of credibility in rural Punjab. While the partly secular approach to politics by Fazl-i-Husain was more the result of political compulsions, the Unionists under Sikander Hayat and Chhotu Ram developed the idea of communal harmony as a important political agenda of the party.

The first elections held under the Government of India Act, 1935 saw the Unionists' form government in Punjab. Chapter 3 deals with the impressive victory of the Unionist Party and the surprisingly dismal performance of the Muslim League. The next chapter discusses the important development work and policies of the Unionist ministry with its emphasis during the period (mainly up to 1942) on improving the available opportunities and the quality of life in rural Punjab. Some important legislative measures which came popularly to be known as the 'golden laws' gave to Unionist leaders Sikander Hayat and Chhotu Ram widespread following in rural areas across the province. The nature of support and goodwill generated by the two was in itself a remarkable phenomena underlined even more by the fact that it usually cut across caste and community lines.

The theme of Chapter 5 is the inherent contradictions and ambiguities that characterized the politics of the Unionist Party in the period 1937-46. The Sikander and Jinnah 'pact' marked the Muslim League's determined fight back into the political scene in Punjab and was in a way the turning point towards its ultimate goal of partitioning Punjab. The Unionist Party's base of support was essentially a gathering of opportunistic elements lacking any ideological adhesive. Typical of parties which are composed principally of feudal elements, intrigue and dissension became hallmarks of the Party.

The last chapter deals with the large number of factors that enabled the Muslim League to uproot the Unionist Party from Punjab by capturing the minds of the Muslim masses. The phenomenal change in the League's fortunes was revealed by the manner in which it won all but two of the Muslim seats in the 1946 Punjab Legislative Assembly elections. The 'two nation' theory had been forcefully propagated by the Muslim League cadres, creating a situation wherein the Unionist Party had become totally irrelevant. Large-scale migration from the Unionist ranks led mainly by the elite left the Party helpless and disintegrated well before it entered the 1946 elections. The process of the Unionist Party's decline had actually started with the Pakistan Resolution in 1940, and was greatly facilitated by the untimely death of the Sikander Hayat in 1942 and Chhotu Ram's two years later. The unanimity with which the Punjab Legislative Assembly voted for partition of Punjab in April 1947 only shows how well the Muslim League had done its work.

The idea of this book developed over the years essentially as a sequel to the extended discussions I was fortunate in having with my late father Kanwar Randhir Singh and his lifelong friend late Rai Sahib Anant Ram, ex-Unionist Party MLA (1937-46). Having been closely associated with leading Unionist stalwarts particularly Sir Chhotu Ram, they provided me a fascinating insight of the Unionist Party and its style of functioning and politics. Their network of friends including some who held important positions in the Unionist government also proved extremely helpful. But for their consistent encouragement this work would never have materialized.

I am also extremely grateful to Ian Talbot, of the Coventry University (UK), an outstanding authority on the history of modern Punjab for having gone through the manuscript and making valuable suggestions which have significantly improved and widened the dimensions of the work. I must especially thank Talbot for having pointed out that politics of the Unionist Party also needs to be studied in the context of 'consociational democracy'. Indeed it also now appears that the 'Jat' and 'peasant based ruralism of Chhotu Ram' as suggested by Talbot has not really disappeared but in fact seems to have persisted in the politics of regional parties.

I would like to gratefully acknowledge the help and guidance provided during the course of this study by K.C. Yadav, formerly of the Department of History, Kurukshetra University, as also for the free access to his valuable library. Yadav has always rendered uninhibited support and earnest help throughout the course of this work and on numerous other projects that I have undertaken. I would like also to especially express a deep sense of gratitude to V.N. Datta, Emeritus Professor of History, Kurukshetra University, who has been a teacher, a revered colleague and a warm friend. I have greatly profited from his sustained interest and insightful observations on my work. I am grateful to Y.P. Bajaj of the Department of History, Punjabi University, Patiala, for having permitted me to draw from some of his research particularly the development and economic policies of Sir Chhotu Ram. I would like to thank Pardaman Singh, formerly of the Department of History, M.D. University, Rohtak for the interest he has always taken in my work. I am grateful to my colleagues in the Department of History, Kurukshetra University for their cooperation and suggestions provided ever so frequently. I am grateful for the assistance provided by the staff of various libraries and archives visited over the years during the course of this work. I would also like to acknowledge the help and assistance of P.D. Gupta in the preparation of the manuscript.

I am also extremely grateful to Shri Ramesh Jain and Shri Ajay Kumar Jain for the publication of this work.

My wife Reicha has been a constant source of inspiration during the course of this study and the various ups and downs it has encountered. This work is truly dedicated to her.

Kurukshetra RAGHUVENDRA TANWAR
February 1997

CHAPTER 1

Origin

LORD CURZON'S belief that the strength of British rule in India depended on the peasantry and on peace and harmony in rural India in a way reflected the true genius of a colonial administration. This view when applied to Punjab assumes a crucial dimension, for a large and important section of the British Indian Army was recruited from rural Punjab. It was also natural therefore for Sir Michael O'Dwyer (Governor of Punjab, 1913-19) to believe that a happy and contented rural aristocracy and peasantry was the surest way to sustain the loyalty of the Indian army,[1] the dependability of which had begun to be tested with increasing frequency. The origin of the Punjab National Unionist Party can be traced to these circumstances under which the colonial rulers initiated a search for loyal, influential and 'respectful' people to support the government, particularly in rural Punjab thereby giving it credibility and an extended lease of life.

From the outset (annexation 1849) but more particularly after the Great Revolt (1857) the British had handled Punjab as a very special possession. Nothing was allowed to go wrong. Over the years, the foresighted administrative measures of some of the more capable civil servants that came from the shores of England to rule India had developed the province into a critical pillar of the British empire. Its political significance notwithstanding, it was a valuable acquisition even in purely economic and commercial terms. With vast fertile plains, abundant water and a hard working population it was ideally placed to suit the requirements of a colonial regime.

Talbot has explained in a remarkable manner how the British sought to provide rural stability to Punjab:

first by associating the 'natural leaders' of the agricultural tribes with their executive authorities; second by ensuring that the rural leaders politically controlled the economic forces set in train by the colonial encouragement of a market oriented agriculture; third by using the resources which this provided to reward the agriculturist population rather than stimulate industrial development; fourth by establishing a framework of political representation which institutionalized the division between the 'agriculturist' and 'non-agriculturist' population.[2]

The distribution of population was for obvious reasons related to the availability of natural resources. As shown in Table 1.1, Jullundur, Amritsar, Gurdaspur and Hoshiarpur districts were densely populated followed by districts like Karnal, Lahore, Sialkot, Gujrat, Rawalpindi and Lyallpur. On the other hand scanty natural resources reflected in the sparseness of population in the districts of Hissar, Mianwali, Dera Ghazi Khan and Kangra.

The predominantly rural character of Punjab as shown in Table 1.2 needs to be underlined.[3] Even after the onset of British rule the situation showed no discernible change towards urbanization. The British had never really been inclined to encourage urbanization; on the contrary, it appears they discouraged the emergence of a infrastructure based industrial economy.[4] Thus, in the rural economy of Punjab, the ownership of land was the most important single parameter which reflected not only an individual's economic status in society but also his social and political influence. The nature of land holdings varied considerably from region to region. For example, land holdings were not only smaller in the eastern districts (now the state of Haryana) but the number of tenant peasants was fewer than in the western districts where over half the land was cultivated by tenants.[5] The size of family land holding units is shown in Table 1.1.

As shown in Table 1.3, 58.3 per cent of the cultivators held less than 5 acres of land. Such meagre land holdings were economically unviable.[6] Of the cultivators 33.2 per cent had less than 25 acres. A large part of these holdings lacked proper irrigation. The remaining 8.1 per cent of the cultivators owned more than 25 acres land or in other words just 8.1 per cent of Punjab's land owning population owned about 45 per cent of its cultivated land.[7] The feudal, social, cultural, economic and political nature of rural Punjab was rooted in this marked disproportionate distribution of land. The fallout of

TABLE 1.1: POPULATION OF PUNJAB, 1921

Natural division	District	Average population per		Number per mile residing in	
		Town	Village	Town	Village
I. Himalayan	Simla	10273	70	680	320
	Kangra	4904	1008	6	994
II. Sub-Himalayan	Ambala	14803	329	174	820
	Hoshiarpur	11617	421	38	962
	Gurdaspur	6873	352	73	927
	Sialkot	21784	385	93	907
	Gujrat	11505	542	56	944
	Jhelum	10244	492	86	914
	Rawalpindi	52217	397	183	817
	Attock	6857	776	67	933
III. Indo-Gangetic Plain West	Hissar	21588	760	106	894
	Rohtak	10765	995	98	902
	Gurgaon	7600	400	89	911
	Karnal	16244	538	298	902
	Jullundur	14606	578	142	858
	Ludhiana	25997	570	137	863
	Ferozpur	24524	655	106	894
	Lahore	50124	695	310	690
	Amritsar	36981	719	199	801
	Gujranwala	15167	450	122	878
	Sheikhupura	4204	559	24	976
IV. North-West Dry	Montgomery	10245	372	43	957
	Shahpur	7214	653	10	890
	Mianwali	7484	875	84	916
	Lyallpur	13600	829	42	958
	Jhang	14253	524	100	900
	Multan	32394	482	109	891
	Muzaffargarh	4804	641	42	958
	Dera Ghazi Khan	7208	619	102	898

SOURCE: *The Census of India, 1921, Punjab, Part II* (Report), pp. 30-1.

TABLE 1.2: PERCENTAGE OF RURAL / URBAN POPULATION 1921

Year	Urban (%)	Rural (%)
1881	11.9	88.1
1891	10.7	89.3
1901	10.6	89.4
1911	9.8	90.2
1921	10.3	89.7

SOURCE: *The Census of India, 1921, Punjab, Part I* (Report), p. 89.

TABLE 1.3: LAND HOLDINGS IN PUNJAB, 1924

Size of holding	Number	Holdings percentage to the total	Estimated no. of acres cultivated	Percentage of total area cultivated
Below 1 acre	525400	17.9	313000	1.0
Between				
acres1 and 3	908400	25.5	126800	4.4
3 and 5	520000	14.9	1935000	6.6
5 and 10	630600	18.0	4400000	15.1
10 and 15	288300	8.2	3353000	11.5
15 and 20	150100	4.3	2444000	8.4
20 and 25	94000	2.7	1967000	6.8
25 and 50	168700	4.8	5887000	20.4
50 acres and over	120900	3.3	7452000	25.7

SOURCE: H. Calvert, *The Size & Distribution of Land Holdings in Punjab* (Lahore, 1925), p. 3.

such a situation was not only profound but was also deeply related to the foundations on which the Unionist Party built its political edifice—the peasantry's problem of debt.

The Punjab had the world's largest canal irrigation system. In 1921 the province produced one-third of India's wheat, and one-tenth of its cotton. The per capita agricultural output per annum had increased by 45 per cent between 1881-1921.[8] Considering its fertile soil, facilities of irrigation afforded by the canals, abundance of dedicated labour and great inherited agricultural skill, the Punjab seemed to have been marked out by nature as a prosperous agricultural region. Yet the condition and the living standard of the average tiller of the soil was pathetic. The existence of debt has been undisputably acknowledged as the principal cause for the plight of the Punjab peasantry. The presence of a huge volume of agricultural indebtedness which was for the most part unproductive, inhibited growth and was one of the more serious problems of the agricultural economy in Punjab.[9]

With 98 per cent of Punjab peasantry in debt,[10] it is important to understand the cause of this malady even more so because in it lay the main basis of the Unionist Party's origin and later its economic policy, an interest sustained from the start by the party's leadership. The issue of debt remained the party's principal political agenda throughout its existence.

Banking in Punjab in the first two or so decades of this century had developed as an instrument to support commercial and trade needs, it was never conceived as a means to meet agricultural requirements. Commercial banking was based on short term lendings whereas farmers required longer period loans. Before the annexation of the Punjab to British India the small peasant's capacity to borrow capital for meeting his various social and personal requirements was strictly limited due to the lack of economic, legal and political security. Land was not considered a safe security for borrowings. However, the development of a strong and stable rule, as well as the reclamation of desert lands by the extension of canal irrigation combined with facilities for marketing agricultural products altered the situation radically and ushered in an era when land became a viable commodity. Growth in earnings from agriculture led to an increase in the value of land.[11]

The stabilized economic and political condition as also the increased value of land encouraged the moneylenders to accept land as a security for loans. This change in a short period of time significantly altered the economic scene in rural Punjab creating in turn a large number of socioeconomic problems. The rapidly growing business of moneylending prompted moneylenders to adopt fair and unfair means supported by high interest to ensure that business prospered.[12] Their effort stood supported by the ignorance of debtors who frequently borrowed capital for unproductive uses and other social purposes like marriages, etc. The peasant fell into the trap of the moneylender primarily because he was not producing enough and he had no alternative source to mobilize financial help in times of need. While cases of unproductive borrowing were common, more generally the peasant borrowed under compulsion. Ready cash for the peasant has been a perpetual problem not only because land is known never to produce enough to meet needs but also because cash becomes available only when the produce is sold. The haphazard manner in which income from the produce was paid to the farmer was almost always at the convenience of the merchant who purchased the produce. The whole exercise further devalued the farmer's financial position. For the small holding peasant the situation has scarcely changed even today.

The all India average ratio of moneylender to population was 1:367, but in Punjab it was 1:100. Although the population of the province was only one-tenth of Indian population, one-fifth of all the moneylenders in India were found in Punjab.[13]

In 1917-18 the North-West Railway earned Rs. 764 lakhs, the major irrigation works earned Rs. 267 lakhs, while the moneylenders in Punjab earned about Rs. 500 lakhs (the actual figure must have been much higher as substantial income had not been officially declared).[14]

The role of the moneylenders affected not only the financial condition of the peasantry but also started a process of change in the socioeconomic structure of rural Punjab. The process of change

TABLE 1.4: GROWTH OF MONEYLENDERS IN PUNJAB

(figure in lakhs of rupees)

Year	Number assessed to tax	Tax	Income subject to tax	Money on loan
1897-8	—	3.8	150	1200
1902-3	8400	4.0	165	1300
1907-8	10300	4.38	188	1500
1912-13	12500	5.13	213	1700
1917-18	15035	7.42	350	2800

SOURCE: Calvert, *Wealth and Welfare*, p. 130.

was influenced by the fact that since indebtedness led to the sale and mortgage of land it became a valuable commodity with its mortgage becoming an expedient measure instead of remaining an exceptional resort. Gradually but surely land was slipping out of the peasant's hand.

This new situation posed a serious threat to socioeconomic stability in the villages of Punjab. Sensitive British officers in fact had warned of the possible danger of unrest as a result of the large scale transfers of land. The urgency in the warnings was adequately reflected in the observations of S.S. Thorburn, Deputy Commissioner of Dera Ghazi Khan, in his book *Mussulumans and Moneylenders in Punjab*.

Initially the government believed that agricultural production was likely to increase by the transfer of land from the poor to the rich farmers and others because the rich had capital which facilitated enterprise. The new owners however did not invest any capital in improvement of the land and contented themselves with the easiest option of the highest rent. As a result the situation became worse.[15]

Discontentment on an extensive scale in the peasantry worried the government mainly because of the fallout that such a situation was likely to have on the most sensitive and important institution of British power in India, the British Indian Army. After the uprising of 1857 the British Indian Army had been reconstituted in such a manner that a large part of it comprised of Punjabis. Most of the soldiers from Punjab were drawn from rural peasant families. From the British point of view this implied that utmost caution was required as an unhappy peasantry meant an important section of the army being discontented.[16]

To check the situation and provide some respite to the peasantry the government passed the Punjab Alienation of Land Act, 1901.[17] In essence the Act forbade the transfer of agriculturist's land to non-agriculturists. The Alienation of Land Act, 1901, like the basic problem of debt, was in due course to become a major issue of debate between the Unionists and their opponents.[18] The basis of the debate emerged from the fact that the Act itself was considered by its opponents as lacking in earnestness and more inclined towards the rich.

Opponents of the Act stressed that it was never really framed with the peasantry's welfare in mind but in fact was conceived by the government to safeguard its goodwill in the rural areas, from where a large section of the British Indian Army was recruited. It was said to be an effort by the government to create in the villages a section of people who would be loyal and grateful to the government.[19] Those opposing the Act also said its provisions were sinister in the sense that it tried to create a division between the urban and the rural elite and even to restrict the spread of nationalistic ideas into rural Punjab. Lord Rivaz, however, left little doubt as to the motives of the Bill when he introduced it on 27 September 1899, saying that it was for those 'who furnish the flower of the native army'.[20]

The character of the administration offered to Punjab since its annexation was a masterly mixture of threats, pressures, punishments, brute power, tactful persuasion, rewards and the gradual extension of political reform. A combination of these measures had kept the province relatively peaceful and hooked to the colonial line. The Reforms Act of 1919 was in fact a symbol of administrative brilliance in that it pretended to give a lot, but it gave only to those who had already been chosen to act as administrative intermediaries for the colonial regime—the elite both rural and urban. Like the Alienation of Land Act, 1901, the Reforms Act of 1919 too was essentially only a part of a pre-planned political-cum-administrative step. It was therefore no coincidence that the first Legislative Council (elected 1920) which was constituted as per provisions of the Act of 1919 was almost totally an assembly of rural and urban elite. It is also not surprising that from within its members was formed the Rural Block later renamed as the Punjab National Unionist Party.

It would however be both historically unsound and unfair to explain the origin of the Unionist Party as merely the result of imperialist scheming and Indian elitist collaboration because there were people who consciously joined the new party with other problems in mind. The number of such people was no doubt small but they did so in the belief that it stood for the development of rural areas and a more equitable distribution of monetary resources and also a bigger share for rural youth in services and educational institutions. The fact that the rural elitist class was able to carry with it a fairly good section of the common peasantry to accept the Unionist Party as a political entity was no coincidence. The poverty-stricken peasant in fact made a conscious choice, explained simply by the fact that he really had no better alternative. Politics in Punjab saw unexpected political partners, the large feudal land owners and families owning a few acres of land.

By the turn of the century the winds of change were flowing strong and clear from the West. However hard the administration may have tried to prevent it, enlightenment and awareness was greatly facilitated and encouraged by soldiers who returned to the Punjab countryside after the end of the First World War. These men brought back not only money but new ideas. Even today a soldier in rural Punjab is a respectable figure and a sort of focal point of ideas and actions which are often followed by the whole village.

The influence of Western education, the print media, and the growth and influence of the middle class also assisted the Punjabi peasant to wake up and seek a better life as did positive aspects of British rule, like justice, law and order and education which served significantly to influence the emergence of new ideas.

The cumulative effect of all this on the peasantry was that it began to aspire for a future free from exploitation, debt, and insecurity. It was this aspiration that led the peasantry to search for a new identity. In more real terms this implied the search for and creation of a new platform which would be bound by common, economic and political aspirations. While initially it was only the big land owners and influential people from rural areas who took the initiative in this direction, the common peasantry followed in trickles later. The irony is that even for its emancipation the poor peasantry of Punjab had no other option other than to follow the very people who in the first place were the cause of their plight.

The large number of political organizations that emerged on the horizon of Punjab in the first two decades of the twentieth century was the result of a growing awareness of both economic and social

TABLE 1.5: EMERGENCE OF POLITICAL PARTIES IN PUNJAB, 1877-1923

Political party/organization	Year of foundation
Lahore India Association by S.N. Banerjee	1877
Indian National Congress branch opened in Punjab	1885
Chief Khalsa Dewan	1902
Muslim League by Fazl-i-Husain	1906
Muslim Association by Mohamad Shafi	1907
All India Muslim League Branch by merger of Fazl-i-Husain and Mohamad Shafi's Parties	1907
Punjab Hindu Sabha	1907
Central Sikh League	1920
Mohammedan Rural Party by Fazl-i-Husain	1921
Communist Party (organizational work started)	1921-2
Swarajya Party	1922
Rural Party as Unionist Party	1923

SOURCE: K.C. Yadav, *Elections in Punjab* (Delhi, 1987), p. 132.

right, of political deprivation, and in most cases a consciousness of nationalism. While the Unionist Party essentially emerged as a party of big land owners it did however differ from other such parties in other parts of India on the ground that it cut across class and communities to represent rural areas as a whole. This basic approach made it an ideal instrument for the British as Talbot says, to isolate the rural population from other streams.[21]

The Act of 1919 was politically an important turning point even though all it did was to go one step forward and two backwards. By the division of the already highly restricted electorate into watertight communal (Hindu, Muslim, Sikh, etc.) and urban-rural constituencies, the forces of nationalism and unity were pushed back, disturbed and weakened considerably. The character and spirit of the franchise as proposed in the provisions of the Act made the whole exercise a political mockery.

TABLE 1.6: TYPES OF CONSTITUENCIES IN THE PLC, 1920

Designation of the constituencies	Urban	Rural	Total
Mohammadans	5	27	32
Non-Mohammadans	7	13	20
Sikhs	1	11	12
Special	—	—	07

SOURCE : K.C. Yadav, *Elections*, p. 11.

The 1919 reforms introduced the virus of communalism and separatism in a highly systemized manner. The division of seats into communal, rural and urban categories further bolstered the division that already existed in a manifested manner in Punjab society.[22] The statutory restrictions contained in the Act deterred and prohibited a large majority of the people from being enrolled as voters. So highly limited was the franchise that just about 3 per cent of the adult population of the state was entitled to vote. For the lucky few who were given the right to vote the opportunity was considered democratic enough. Those who aspired for political influence and posts, the restrictive provisions notwithstanding, believed that the reforms enabled Punjab to move forward politically.[23] The new elite and upper middle class used the opportunity to secure political recognition. There is little doubt that as a result of this limited political exercise the British succeeded to a great extent in winning the support and goodwill of an influential section of Punjab's rural elite, in particular the Muslim community.

This policy of distributing people into compartments drew strong criticism, among others, from Lala Lajpat Rai who considered the policy as an attempt to create an economic wall between the rural and urban people.[24] The politically conscious urban Hindu elite was further distanced by this policy from the rural elite particularly the Muslims. The net result was that the advent of nationalistic awareness into rural Punjab received a setback and was temporarily slowed down.

A study of the Unionist Party's origin must also bear in mind the special character of Punjab's society. Talbot has very rightly

TABLE 1.7: PROPERTY/STATUS QUALIFICATIONS OF PUNJAB LEGISLATIVE COUNCIL VOTERS, 1920

Rural Constituencies

(i) Owner/tenant/lease of land assessed to land revenue not less than Rs. 27 p. a.
(ii) Zaildar/Safedposh/Lamberdar.
(iii) Income Tax Payee.
(iv) Retired (Pensioned/discharged) officer/O.R. of H.M.'s regular forces.

Urban Constituencies

(i) Owner/tenant of immovable property not being land, assessed to land revenue but including any building, etc., on it of the value of not less than Rs. 4000 or of rental value of not less than Rs. 96 p. a.
(ii) Payee of Municipal or Cantonment tax amounting to not less than Rs. 50 p. a.
(iii) Income Tax Payee.
(iv) Retired (Pensioned or discharged) officer/N.C.O., soldier of H.M.'s regular forces.
(v) Possessing the qualifications of a rural voter.

Special Constituencies

(i) Landholders' Constituency
Owner of land assessed to land revenue not less than Rs. 500 p. a.
(ii) Punjab University Constituency
Fellow/Hony. Fellow Graduate of the University of not less than 7 years' standing.
(iii) Industries Constituency
Owner or representative/partner of a factory in Punjab or corporation with a paid up capital of Rs. 25,000.
(iv) Member of the Chamber of Commerce in Punjab.

SOURCE: *Punjab Government Gazette Extraordinary*, 7 August 1920.

suggested: 'two overriding characteristics of the colonial Punjab were its rural nature and co-existence of vigorous Muslim, Hindu & Sikh communities'.[25] The cardinal principle, as pointed out by David Ludden,[26] that peasant societies are influenced by four types of networks—kinship, religion, state and market interactions—can well be applied to rural Punjab. It needs also to be pointed out that the highly compartmentalized state of Punjab's society was not a result of the attitudes and policies of the British alone, there were in fact many other important factors responsible as well.

The uniqueness of Punjab's social system was that while religion divided society, tribal and caste ties created an undercurrent of affinity and affiliation. In political developments these ties played an important role, the origin and growth of the Unionist Party being one good example. While common cultural legacies were probably the more significant binding force, yet since people belonging to similar castes usually had the same type of profession, there also emerged an economic bond. This economic bond helped people to transgress barriers of religion and caste.

The circumstances that enabled the consensual kind of politics that was practised by the founding and important members of the Unionist Party also needs to be understood and properly assessed in the context of the commonly shared cultural roots and values. The cross-cultural commonness is so easily evident, as Talbot[27] points out, for example, in songs, proverbs and folklore. The richness of Punjabi literature is associated in a considerable measure to *Sufism* and *Sufi* verses. But for some pockets in the eastern (mainly the Hindu Jat belt of Haryana) region, Sufism spread out well beyond the sway of Islam. It is true that as revivalist movements began to show their teeth in the nineteenth century cultural values that had been shared by people for centuries were exposed to undercutting. The tendency among revivalist religious leaders to assert the exclusiveness of their own communities in fact did irreparable harm to the cultural health of Punjab's people. However, even while the cultural bonds were considerably weakened they did not totally disintegrate and thereby allowed the propagators of consensus politics a fair chance of seeking support across community lines. Cultural links among different communities had developed over centuries and could not easily be washed away however hard the segregationist leaders might have tried. Herein lay the genesis or at least a part of it, of the significant divide that developed in the political culture of rural and urban Punjab.[28]

The important cultural differences that manifested themselves between the rural and urban population in political as well as other walks of life were considerably related to the response of concerned communities to the appeals of revivalist leaders. As the impact of the print media represented mainly by community-based provocative newspapers of the time was rather limited in rural areas it took a far longer time for cultural links to fade. Quite the opposite happened in important urban centres where such newspapers played an important role in highlighting differences among communities. This partly explains why the cross-cultural and inter-community politics practised by the founding leaders of the Unionist Party got a far greater response in rural Punjab. In the initial years Unionist Party politics groomed itself on the common cultural ethos as well as social attitudes, for example, the significance of land ownership, the predominance of 'self-respect', *izzat* as a way of life. Such cultural and social attitudes cut across community lines in rural Punjab and helped not only in diffusing the effects of caste and communal differences but giving to the peasantry of rural Punjab a sense of belonging to a 'common stock'.[29]

The significance of tribal politics and affiliations came centre stage after the British accepted the crucial nature of support rendered by tribal chiefs in the British hour of crisis in 1857[30] and decided to reciprocate. The tribal chiefs were considered a safeguard of the Raj apart from being important intermediaries. The policy of accepting the tribe as the focus of rural identity had far-reaching implications. To quote Talbot: 'the maintenance of tribal structure of rural society became the legitimizing principle of British rule, thereby obscuring realpolitik imperatives'.[31] The Unionist Party in a way was used as a tool to justify the 'goodness of British' rule particularly in the context of its 'keenness to develop rural areas'. By retaining their old tribal dispositions, beliefs and bonds intact in spite of the fact that in the course of time some people had embraced different religions and got divided into them, tribal and caste attitudes lent stability to Punjab society. The major castes, most of which were common to all the three major religious communities in Punjab (listed in Table 1.8) adequately show the role of inter-religious caste bonds.

The circumstances within which the Unionist Party was born also reflect an interesting paradox, that while caste and kinship affiliations tended to dilute differences between social groups which were common to different religions but on the whole they were unable to override the differences that different religious leaders invariably encouraged among their followers. It was this inherent contradiction with which the Unionist Party had to live throughout its not too long life. Since Unionist Party politics essentially revolved around caste, kinship, *biradari* and of course religion, every decision or issue appeared to get influenced by these parameters. The demographic distribution of Punjab's population into the various religious groups however has remained through the region's history

TABLE 1.8: HINDU, MUSLIM, SIKH CASTES IN PUNJAB, 1921

Caste	Hindu	Muslim	Sikh
Jat	1035405	2582495	1822881
Rajput	499251	218319	32579
Gujjars	157959	465676	—
Saini	66359	—	—
Kamboh	—	76829	64194
Khatri	390253	—	61234
Arora	591230	—	116175
Sunar	77251	28798	—
Tarkhan	161833	312125	—
Kumahar	155879	383952	—
Lohar	83385	217459	—
Nai	106720	218319	32579
Jhinwar	215210	36720	48456
Julaha	56593	579404	—

SOURCE: *The Census of India, 1921, Punjab, Part II* (Report), p. 132.

as it does even today an important deciding factor in the choice of political options and action.

The Muṣlims as Table 1.9 shows, constituted just over 50 per cent of Punjab's population, with the Hindus forming 35.7 per cent and the Sikhs about 12 per cent. Muslim society in Punjab like the Hindus and Sikhs far from being homogeneous was fragmented into obvious demarcations of educated elite, illiterate and petty land owners, vast landless and ignorant masses and a section of people

TABLE 1.9: RELIGIOUS COMPOSITION OF PUNJAB, 1921

Religion	Actual number	Number per thousand of the total population
Musalmans	12,955,141	506
Hindus	9,125,202	357
Sikhs	3,110,060	121
Christians	346,259	13
Jains	46,019	2
Buddhist	5,918	—
Parsi	518	—
Jews	36	—

SOURCE: *The Census of India, 1921, Punjab, Part I* (Report), p. 172.

somewhat unique only to the Muslims, the *pirs* and *sajjda nashins*,[32] who went on later to play a major role in Unionist Party politics and the rise and decline of its fortunes.[33] The Muslim population was mainly concentrated in the western districts, for example in Muzaffargarh, Dera Ghazi Khan, Mianwali, Attock, Rawalpindi, Jhelum, where more than 80 per cent of the population was Muslim. In the eastern and central districts the proportion of Muslim population ranged between 15 to 45 per cent, the lowest being in Rohtak where Muslims were less than 10 per cent.[34] Muslim society was predominantly rural. In the western districts where large sections of Muslim population was concentrated, only one out of twenty people lived in towns.[35] In the eastern districts the ratio was somewhat higher with one out of six living in towns.[36]

The roots of a typical feudal society like that of Punjab lay deeply embedded in ignorance and the lack of education, particularly among the disadvantaged. While the Hindus and Sikhs (Table 1.10) were almost at par in the field of education, the Muslims, who were in majority, were however far behind. The Unionist Party's early politics can also be traced to this unfortunate fact. The backwardness of the Muslims in education was the single most important factor for the deprivation of the community in economic activity. This fact partly explains why internal contradictions tended to manifest themselves more frequently among the Muslims and the Unionist Party of which the community was the major constituent. Table 1.10 shows the significant gap that existed between the Muslims and other communities in the field of education.

A large number of contributing causes have often been suggested as explanations for the age old distrust among Muslims in general towards Western and modern education. But in sum, it could be said that the main cause was the belief in Muslim society and with sufficient basis that modern Western education was significantly short of Islamic religious content. As a result the Muslim masses developed a tendency to stay aloof from schools imparting Western education and opted only for those institutions that were inherently Islamic in culture and educational content. This separatist attitude which of course did have remarkable exceptions put the community to considerable educational and economic disadvantage,[37] leaving it way behind others.[38] The inward looking attitude

TABLE 1.10: LITERACY LEVEL OF MAJOR RELIGIOUS COMMUNITIES, 1921

(Number of literates per thousand)

	Hindu		Muslim		Sikh		Christian		Jain	
	Male	Female	Male	Female	Male	Female	Male	Female	Male	Female
Punjab	113	11	37	4	93	13	140	93	506	47
Hissar	64	3	27	2	51	3	236	226	170	35
Rohtak	59	3	50	4	347	75	31	14	505	28
Gurgaon	71	3	33	2	177	23	266	187	529	46
Karnal	50	3	36	4	72	9	60	51	424	17
Jullundur	133	19	59	10	74	7	312	154	593	130
Ludhiana	194	24	60	13	103	16	415	433	521	39
Ferozepur	125	15	32	5	65	7	382	161	517	102
Lahore	215	56	74	15	89	13	171	126	536	78
Amritsar	144	12	43	4	82	11	103	95	461	63
Gujranwala	207	39	33	7	136	30	22	15	339	48
Sheikhupura	127	9	28	2	80	8	27	31	605	605
Simla	441	15	259	87	498	216	795	941	881	316
Kangra	86	5	54	8	283	11	573	515	38	83
Ambala	91	9	69	10	112	12	703	796	640	117
Hoshiarpur	106	9	55	5	118	10	84	59	561	78
Gurdaspur	108	12	48	7	56	8	32	31	—	—
Sialkot	105	12	41	5	89	15	76	21	544	59
Gujrat	269	32	34	3	323	41	102	98	1000	1000
Jhelum	413	62	54	2	449	79	596	486	432	22
Rawalpindi	359	77	62	3	438	119	757	675	568	58
Attock	403	64	30	1	413	54	828	616	1000	—
Montgomery	194	25	22	2	118	14	45	30	600	—
Shahpur	269	50	28	2	279	100	28	18	1000	—
Mianwali	273	11	22	—	344	23	690	700	—	—
Lyallpur	137	19	31	3	54	9	18	7	669	48
Jhang	412	39	24	2	404	68	165	65	1000	333
Multan	279	22	24	3	262	38	431	182	462	250
Muzaffargarh	312	17	22	2	122	28	779	127	500	—
Dera Ghazi Khan	378	30	25	1	188	41	600	438	496	95

SOURCE: *The Census of India, 1921, Punjab, Part I*, p. 299.

of the community had a telling impact not only on economic growth but also on political options. With scarce education, limited economic opportunity the community was left to the mercy of self-seeking feudal leaders.

It was this natural handicap that influenced the course of Muslim politics and the community's political attitudes in Punjab, emerging in the form of a very significant grip on the Muslim population by feudal lords, traditional socioreligious leaders like *pirs*, *sajjada nishins* and *biradari* leaders. The level to which such influentially placed people were able to control the political destinies of a vast section of Punjab's Muslim[39] population particularly in rural areas was a remarkable phenomena that significantly influenced the Muslim community's response to other sections of Punjab's society.

When the British in the beginning of the twentieth century tried to give political cohesion to a class of rural landed intermediaries, loyal to the government, the *sajjada nishins* and *pirs* were recognized as being ideal for the job. In a decision of administrative politics that showed foresight they were encouraged to take on a new identity and status which further added to their economic social and political influence. It was a mutually benefiting understanding. Similar was the case with the *biradari* leaders. In most cases such leaders owned vast lands and acquired often unmerited socio-economic status. Together with the *pirs* and *sajjada nishins* the *biradari* leaders had a firm grip on the destiny of the Muslim masses. While aversion to Western education came in due course to be gradually diluted, Muslim society in Punjab could never really free itself from the hold of these highly vested class leaders. The hold of such reactionary socioreligious institutions was of course not restricted to the Muslim society but its manifestation seemed more alarming because of the majority character of the Muslims in Punjab.

The tendency of separatist education as we have seen was a predominant trend among Muslims, but it was not unknown even among the Sikhs and Hindus. There were a large number of institutions catering to the religious requirements of different communities. The atmosphere in such institutions was necessarily that of a social system and culture associated with only one community. As a result the education imparted had the effect of isolating their students from those of other communities.[40] With a large number of children going to such institutions a natural process of division got underway.

Institutions that specialized in catering to the needs of specific communities by their very nature did considerable harm to the concept of a homogeneous society. Ahmad Yar Khan Daultana, member of the Punjab Legislative Council, deposed before the Punjab University Enquiry Committee (1932-3) that 'students from such institutions finished their education with the impression that there was a very severe rivalry between various religions. It was their deep rooted feelings that laid the foundation of a great communal strife.'[41]

Like in education, in economic and commercial activity too, most sections of the Muslim population were way behind the Hindus and Sikhs. The Hindus, for example, owned more than 60 per cent of registered factories in Lahore and paid eight times more sales tax than the Muslims.[42] The situation was similar all over Punjab: whether it was in banks, factories, shops, trade organizations, a majority were in the hands of people belonging to the Hindu community.[43]

The rapidly growing differences between communities were not limited to just between Hindus and Muslims or between Sikhs and Muslims. To a less marked degree there was growing tension even between Hindus and Sikhs. The turn of the century in fact witnessed a passionate debate between provocative proponents of the Hindu and Sikh communities, centered mainly on the assertion that the Sikhs were a separate religious faith and as such could not be covered under provisions of the Hindu Law of Inheritance,[44] only to be countered with contrary claims by those claiming to represent the Hindus.

The fact that the Hindus and Sikhs dominated most activity having monetary implications may partly have been due to the fact that both these communities were way ahead of the majority community, the Muslims, in the field of education (Table 1.10). Being in an advantageous position in education obviously provided greater opportunities in avenues of employment. The educational and economic disadvantage with which the Muslims of Punjab were faced not only reflected itself in the formation of the Unionist Party but the peculiar circumstances in which the majority community found itself considerably influenced the political and economic attitudes of some leading Unionist Party leaders.

The Hindu population of Punjab was concentrated in districts east of the river Ravi with the exception of the Sikh dominated districts of Jullundur, Ludhiana, Ferozepur where the Hindus were less than 40 per cent. In some districts like Rohtak the Hindu population exceeded 80 per cent, whereas in the western districts it was scattered and scarce. For example in Dera Ghazi Khan it was less than 12 per cent and in Attock it was less than 5 per cent.[45] The Sikh population likewise was concentrated mainly in the fertile central districts of Ludhiana, Amritsar, Jullundur. In 18 of Punjab's 29 districts the Sikh population was below 10 per cent.[46] The Sikh population showed a remarkable increase of over 13 per cent during the years 1891-1901 and a phenomenal increase of almost 50 per cent between the years 1901-11.[47] This increase was obviously more in the form of statistics and not so in real terms. The emphasis placed by leaders of the Hindu and Sikh communities on maintaining distinct identities got reflected in the Census figures.

By the 1920s the Sikhs of Punjab had managed to attain a level of political influence which was somewhat disproportionate to their share in Punjab's population. This was not surprising keeping in mind the dynamic nature of the community, the economic affluence, the share in government jobs and armed forces as also the religious and cultural zeal which was synonymous with the community. Various Sikh organizations were concentrating during the period, 1911-21 to bring together the divergent Sikh sects that tended to dilute the political force of the community. For example, the Singh Sabha of Amritsar (founded 1873) concentrated mainly on the spread of education and cultural preservation. At the turn of the century the Singh Sabhas were merged into the Chief Khalsa Diwan which was formed to represent the political demands of the Sikhs to the government.

The political behaviour of the three major communities in Punjab in the years 1900-21 can briefly be summarized as each one trying to belittle the other. Points of dispute were numerous but the result was always the same, tension and strife. The factors leading to communal tension and divisive attitudes were numerous and widespread. Some of these factors had a direct bearing on the nature of the Unionist Party as also on its origin; a brief reference would therefore be in place.

The caste and tribal leaders who had begun to play an important role at the turn of the century derived their strength by highlighting differences rather than diluting and erasing them. In the effort to establish their individual identity and status such leaders worked to divide people.[48] Even the information supplied by such useful exercises like the Census for example, was used as an instrument by educated public men to generate awareness of the growing numbers of the other communities. In doing so such 'leaders' attempted to bring closer their own co-religionists and thus went on to project themselves as 'saviours of the community'.

The print media[49] was another instrument used effectively by vested interests to increase communal differences[50] during the first two decades of this century. Most of the periodicals and newspapers[51] served as aggressive mouthpieces of communalist movements and viewpoints. Journalism in Punjab in the 1920s was truly 'yellow', with newspapers competing with each other to ferment trouble, tension and to belittle the 'other' community merely to sell a few more copies. This war in 'print' was not a phenomenon of the twentieth century but had actually started in the late nineteenth century, a fact well represented in the writings of Lekh Ram of the Arya Samaj and Ghulam Ahmad of the Ahmadiyah Movement.[52] The redeeming feature of this campaign of hatred and vilification was that its area of influence was restricted mainly to major urban areas, for example, Amritsar, Lahore and Rawalpindi, where the level of literacy was higher. This was one reason as we shall see later as to why the Unionist Party's appeal of communal harmony struck quicker roots among the peasantry of rural Punjab and failed to attract much attention in the larger cities.

The growing distance between the three major communities of Punjab within the context of the Unionist Party's origin can also be linked to the tendency to spread the message of the fight for freedom by slogans like 'Ram Rajya' and even 'Swaraj', which came to be interpreted in religious terms by Muslims in Punjab.[53] It needs to be noted, for example, that Lala Lajpat Rai the great nationalist who personified the fight against British rule in Punjab was at the same time an active and leading worker of the Hindu Mahasabha, a frontal Hindu organization operating in confrontation with the Muslims in Punjab.[54] For as long as he was alive Lajpat Rai was able to contain the passionate anti-Muslim stance of 'hawks' in the Hindu Mahasabha but after his tragic death the situation deteriorated rapidly. Not only did the Congress and India lose a great leader but more importantly, his absence enabled extreme viewpoints to take centre stage.

The call by Mahatma Gandhi in 1920 to non-cooperate was a milestone in the fight for freedom; in Punjab however, it had an unexpected fall out. Of the province's leading Congressmen two quit the party. One of them, was Mian Fazl-i-Husain.[55] He resigned from the Congress on the ground that not only was the ideology of the Non-Cooperation Movement unacceptable to him but he felt such a policy would harm the overall interest of the Muslim community in Punjab. Fazl-i-Husain was a leading figure in the political circles of Punjab but his early career presents a contradictory and unstable political attitude. For example, in 1917, his speech at the Punjab Provincial Congress (October 1917) is described by the governor of Punjab as 'pure sedition'.[56] But in the very next year (1918) he is honoured by the government for his cooperation in the war efforts.[57] Then again he plays an important role in the anti-Rowlatt Act agitations.[58] But it seems the harassment he suffered during the Martial Law regime[59] had a sobering effect on him which finally manifested itself in 1920 when he decided to quit the Congress. This complete change of political heart proved a boon for him personally. For politics in Punjab Fazl-i-Husain's change of heart was destined to give a totally new direction and dimension.

The other important Congressman who deserted the Congress on the pretext of non-cooperation was Chhotu Ram.[60] He was Congress president for Rohtak district at the time of his exit from the party. Like Fazl-i-Husain's decision of leaving the Congress Chhotu Ram's too was linked to the issue of the Non-Cooperation Movement. And like Fazl-i-Husain the political inclinations of Chhotu Ram in the early years too appear somewhat unstable.

During the First World War like many other eminent and influential men he helped the government in the soldier recruitment effort. While remaining an active Congress man he founded the *Jat Gazette* with effective help from Harcourt Butler, the Deputy Commissioner of Rohtak, and in return even expressed a sense of gratitude and loyalty to the government.[61] There has as a result been a fair amount of controversy on the political role of Chhotu Ram in the formative years of his political career. The other explanation for his leaving the Congress is based on the ground that the peasantry and the ignorant rural population which was overburdened by debt was in no position to confront the government on political issues particularly at a time when the immediate problem that required attention was the economic plight of the peasant, particularly the question of debt.[62] His humble background and experience of poverty in his early years not only left a lasting impression on him but appears to justify his exit from the Congress.

It was politically obvious for aspiring and ambitious public men to build an alternative political platform. The birth of the Unionist Party must be viewed in the context of the combination of these peculiar circumstances as also with the British colonial policy in Punjab in the preceding fifty years, which in sum revolved around placating Muslim sentiment and building a loyal buffer of landlords and influential *biradari* leaders between themselves and the masses. In any case there were no options for politically ambitious men who had opted to desert the Congress at a critical juncture other than that of the floating of a new political organization.

Apart from the Congress the other important political organizations that were relatively active in Punjab in the years of the Unionist Party's origin were the Muslim League, Swaraj Party, Central Sikh League and the Akali Dal. The Congress in Punjab had somehow come to be identified in the 1920s with the urban educated classes and unlike in the neighbouring U.P. it failed generally speaking to attract the rural masses. Another reason for the Congress Party's lack of mass rural appeal among Muslims was that it was considered a political organization having closer relations with the Hindu community. This factor, whatever its basis, went a long way in making a large number of Muslims seek alternative political options.

The Muslim League on the other hand had only a superficial presence comprising mainly of urban Muslim elite being practically unacknowledged among the rural Muslim population of Punjab at the time. This fact partly explains why Fazl-i-Husain opted to float a new organization rather than join the Muslim League which without doubt would have welcomed a leader of his stature. The creation of the Unionist Party may never have been even necessary had the Muslim League some element of popularity and support among the Muslim masses of rural Punjab. The League's almost total urban character in the 1920s in Punjab appears to have worked as a subconscious motivating factor which gave to the Unionist Party its totally pro-rural bias.

Sikh politics during the period had come to be centred around the Akali Dal, the emergence of which as a political force was an important milestone in Sikh political history. While the Akali Dal came in the course of time to represent the Sikh peasantry, the Khalsa National Party was able to woo some influential Sikhs to its cause. However, with the birth of the Unionist Party a fairly large section of Sikh peasantry, particularly the Jats began supporting it. The Hindu Mahasabha also had a formidable presence in Punjab during the period. In many ways it was a sort of Hindu answer to the Muslim League. Lala Lajpat Rai's association with the organization gave it considerable credibility.

In the early 1920s the Swaraj Party was also able to attract some influential Congressmen to its fold. But like the Congress it too was considered as an organization of rich and influential urban elite including a fair number of leading barristers, mostly Hindu.

The elections to the Central and Provincial legislatures as provided under the Act of 1919 were held under the shadow of the Non-Cooperation Movement. Congressmen had withdrawn from the elections on the ground that participating in such restrictive elections was against the nation's interest.[63] On the whole the elections were a low key affair in which only about 50 per cent of the enrolled voters turned up to cast their votes.[64] The elite however got a chance to go to the legislature and have a feeling of democracy, however superficial it might have been. Most of those who were elected did not belong to any specific political party but were mainly big landlords, traders, lawyers, *biradari* leaders, in sum, rich, shrewd, enlightened and politicized. Above all, most of them had deep vested interests associated and dependent in some form or the other on the colonial government's goodwill.

The council that was constituted was in keeping with what the British rulers had expected, loyal and obedient.[65] Fazl-i-Husain was the most influential member of the newly formed council. He was returned from the Punjab University Constituency. His influence and stature having derived from the fact that besides being a barrister he had been the most important leader of the Congress, and was also credited with having founded the Muslim League in Punjab. For the British in Punjab the composition of the new Legislative Council and more importantly the nature of leadership that was likely to emerge presented a unique and golden opportunity. Fazl-i-Husain was not only appointed a minister,[66] but even the choice of the second minister was left to him by the Governor Sir Edward Maclagan. Fazl-i-Husain chose Lala Harkishan Lal.

Fazl-i-Husain's political clout with the administration and influence among the Muslim members in the council enabled him to bring together thirty-five Muslim members and form a superficially united group, the 'Rural Block'.[67] Most of the 'Rural Block' members were from rural Punjab. The formation of such groups within the legislature was a common practice even in the British Parliament where groups of specific influence and interest tended to push together measures and issues which suited defined objectives. So Fazl-i-Husain's objective of bringing together members belonging to rural areas was perhaps guided by British intellect.

The manner in which Fazl-i-Husain attempted to form a vaguely defined coalition to operate on the floor of the council with common objectives was not a chance attempt but a well calculated political strategy. The exercise to bring together on a common platform elite leaders from different communities was in fact a conscious attempt to exploit the common cultural and social linkages that made the appeal of Fazl-i-Husain fairly attractive. The 'Consociational system'[68] of politics that the founder of the Unionist

Party visualized proved to be successful only because the substantial degree of common cultural and social ethos provided a receptive or rather fertile ground for such views.

This point can be further stressed by a hypothetical observation that a similar appeal to urban members of the council, for example, would not have yielded a similarly fruitful response. This can be explained by the fact that in urban areas of Punjab a great measure of the common cultural and social roots had been considerably damaged by sectarian and divisionist views propagated by leaders and conveniently facilitated by the press. In this context it appears the widespread illiteracy of rural Punjab may in fact have had a 'silver lining', because the fences created by the print media between communities in urban areas still remained tresspassable in rural areas. In this sense Fazl-i-Husain's attempt to lay the foundations of his new party essentially on 'rural' support was well conceived. The level to which this simple political agenda proved successful needs to be appreciated not only in terms of the support secured by Fazl-i-Husain from Muslim members of the council but also the growing enthusiasm that this approach generated among the Hindu Jat peasantry of eastern Punjab[69] as reflected in the response that leaders like Chhotu Ram received.

The basic compositional character of this 'Rural Block' was such that internal dissension and intrigue became an integral part of it as a result of varying vested interests. From the outset this group of legislators was generally divided in two, with a history of recurring strong political and non-political rivalry. One of the factions was led by the Daultana clan and the other by the Noons and Tiwanas.[70] Even Fazl-i-Husain could manage to bring them together only temporarily. This fundamentally flawed inherent feature of the 'Rural Block' would prove in due course to be the most diseased legacy that would be transmitted to Punjab politics in general and the Unionist Party in particular.

It was with such support that Fazl-i-Husain initiated the process of consolidating his hold over the members of the 'Rural Block'. He initiated the process by seeking favours for the Muslim community of Punjab[71] in general, but more specifically in matters like recruitment and ensuring that Muslim employment and other quotas were not misused or left vacant.[72] In his effort to gather political support for his new political platform he had to pursue various influential sections of Muslim society most of whom had come to be well represented in the 'elitist' legislature.

One such section of Muslim leaders who supported Fazl-i-Husain and also played an important role in establishing the credibility of the 'Rural Block' and later the Unionist Party were the *pirs* and *sajjada nishins*. Being a typical feudal society the influence of such traditional leaders in Punjab's society was profound. With their large landed estates and because of their extensive social, religious and more importantly economic clout the masses willingly accepted them as their leaders even in matters which were not associated with religion. The British bureaucracy in Punjab for obvious reasons had no reservation in accepting and supporting this small group as the natural leaders of Punjab's people. The colonial government as such successfully created a new leadership which went on to play a leading role in the administration as *zaildars*, honorary magistrates and district board members. For Fazl-i-Husain it was imperative to woo these influential leaders to his newly formed political platform. The *pirs* too were happy with the new emerging political alignment because in any case most of the legislators associated with Fazl-i-Husain were Muslims. They were impressed by the 'Rural Block's' efforts of seeking advancement of Muslims through reservations in the government services and schools and even the protection of the economic interests of the rural Muslims from the Hindu moneylenders. But more important was the fact that most of the Rural Block members were big landlords, thereby underlining the strong common economic bond that was to emerge in due course.

The early success of Fazl-i-Husain was rooted in his ability to gather under his influence a fairly large section of the politically active among the Muslim community of Punjab. His shrewd political foresight made him realize that this support if restricted exclusively to the Muslims could not have sufficed if a worthwhile political organization was to be created in the state. The search for broader credibility, social acceptance and perhaps the requirements of real politik prompted him to start the process of associating Hindus and Sikhs with the 'Rural Block'. This process of assimilation was initiated in the Legislative Council itself when Muslim members of the 'Rural Block' and Hindu and Sikh members from rural Punjab began pursuing issues and participating in debates in the council in a united manner.

Under the guidance of Fazl-i-Husain the 'Rural Block' began to align with the Hindu and Sikh rural leaders in the council whenever the issue of discussion involved rural Punjab or the peasantry. This policy of adopting a unified approach on common problems concerning rural areas irrespective of the community or religion that the members belonged, directly initiated the process that led to the birth of the Unionist Party. The elections to the Punjab Legislative Council in 1923 later presented to the 'Rural Block' members and others who gradually and loosely merged with it on the first occasion to present a united front.

The actual renaming of the 'Rural Block' as the Punjab National Unionist Party took place only after the 1923 Punjab Legislative Council had been formed. Yet for all practical purposes the alliance of common political and economic interest between Muslim members of the 'Rural Block' and like-minded Hindu and Sikh legislators from rural Punjab had come into existence in 1922.

The elections to the second Punjab Legislative Council (1923) were thus fought by the 'Rural Block' in alliance with rural leaders of the Hindus and Sikhs. Common views were presented, a joint manifesto was released and even votes were sought for candidates on party basis.[73] The fact that the 'Rural Block' had decided under the leadership of Fazl-i-Husain to partly shed its predominantly Muslim character and adopt a more apparently secular and economy based front is underlined by the election manifesto issued by Fazl-i-Husain for the 1923 Punjab Legislative Council elections. Some important points of the manifesto were:[74]

1. To attain dominion status within the British Commonwealth of Nations by constitutional means at an early date.
2. To demonstrate by a statement like working of the Reforms, that given suitable opportunities and reasonable facilities, Indians are capable of shouldering the responsibilities of self-government.
3. To prove that constructive effort, if directed in a spirit of good-

will and earnestness to the working of Reforms can produce results of greater benefit to the community than a case of disdainfulness and destructive criticism.

4. To provide equal opportunities of advance to all and to direct in an increasing measure, the beneficient activities of government to backward classes and areas with a view to enable them to make good the leeway produced by an ill-conceived or inadvertent policy of neglect in the past.
5. To secure a fair distribution of the burden of provincial taxes between agricultural and other classes.
6. To secure a just and fair representation of all classes and communities in the public services of the province.
7. To check the exploitation of economically backward classes by economically dominant classes.
8. To promote indigenous industries and to encourage the use of Swadeshi articles.
9. To banish illiteracy from the province.
10. To encourage a policy of decentralization.
11. To encourage the growth of local self-governing institutions.
12. To diminish litigation.
13. To secure economy in the administration.
14. To suppress corruption and bribery.
15. To promote temperance.
16. To preserve intact the Punjab Land Alienation Act as a measure of protection to backward classes.

The election 'manifesto' issued by the 'Rural Block' leaders was a usual political gimmick in the sense that the rules and procedures of 'dyarchy' scarcely provided an opportunity to any so-called elected representative to effectively influence the course of decision-making. Notwithstanding this fact, the main contribution of the manifesto was the fact that Fazl-i-Husain acknowledged the need to associate non-Muslims with his political fortunes.

The other important point that emerged from his political statements preceding the 1923 elections to the Punjab Legislative Council was a conscious effort on the part of Fazl-i-Husain to project himself and his early associates as leaders who were concerned for the welfare of the rural inhabitants of Punjab. As a sequel to this policy, by the eve of the 1923 elections Fazl-i-Husain had created a clear demarcation of urban and rural interests. His staunch ally and close associate in these early years Chhotu Ram provided to Fazl-i-Husain and his new organization the image and credibility of being secular, thereby greatly extending the area of impact and appeal. Chhotu Ram grew rapidly in political stature and came to personify the political will and aspirations of the south-east Punjab.[75]

The elections of 1923 was thus in a way the first real test of the new political ideology and political programme floated by Fazl-i-Husain. While the elections were once again boycotted by the Congress, a breakaway faction of the party in the form of the Swaraj Party represented by C.R. Das, Moti Lal Nehru, Hakim Ajmal Khan at the national level and mainly Dr Kitchlu in Punjab chose to participate in the elections. Of the total of thirty-seven All India Congress Committee members from Punjab twenty-three supported the Swaraj Party's proposal of participating in the elections.[76] The other local parties that entered the contest included Raja Narender Nath's Hindu National Party[77] and the Shiromani Gurudwara Prabandhak Committee. The Muslim League in 1923 was of no political significance in Punjab. The Sikh community was well divided among the Congress and the SGPC, with a fair section of the Sikhs being under the influence of the 'Rural Block'. Sir Sunder Singh Majithia[78] for example, actively cooperated with the 'Rural Block' and later on its conversion into the Unionist Party continued the support.

Notwithstanding the fact that the franchise was highly restricted and also that the most important political organization in the country, the Indian National Congress, had boycotted the elections, the exercise turned out to be fairly lively. Some important national leaders by touring the province for electioneering[79] gave to the elections some much needed element of credibility.

Fazl-i-Husain derived considerable political advantage from the fact that the 'Rural Block' pursued a policy of emphasizing the development of rural Punjab and showering numerous benefits on the peasantry. The fact that the election was highly restrictive in terms of eligible voters excluded the masses almost en block, leaving the 'Rural Block' to gather support from divergent elite sections of society. Just about 2,50,000 people cast votes in 1923, as compared

TABLE 1.11: PARTY POSITION IN THE PUNJAB LEGISLATIVE COUNCIL, 1923

Party	No. of candidates won
Rural Block (Party)	33
Swaraj Party	12
Gurudwara Prabandhak Committee	9
Independents	17
(Hindus = 11	
Muslims = 5	
Europeans = 1)	
Total	71

SOURCE: Yadav, *Elections*, p. 52.

to 1,30,000 in 1920.[80] This was partly due to the fact that in 1923, some elements of the Congress participated under the Swaraj Party's influence. Such was the political environment and the election procedures that the whole exercise of the elections appeared not only meaningless but the success of Fazl-i-Husain and his party was a forgone conclusion.

The relative success of Fazl-i-Husain and his 'Rural Block' was mainly dependent on his ability to gather onto one political platform, divergent but politically influential people, most with feudal backgrounds, for example, the big landlords, *pirs*, *biradari* leaders, besides important urban elite. The tactful manner in which Fazl-i-Husain wooed to his cause the Hindu Jats of south-east Punjab chiefly through Chhotu Ram not only won for him support in terms of seats in the council but did much to project him as a secular leader.

Fazl-i-Husain's success can also be seen in light of the British policy of creating a dependable political mechanism in rural Punjab. The most important feature of the political mechanism that emerged as a result of the 1919 Act was that political rules and norms that came to govern Punjab's politics were focussed almost totally for the benefit of the financially and socially important sections of society. As already seen the people who composed the 'Rural Block' belonged exclusively to the highly privileged sections of Punjab society. For representatives of any mass-based party like the Congress to compete for the votes of the elite of Punjab who also had the support of the powerful British bureaucracy was pre-ordained to failure.

The Unionist Party as we have seen was born soon after the formation of the 1923 Legislative Council.[81] Of its 39 initial members, 32 were Muslims, the remaining 7 were Hindus and Sikhs. The reality of having been born far away from the ground political actualities of Punjab and within the 'sacred' confines of the Legislative Council gave to the Unionist Party a flawed foundation. This elitist and feudal image as we would see stuck to the party for the rest of its short life. It would prove an important impediment in the course of its attempt to become a popular, mass party.

The party having been formally launched was guided by its two important leaders, Fazl-i-Husain and Chhotu Ram. The new political programme and ideology which was launched briefly said:

> the new party would improve the condition of the peasantry, backward classes and backward communities living in rural Punjab. It would stand against the exploitation of moneylenders and strive to improve the life in rural areas and by opening rural dispensaries, primary schools, high schools, cooperative societies, intermediate colleges, veterinary dispensaries, panchayati system and small committees.[82]

The early emphasis of the Unionist Party leaders on rural development was a foresighted decision, keeping in view the demographic composition of Punjab's population which was 89.7 per cent rural as already seen in Table 1.2.

That the Unionists benefited significantly in many elections that followed on the rural development card stands clearly established. However, it also appears that even the British were bound to benefit from a rural bias in development because the more informed and politically conscious urban population would get further estranged from the rural leaders. There is also some evidence to believe that Fazl-i-Husain himself was critical of Sir Michael O'Dwyer's attempts to encourage the rural versus urban syndrome which aimed to reduce the political importance of the educated classes of urban Punjab.[83] The situation must have been fairly alarming, leading Fazl-i-Husain to comment:

It was not their intention or objective to pull back the urban areas but to improve the condition of the rural areas and bring them at par with the urban areas. It was never intended to stop urban progress. It (Unionist Party) could not be anti-urban, merely because it was their policy that when there was little money for developmental activity and there were two rival schemes, one for urban progress and the other to take the first step towards development in rural areas, a preference was to be shown to the rural scheme. No urban area could remain to be bad. Neglect of one was bound to show on the other as they are interdependent.[84]

That a large section of important urban elite particularly among the Muslims accepted Fazl-i-Husain's point of view is evident from the fact that influential urban leaders like Abdul Qadir, Sheikh Din Mohammad, Sheikh Abdul Ghani, Sheikh Muhammad Sadiq, Khwaja Mohammad Yusuf, and Sheikh Faiz Mohammad joined his party.[85]

The second important feature of the Unionist Party's early and formative political ideas was its emphasis on making Punjab a cradle of communal harmony.[86] Such a policy from Fazl-i-Husain's point of view may possibly have been dictated by political compulsions at the outset. But later intended or not, this image somehow managed to stick to the party right up to the end. In the turbulent decade of the 1940s this secular and well meaning harmonious image of the party was all that was left with it in terms of achievement.

In the broader perspective the political ideology projected by the Unionists in these early years was to attain dominion status, not by confrontation and disruption, but by constitutional methods. It demanded provincial autonomy. It stood for economy in administration in the province and at the centre. It favoured freedom of speech and thought. It wanted the tax network not to be broadened, essentially meaning that the rich in the rural areas should not be covered by taxes. It also stressed that income from taxes must be fairly and equally spent.[87] In this sense the very fact that economic issues came on the political agenda and even started taking priority over communal issues was perhaps the most significant contribution of the Unionist leaders in these early years of the party's existence.

Fazl-i-Husain was appointed Minister (Education) on 20 December 1923, but after Sir Malcolm Hailey joined as Governor of Punjab (31 May 1924) his influence was considerably contained because the governor was surprised to note that, 'a minister who was merely incharge of a few departments and who should be behaving as an obedient driver of the state vehicle, should behave as if he owned it'.[88]

The tussle between the governor and Fazl-i-Husain came out in the open on the issue of the election of the first President of the Legislative Council. Following some political manipulation, Fazl-i-Husain's candidate Abdul Quadir outvoted Gokul Chand Narang who was believed to have had the concealed support of the governor.[89] The incident merely underlines the fact that Fazl-i-Husain's influence and position in the politics of Punjab was well established.

The 'Rural Block' which was later renamed as the Punjab National Unionist Party was the brainchild of a leading and influential Muslim Rajput barrister of Punjab, Sir Fazl-i-Husain . The 'Rural Block' was a superficially united body of 35 Muslim members of the first Punjab Legislative Council (1920). Far from acting or working as a political party, members of the 'Rural Block' were together initially only in the sense that most of them were from rural Punjab and had common vested interests, chiefly, the preservation of the existing economic and political power structure in rural Punjab. The political formation also enjoyed the support and the goodwill of the British administrative system.

This goodwill and support for the big landlords, influential *biradari* leaders and other feudal lords was generously provided, partly to establish a loyal, effective and influential buffer between the administration and the masses as also to keep the peasantry of rural Punjab within satisfied control because a large section of the British Indian Army was recruited from Punjab.

The 1919 Act which led to the creation of the Legislative Council, actually pretended to provide substantial political relief, but in reality it simply prompted forward those sections of society who were already in some form or the other indebted towards the colonial state.

The genesis of the Unionist Party can also be traced to the changing scenario, economic and political environment of Punjab during the first two decades of the twentieth century. This change was initiated by a network of complex and interwoven factors, among the important ones being the influence of ex-servicemen who returned from the West after the First World War. Western education, growth of middle class, the print media, impact of the national movement all combined to spread awakening in rural Punjab.

The gradual but increasing association of the common peasantry with the elite of rural and urban Punjab society presented a remarkable paradox. This happened only because the peasantry of Punjab in its search for a secure future, free from the exploitation of the moneylender really had no other choice. It must have been a comic spectacle to see the leaders of a feudal society proclaiming their intention in the Legislative Council to uplift the downtrodden masses. But then the Act of 1919 had made sure that no one but the elite could enter the council. The Unionist Party was in fact born at the top and had little to do in its origin with the 'pains of labour' and the ground realities. In the years of its origin the most remarkable aspect that comes to mind is the impossible ability and nerve of its leaders to bring on one platform the exploiters and the exploited.

The political character of the Unionist Party in the early years swung between open and concealed collaboration. Yet with considerable conviction the principal message transmitted was of a party united on the basis of economic ideas. In spite of its inherent contradictions it created a new political agenda in Punjab, that of rural development, an issue that was destined to influence the politics of Punjab until its partition in 1947.

NOTES

1. Michael O'Dwyer, *India As I Knew It 1885-1925* (London, 1926), pp. 22-70.
2. I. Talbot, *Khizr Tiwana: The Punjab Unionist Party and the Partition of India* (Richmond, 1996), p. 53.
3. The rural emphasis in Punjab's demographic character was not unique to the province, the same was the trend all over India. As for Punjab it can but only partly be explained as being based on a tradition which in turn had its genesis in the fact that Punjab lay on the route of frequent invasions from the north-west. The invading armies during ancient and medieval

times followed tried and tested routes. The vast network of rivers made the opening of new routes not only difficult but risky. The frequent movement of troops after the British took over (in 1849) also discouraged people from moving towards developed urban centres. In the forty years 1881-1921, the urban percentage of population in Punjab in fact showed a decline from 11.9 per cent to 10.3 per cent of the total. The trend of settling beyond the limits of inhabited areas and establishing independent dwelling units outside the villages on the land owned by the family is a common feature in rural Punjab even to-day.

4. See, for example, B.S. Saini, *Social and Economic History of the Punjab 1901-39* (Delhi, 1975).
5. The extraordinarily large size of some individual family landholdings was perhaps the single most important factor for influencing the collaborative attitude of leading political personalities of Punjab. The larger the size of land owned the more dependent the concerned family was on government patronage and support. At the same time the extensive economic clout that was generated by such landholdings enabled the landlords to contain in their influence the people who subsisted on such lands. In some of the western districts of Punjab for example over 90 per cent of the available cultivable land was owned by selected feudal families. See for example, I. Talbot, *Punjab and the Raj 1849-1947* (Delhi, 1989), p. 16.
6. The question of what the ideal size of a landholding is to be economically viable remains unresolved. The viability of agricultural land is greatly, or in fact totally dependent on availability of water and the type of soil. For a province like Punjab with vast variation in the geographical conditions no single parameter could be applicable. In 1921 for example a land holding of even 15 acres on an average was considered insufficient to support a medium sized family. See M.L. Darling, *Punjab Peasant in Prosperity and Debt* (Bombay, 1925, rpt., New Delhi, 1977).
7. H. Calvert, *The Size & Distribution of Land Holdings in Punjab* (Lahore, 1925), p. 206.
8. See Talbot, *Punjab and the Raj*, p. 39; also N. Charlesworth, *British Rule and The Indian Economy* (London, 1982), p. 26. While statistically as suggested here there was a marked growth in the per annum agricultural output between 1891-1921, yet and quite paradoxically this increase does not reflect itself in real terms. This contradictory phenomenon can perhaps be explained by the fact that since about 46 per cent of the total cultivable land was owned by only about 8 per cent of the province's population (as suggested by Calvert) obviously the benefit of increase in annual agricultural output did not benefit about 90 per cent of Punjab's population.
9. While the small size of land holdings was an important factor for the economic plight of the peasantry other causes included poor seeds, system

of crop rotation, etc. According to an enquiry into the causes of debt (Darling, *Punjab Peasant*, pp. 17-20), concluded that in Punjab, debt which averaged Rs. 31 per cultivated acre amounted to Rs. 76 per head of the agriculturist population. It was as much as nineteen times of the total land revenue demand of the province. Money lending in Punjab had grown to become the second most important industry after agriculture. Calvert suggested that the Punjab peasant paid 4 to 5 times more as interest on debt than what they paid as land revenue and water charges, etc. See, his *Wealth and Welfare of the Punjab* (Lahore, 1922), p. 8.

10. Calvert, *Wealth and Welfare*, p. 8.
11. Ibid., pp. 125-8.
12. Ibid., p. 130.
13. Ibid.
14. Ibid.
15. Ibid., p. 271.
16. Ibid., pp. 242-6.
17. For the background of the administrative tradition which produced the Land Alienation Act, see, P.H.N. Vanden, *The Punjab Tradition* (London, 1972); Gurcharan Singh, 'The Punjab Alienation of Land Act 1900: Its Background', *Proceedings Punjab History Conference* (November 1965), p. 175; also N.G. Barrier, 'The Formation and Enactment of the Punjab Alienation of Land Bill (1900)', *The Indian Economic and Social History Review*, vol. II (April 1965), p. 160. The Act, in spite of all the controversy it generated opened an era in the economic history of the Province. See *Punjab Administration Report*, 1901-2, p. 37 (hereafter *PAR*).
18. Throughout the Unionist Party's existence the Act remained the focul point of dispute. Till 1940 it was amended ten times, by Act I of 1907, Act XVIII of 1920, Act I of 1931, Act VII of 1936, Government of India Adoption of Indian Laws Order, 1937, Act II of 1938, Act X of 1938, Act V of 1938, Act VIII of 1938 and Act VIII of 1940.
19. See Shadi Lal, *Commentaries on the Punjab Alienation of Land Act* (Lahore, 1933), p. 1. It provided that agricultural land could not be transferred from an agricultural tribe to a non-agricultural tribe in the execution of a decree. Mortgage which included conditional sale was banned. The Act further provided that all mortgages by agricultural to non-agricultural tribes were illegal excepting in cases where automatic redemption was provided for in the deed of mortgage. It also provided that land could not be leased for more than five years.
20. *Indian Legislative Council Debates*, 27 September 1899, p. 237.
21. Talbot, *Khizr Tiwana*, p. 52.
22. *Punjab Legislative Council Debates*, vol. I, 1921, pp. 455-509 (hereafter *PLCD*).
23. For references to this view see, Azim Husain, *Mian Sir Fazl-i-Husain: A*

Political Biography (London, 1946), pp. 168-9. This being a biography of a father by a son it contains the flaws that must necessarily be overlooked in such a work. But at the same time this very close relation between the biographer and his subject also provides an insight and view that may otherwise not have been possible. I have drawn from this book more specifically because it remains the most authentic work on the founder of the Unionist Party and also because no other work has dealt with the earlier phases of Fazl-i-Husain's life in such detail.

24. *The People*, 12 July 1925.
25. Talbot, *Khizr Tiwana*, p. 4.
26. D. Ludden, *Peasant History in South Asia* (New Delhi, 1989), p. 9.
27. Talbot, *Khizr Tiwana*, p. 5.
28. Ibid., p. 6.
29. Rai Sahib Ch. Anant Ram, a Unionist Party member of the Punjab Legislative Assembly (1937-46) explained how among agrarian communities the cultural and social bond that developed from the ownership of land often overshadowed the differences that emerged from belonging to different communities. He mentioned how Chhotu Ram mastered the art of projecting the cultural common ground of the peasantry. Interview 16 January 1988.
30. Talbot, *Khizr Tiwana*, p. 26.
31. Ibid., p. 53.
32. D. Gilmartin, 'Religious Leadership and the Pakistan Movement in Punjab', *Journal of Modern Asian Studies*, 13, 3 (1979), presents an interesting explanation of how traditional socioreligious leaders like *sajjada nishins* and *pirs* were able to develop important political control over the common Muslim masses more particularly in rural Punjab.
33. Talbot, *Punjab and the Raj*, pp. 21-6, has discussed the effectiveness of the system that enabled *sajjada nishins* and *pirs* to build powerful political clout. He has shown how the objective of building political influence was considerably facilitated by the fact that the place of operation or the headquarter of the *pir* was a highly revered place where ordinary and important material blessings were believed to be securable. The relationship between the *pir* and the *murid* (people) was akin to that of a patron and client, where the latter took an oath of obedience and loyalty to the *pir* and in return was provided access to the *baraka* (charisma).
34. *The Census of India, 1921, Punjab, Part I* (Report), p. 173.
35. Ibid.
36. Ibid.
37. S. Nurullah and J.B. Naik, *A History of Education in India* (Bombay, 1951), pp. 580-1.
38. W.C. Smith, *Modern Islam in India* (London, 1946), p. 193.
39. Ibid.

40. *The Report of the Indian Statutory Commission*, 1929, pp. 247-8.
41. *The Report of the Enquiry Committee on the University of Punjab*, 1933, p. 150.
42. *The Census of India, 1921, Punjab, Part I* (Report), p. 177.
43. Ibid.
44. For detail see K.W. Jones, *Arya Dharma: Hindu Consciousness in 19th Century India* (Berkeley, 1976), pp. 205-11. A passionate debate in the regional press followed the Punjab High Court's pronouncement that the provisions of the Hindu Law of Inheritance were equally applicable to the Sikhs. See for example, *The Tribune*, 7 February 1899. The High Court's intervention followed a petition of the widow of Dayal Singh Majithia (died in 1899) who said the law did not apply to her as she was a Sikh.
45. *The Census of India, 1921, Punjab, Part II* (Report), p. 30.
46. Ibid.
47. Jones, *Arya Dharma*, pp. 205-11. There seems to be some error in the way Jones has calculated the 50 per cent growth in the Sikh population of Punjab between 1901-11. Surely it could not have been so in real terms.
48. G. Pandey, *The Construction of Communalism in Colonial North India* (Delhi, 1990), has discussed revealing how the roots of communal politics were facilitated. While the focus of his work is on Uttar Pradesh in particular, it is equally applicable to Punjab. P. Brass, *Language, Religion and Politics in North India* (Cambridge, 1974), has also dealt with the subject in some detail.
49. See N.G. Barrier and Paul Wallace, *The Punjab Press* (Michigan University, 1970).
50. Talbot, *Punjab and the Raj*, p. 77.
51. Of the 276 newspapers and periodicals in Punjab (1920), 178 were in Urdu, 58 in English, 26 in Gurmukhi and 10 in Hindi. Only 22 of these were dailies, 79 were weeklies and 141 were monthlies. Of the total publications, 162 were published in Lahore alone. Other centres of publication included Simla, Rawalpindi, Lyallpur, Sialkot, Gurdaspur. See *PAR*, 1920, p. 146.
52. The viciousness of the attack often reached fanatical levels. For detail see Jones, *Arya Dharma*, pp. 148-50.
53. See for example Jamail-ud-Din Ahmad (ed.), *Some Recent Speeches and Writings of Mr. Jinnah* (Lahore, 1943), p. 69.
54. For this view see, F.K. Durrani, *The Meaning of Pakistan* (Lahore, 1944), pp. 67, 97.
55. Fazl-i-Husain was born on 14 June 1877 in a Muslim Bhatti Rajput family of Peshawar. His father was Mian Husain Baksh and mother Bibi Ami-ud-din Nisa. He graduated from Government College, Lahore in 1897 and passed the Barrister at Law Examination, joining the Bench in 1901. He later started practice at the High Court in Lahore. For a sketch of career

see Azim Husain, *Mian Sir Fazl-i-Husain: A Political Biography*, pp. 10-125; also Jahanara Shah Nawaj, *Father and Daughter* (Lahore 1971); D.C. Sharma, 'The Truth About Mian Fazl-i-Husain', *The Modern Review*, January 1937. For details of political rise and ideological inclinations see Syed Nur Ahmad, *Mian Sir Fazl-i-Husain* (Lahore, 1936); also Waheed Ahmad (ed.), *Letters of Mian Fazl-i-Husain* and his, *Diary and Notes of Mian Fazl-i-Husain* (both by the Research Society of Pakistan, Lahore, 1976). Extended references are also available on Fazl-i-Husain in numerous other works relating to the period for example, Firoz Khan Noon, *From Memory* (Lahore, 1966), and the numerous works of Talbot on the period including his *Punjab and the Raj*.

56. See Azim Husain, *Mian Sir Fazl-i-Husain: A Political Biography*, p. 124; also Ravinder Kumar, *Essays in the Social History of India* (Delhi, 1983), p. 190.
57. Azim Husain, *Mian Sir Fazl-i-Husain: A Political Biography*, pp. 100-24; also Noon, *From Memory*, p. 98.
58. Azim Husain, *Mian Sir Fazl-i-Husain: A Political Biography,* pp. 100-24.
59. Ravinder Kumar, *Essays in Social History*, p. 190.
60. Noon, *From Memory*, p. 98.
61. Chhotu Ram (1881-1945) was born in village Garhi Sampla, 45 km from Delhi (on Rohtak Road). Being a good student from the very beginning he graduated from the prestigious St. Stephens College, Delhi. He later passed the Law examination and started practice at Rohtak. The period also saw an early association with the Congress and the start of a successful political career.
62. See Y.P. Bajaj, 'Sir Chhotu Ram and His Work' (Ph.D. thesis, Kurukshetra University, 1972), p. 7. This work is essential reading for an insight into the socioeconomic ideas of Chhotu Ram.
63. *The Tribune*, 26 April 1921.
64. Ibid.
65. Ibid., 10 December 1920.
66. *PAR*, 1922, p. 17.
67. Azim Husain, *Mian Sir Fazl-i-Husain: A Political Biography*, p. 125.
68. See Talbot, *Khizr Tiwana,* p. 180.
69. Interview with Ch. Hardwari Lal, 20 December 1995. Hardwari Lal joined the Punjab Civil Service during the Unionist period and worked on various important positions. After independence of India he worked as vice-chancellor of Kurukshetra University and M.D. University, Rohtak and had also been elected to the Haryana Legislative Assembly and the Parliament of India.
70. *PAR*, 1922, p. 17.
71. For details of the complexities that governed these factional ties and feuds see Syed Nur Ahmad, *From Martial Law To Martial Law*, ed. by Craig Baxter (Lahore, 1985), pp. 53-5.

72. *The Tribune*, 11 February 1923.
73. Syed Nur Ahmad, *From Martial Law*, p. 52.
74. *Unionist Party Manifesto*.
75. Interview with Ch. Hardwari Lal, 20 December 1995.
76. *Unionist Party Manifesto*.
77. *The Tribune*, 17 May 1923.
78. Ibid., 6 June 1923.
79. Sir Sunder Singh Majithia (1871-1941) had a long political stint in Punjab. He was first nominated to the Punjab Council in 1909. From 1915 to 1921 he was a member of the Imperial Legislative Council. From 1921 to 1926 he was Member Revenue, of the Executive Council of Punjab. In 1937 he was elected to the Punjab Legislative Assembly as a member of the Khalsa National Party and remained Revenue Minister in the Unionist Government up to his death in 1941.
80. *The Tribune*, 22 May 1923.
81. *PLCD*, vol. VI, 1924, p. 3.
82. Azim Husain, *Mian Sir Fazl-i-Husain: A Political Biography*, p. 153.
83. Ibid.
84. Fazl-i-Husain's testimony to the Hunter Commission, see ibid., p. 157.
85. Fazl-i-Husain, 'Punjab Politics' (rpt.), *Punjab Past and Present*, vol. V-I, April 1971, p. 128.
86. Syed Nur Ahmad, *From Martial Law*, p. 148.
87. *The Indian Quarterly Register*, 1928, vol. II, p. 122.
88. *Jat Gazette*, 15 June 1927, p. 4.
89. Syed Nur Ahmad, *From Martial Law*, p. 54.

CHAPTER 2

Growth of the Unionist Party, 1924-1936

THE ADMINISTRATIVE process witnessed in Punjab during the period 1924-36 was a complex system of supposedly shared authority, more commonly known as 'dyarchy'. The rules of governance laid down by the Act of 1919 provided to the British administrators total discretion of picking and choosing the people with whom they wished to share power. This feature of 'dyarchy' alone implied that the concept of shared power was in fact nothing but a medium through which the British patronized those who supported the colonial edifice. It is amusing to see Unionist Party leaders demanding a more assertive and authoritative share in power, particularly so when we keep in mind the fact that the Unionist Party was itself born under watchful British eyes and supervision. For a political party born under colonial influence and composed chiefly of privileged sections of society with deep vested interests, whatever little sharing of power was offered by the British in Punjab it was accepted by the recipients with gratitude.

The basic objective of the British through the new political scheme was to ensure that political power was enjoyed only by landowners. Only members of agricultural tribes were eligible to stand from rural constituencies. This policy clearly divided the people into rural and urban compartments.[1]

Notwithstanding the limitations that emerged from the inherent character of the Unionist Party as also those that were imposed by the operational rules of 'dyarchy', its leaders continued their efforts in search of political responsibility and authority. The first important step taken in the direction was on 11 July 1924, when Firoz Khan Noon[2] explained the political programme and objectives of the

Unionist Party. He said that in principle the party was not against the continuance of British rule but wanted autonomy at an early date. The cornerstone of the party's political programme Noon stated was the development of rural areas and the enhancement of the rural population's interests. He said that there must be economy in administration and a judicious and proportionate distribution of developmental expenditure and growth of self-governing bodies. There was also a reference in Noon's statement to the desire of the party to grow as a secular political organization.

The views of Firoz Khan Noon are significant because from them it appears that even in the early years the Unionist Party was projecting an image and ideology that appeared to be crystallized. The reduction of revenue, the burden of debt, rural development, protection of economic interests of small and big agriculturists were agenda issues on the basis of which the Unionist Party chalked out its political future.

Even though the level of success that the Unionist Party managed under the electoral provisions of the Act of 1919 was no indicator of its popularity yet it is evident that the Unionists were able to strike a warm note in the heart of the Punjab peasantry. The single most important cause for this early popularity was the pro-rural politics adopted by its leaders. A brief reference to some of the important work taken up and issues raised by the Unionist Party during its early period (1924-36) is thus being made in order to understand in a better perspective the background of the party and the factors that were mainly responsible for its progress and popularity.

Education received special attention of the Unionist Party leaders during the early years.[3] The overall expenditure on education by the Punjab government increased from Rs. 215.5 lakhs in 1922 to Rs. 288.00 lakhs in 1926-7.[4] The number of students in primary and vernacular schools increased from 5,46,130 and 1,31,475 respectively in 1922 to 7,97,713 and 3,42,841 in 1926.[5] The growth in the number of adult students was from 1,72,776 in 1922, to 98,467 in 1926. The number of such schools showed a remarkable increase from 630 in 1922 to 3,900 in 1926.[6] Punjab came to be ranked the third highest in the country in the context of school education after Madras and Bombay.[7]

Institutions of local government like the Panchayats and the Municipal Committees too received special attention. Panchayats were made statutory.[8] In 1925, District Boards came to have elected chairmen in place of nominated ones. Four Acts were initially passed to raise the number of elected members, to provide more powers and have elected chairmen of these committees.[9] The result of these amendments was that by 1926, 72 per cent members in the 105 municipalities of Punjab were elected. The percentage of people working as official chairmen came down from 86 per cent in 1923 to about 41 per cent in 1926.[10]

The period also saw considerable increase in public and medical care expenditure in rural areas. Most of the increased funds were allocated to new health facilities and drinking water. One civil and veterinary dispensary came to be provided in a radius of 5 km of every village.

The burden of debt on the Punjab peasantry was an issue used by the Unionist Party leaders to woo large sections of people to their cause. The support received on this basis provided the material to help it build its political platform. According to an estimate the prevalence and quantum of debt in Punjab was the highest in India during the period 1923-6.[11] Another estimate shows that capital invested in the business of money-lending in Punjab was greater than what was invested in trade and industry.[12] The government on its part did not help, in fact its taxation policy which was especially harsh only served to worsen the situation. Almost 90 per cent of government revenue came from agriculture.[13] In 1925-6 the peasants of Punjab paid Rs. 13.5 crores as interest alone on his debt. This pathetic condition is further underlined by the fact that a large section of the debt was incurred by the peasantry for the payment of revenue.[14]

The first important step towards decreasing the burden of debt was taken in 1924 with the introduction of the Punjab Moneylenders' Bill, 1924.[15] This Bill proposed to provide protection to the agriculturists against exploitation by unscrupulous moneylenders. The Bill provided for a statutory maintenance of account books and a penal clause for violations of the provisions. The Bill attracted much opposition, discussion and controversy.[16] Lala Lajpat Rai called it 'mischievous'.[17] Gokul Chand Narang said it would destroy legitimate trade.[18] However, the Act received widespread support from rural members of the council. It was later reintroduced as 'The Punjab Borrowers Protection Bill', in December 1925. This time the Bill was attacked by its opponents as a communal measure. The Unionists defended it by saying it had no bias against any community, and was a long over-due economic and political necessity.[19] The Bill had, once again to be reframed as the 'Punjab Regulation of Accounts Bill', so as to be finally passed by the council on 7 July 1926.[20] It could not be implemented however as the Governor vetoed it on the excuse that he would enforce the important provisions of the Bill in some other way.[21]

For the Unionists, even though it was a setback on the floor of the council, but politically it won the party sympathy in rural Punjab. But even more importantly in the political context the content of debates and other developments related to the Bill proved to be a sort of pointer to the future trend of politics in Punjab which was gradually assuming on most issues the colour and dimension of a urban versus rural divide. This was a trend perhaps encouraged consciously by some of the important Unionist leaders as the political fallout from such a division was bound to favour the Unionist Party.

An important measure that drew the Unionist leader's attention during the period 1923-6 was the need to augment irrigation facilities. Though nothing concrete was to emerge for a long time, the process was started when Fazl-i-Husain accompanied by Firoz Khan Noon and Sunder Singh Majithia visited Rohtak during 1925-6.[22] The farmers presented them a memorandum urging them to start the Bhakra Project.[23] They got the proposal scrutinized and were able to persuade the government to send a special officer to the USA in 1926 to study the feasibility of the project.[24] Even though the scheme took a long time to be implemented, the Unionists, mainly Chhotu Ram kept the issue alive.[25] Similar was the case of the Thal Project which was first conceived of in 1901. It was through the efforts of the Unionists that the government agreed to pursue this project. A sum of cost Rs. 2.95 crores was spent on it in 1924.[26] The project was finally completed in 1942 and irrigated almost 1.5 million acres.[27]

The Unionist members of the council also put pressure on the government to create infrastructure to assist the agriculturist in disposing his produce.[28] Unfair practices in the trade of agricultural commodities were fairly common.[29] The result was the introduction of the Punjab Agricultural Marketing Bill in 1925. Through the Bill it was proposed to check corrupt trade practices by imposing penalties on violations. The Bill was, however, vetoed by the governor[30] and could be adopted after reintroduction only after 1937.

Like the Punjab Regulation of Accounts Bill (1926) the introduction of the Punjab Land Revenue Amendment Bill (1926) too was of considerable significance from the agriculturists' point of view. It was a major initiative demanding reduction in land revenue from 50 per cent to 25 per cent. The Government of India opposed the proposal of the Punjab Legislative Council on the ground that it was biased towards the rural areas. Finally, the Bill was moved as the Punjab Land Revenue Bill, with provision of reducing the demand of revenue from 50 per cent to 33 per cent. Later with some modifications like the essential involvement of the legislature in the future framing of any such legalizations,[31] the Bill was passed by the council but was vetoed by the Governor Sir Malcolm Hailey mainly on the ground that the Government of India was not inclined to accept it.

As can be seen from the issues raised by Unionist Party Legislative Council members in the 1923 Council and also from the nature and content of the debates that the council stood divided on the basis of a strong pro-rural bias among Unionists on one hand and those opposed to them on the other. This coalition of economic interests revolved around the big landholders. It is significant to note that such policy stands won the Unionist Party friends even among the small landholders and self-cultivating peasants. Even while the party was being led by feudal lords and landholders, its pro-rural bias, however, vested it might have been enabled the Unionist Party to strike root in the hearts of rural Punjab. This peculiar and paradoxical factor alone was to go a long way in assisting the Party in future trials of political strength and conflict in the 1930s.

Some other developments during the period 1923-6 also highlight the growing influence of the Unionist Party. The defeat of the governor's nominee for the council president's position as also the strong coalition on economic issues reflected in the debates over the 'Moneylenders' Bill and the Revenue Bill were pointers to the new power of the Unionist Party. Henceforth, politics in Punjab, whatever its character, collaborative, casteist, region-based or opportunistic, was to remain dominated by the Unionist Party right through to 1944-5. In many ways the type of political system that the Unionist Party initiated during the years 1923-6 ultimately provided a counterbalance to the Indian National Congress in Punjab. It was a condition that the British effectively exploited to their advantage.

The 1923 Punjab Legislative Council was dissolved in October 1926 and was reconstituted after fresh elections held in November 1926. Fazl-i-Husain had in between joined the Viceroy's Executive Council. His absence was a serious handicap for the Unionists in the elections that ensued. Internal dissension and intrigue created a situation in which the candidates were left to resolve their disputes among themselves. Quite in line with its opportunistic character, the winning candidates were often accepted as the party's own candidates.[32] The party had little place for policies, programmes and ideologies with its politics being dominated by individual personalities with subjective aims and vested interests. The main reason for the Unionist Party having done well in spite of major flaws was that political parties opposing it in Punjab were scarcely better.

The Congress in Punjab, for example was overshadowed with serious internal differences. From amongst its leading stalwarts, Lajpat Rai and Neki Ram Sharma formed the independent Congress Party (Nationalist Party).[33] Even otherwise leading Congressmen were frequently involved in opposing each other. Lala Lajpat Rai and Neki Ram Sharma both strongly criticized the Swarajists. Lala Lajpat Rai in his speeches, for example, exhorted voters not to support the Swarajists as they did not have a clearcut policy[34] and even charged Moti Lal Nehru with having collected money for the Swaraj Party by improper means.[35] Madan Mohan Malaviya also dwelt on similar themes in his election speeches. On the other hand Moti Lal Nehru criticized Lala Lajpat Rai for misleading the Hindus.[36]

With leading Congressmen having chosen different political platforms and perpetually attacking each other, the condition of the party could not have been worse.

The Congress was in such a pathetic condition mainly due to internal bickering and dissensions, but it was also because of a total lack of understanding of the ground realities that prevailed in rural Punjab. The influence of the party was almost totally restricted to the interest of the urban middle class. Its stand vis-a-vis The Punjab Regulation of Accounts Bill in particular, enabled and encouraged the rural legislators who had come to be associated with the Unionist Party to brand the Congress as a party of 'Banias' (businessman). It was more a crisis of identity, an identity of which the Congress in Punjab could never rid itself. In any case this peculiar situation of being mistrusted totally by the peasantry and somewhat reservedly by the urban business classes was essentially of its own making.

With little political significance, the condition of the other political formations was as bad. The Sikh League had aligned with the Congress. The Khilafat Committee could put up only six candidates in the election including Dr Mohammad Iqbal.[37] The Hindu Mahasabha however participated in the election in full strength though its influence was essentially restricted to urban areas.

The election results clearly showed that the elitist electorate had rejected the Congress with the Hindus going almost en masse to the Hindu Mahasabha leaving the Congress to win only two seats. Almost likewise the Muslims voted for the Unionist Party. In a way the election was meaningless in the sense that as already seen the

TABLE 2.1: PARTY POSITION IN PUNJAB LEGISLATIVE COUNCIL, 1926

Party	No. of seats won
Unionist Party	31
Hindu Mahasabha	12
Central Sikh League	11
Khilafat Committee	3
Congress	2
Independents	12
Total	71

SOURCE: Yadav, *Elections*, p. 61.

electoral college was highly restricted and those involved in this particular election formed less than 4 per cent of the adult population of the state. Even so, for the Unionists it was a step forward. Their success can be attributed mainly to the support of the 'traditional' Muslim leaders. The Hindu votes polled by the Unionists Party were mainly from the areas of south-east Punjab where Chhotu Ram's influence was growing rapidly.

The council that was formed comprised a number of leading landlords[38] and other influential men with a record of proven loyalty towards British rule. The urban *versus* rural division which had manifested itself in the previous council (1923), was further underlined by the election results of the 1926 council. Likewise the highly surcharged communal atmosphere in which the elections had been fought appeared to influence the compositions of the new council as well as the political attitude of some of the new members. The fact that just two of the Unionist Party's thirty-one members in the council were non-Muslims further added to the problem.

The most notable feature of this council's functioning was the partisan and remarkably negative role of Malcom Hailey, the Governor of Punjab. He deviated from the accepted norm of nominating ministers from one (largest) party, and instead, on a technical pretext of fair communal representation appointed Firoz Khan Noon, Sardar Joginder Singh[39] and Sir Manohar Lal,[40] as ministers thereby including representatives of the three major communities in Punjab. While Fazl-i-Husain was keen for Chhotu Ram's inclusion in the cabinet, some Hindu members of the council for different reasons were against his inclusion. Some considered him too secular and even pro-Muslim, others thought of him as casteist, finding fault with him for his pro-rural attitude.[41] In sum, Hailey managed to keep out of the cabinet a man who rarely hesitated in opposing anything that was anti-rural or anti-agriculturists. Chhotu Ram had also developed a reputation of fearless frankness and frequently caused embarrassment to the government as also to his colleagues in the party.

The manner in which the governor nominated the ministers to the cabinet made a mockery of the principles of party government and served to further aggravate the divisions on communal lines in the council. A disgusted Fazl-i-Husain wrote later that government policy was responsible for there being no leader in any community. 'As soon as government officials found an Indian wielding influence, the tendency is to counteract his influence. This has come to be a government policy. Ministers cannot really be useful if their position is no better than that of a glorified Tehsildar, to do the bidding of the government.'[42]

The policy followed by Hailey was in line with British interest. By appointing Sir Manohar Lal for example, the govenrment won over the urban Hindus, thereby weakening the Congress. In a way, in doing so he reciprocated the softer and more conciliatory policy adopted by the Hindu National Party towards the government. Hailey was also perhaps aware that a large section of the Unionists were in any case greatly dependent on the government's patronage and support and would therefore be disinclined to annoy the government. The third Punjab Legislative Council was thus in essence successfully converted into a 'loyal council' with most of its members being taken for granted. The Unionists were left with the option of only working as a 'friendly' opposition in the council, with Sir Chhotu Ram as chief spokesman. On the political status of the party in 1927, Chhotu Ram, commented: 'the party was neither in power nor out of power'.[43]

Even though the influence of the Unionist Party members in the council was considerably curtailed by the policies of Governor Hailey, some Unionist members frequently raised important issues and often managed to secure some measure of relief. Like in the previous council, they pursued the government to improve the quality of education by opening more primary and secondary schools.[44] Demands were also raised in the council to curtail the funds of the Public Library, Lahore so as to divert more funds for rural libraries.[45] Some of these legislators put pressure on the government to be more considerate towards the facility of education in rural areas. In 1927 for example, Chhotu Ram demanded proportional admission to Medical College, Amritsar, for rural boys particularly from the backward Ambala division.[46] They also opposed the proposal of the government to increase the duration of the medical course from four to five years on the plea that rural students would find it even more difficult to bear the cost of longer stays in the colleges.[47] The Unionists further urged the government to grant half fee concession to students of backward areas.[48] Such proposals evoked strong opposition and heated arguments not only in the council but even outside. Lala Lajpat Rai for example said, 'medical colleges cannot be started in villages, villages cannot be preferred to cities in the spread of education'.[49]

Reduction in land revenue, however, remained the main agenda of Unionist politics in this council. A resolution moved by Sikander Hayat proposing among other things the abolition or reduction of revenue on very small holdings, relief to *barani* lands and categorization of lands as *barani* was an important initiative towards providing relief to the small peasant. This proposal was however defeated in the council by one vote,[50] after a prolonged and enthusiastic debate.

Unionist legislators also demanded that agriculturist revenue payers have a say in its spending in proportion to their contribution.[51] By implication this meant more financial resources for rural development. Some Unionists also opposed provincial contributions to the central exchequer as this practice starved the provinces of funds.[52] The Unionist members frequently raised many other issues, for example better rural representations in services, more medical facilities and sanitation facilities for rural areas, more banks and societies for development of agriculture and the consolidation of landholdings.

Perhaps the most important achievement of the Unionists in this council was the passage of the Punjab Land Revenue (Amendment Bill). This Bill had been vetoed by the governor in the previous council but this time it was introduced in the council as a Government Bill. In essence the Bill proposed reduction of land revenue from 33 per cent to 25 per cent. Chhotu Ram wanted to add a clause that would enable the government to exempt the small farmer from revenue. His suggestion was however opposed and defeated by the big landlords in the council. The debate on the Bill exposed for the first time in a significant manner the self-seeking approach of some components of the Unionist Party. So much so that Chhotu Ram's proposal was opposed even by his friend and senior colleague, Fazl-i-Husain, while ironically Chhotu Ram's arch opponent Lala Lajpat Rai, found his suggestion 'fair and just'.[53] The myth that big landlords mainly belonging to the Unionist Party were keen to improve the monetary condition of the common peasantry was set aside by this debate in the council. The Bill was passed on 11 May 1928,[54] mainly backed by the Unionists, it secured the governor-general's assent on 12 February 1929, after a strong recommendation of the Punjab government. The Bill was a boon to the farmers of Punjab.[55]

Another important legislative measure that had far-reaching implications and that proved of great benefit to the debt-ridden agriculturists of Punjab, was the passage of the Punjab Regulation of Accounts Bill. A similar Bill had earlier been refused assent by the governor after being passed by the previous council. It was reintroduced by the government on 26 July 1927. Once again the Bill was opposed mainly by leaders of the business community in the council but it was however passed in December 1929 and was enforced from July 1931. The delay in its implementation was partly due to pressures of the moneylenders' lobby.

It needs to be emphasized that while Unionist legislators frequently gave the impression of assertively seeking benefits for the people but in fact their effort was to a great extent motivated by personal benefits. In no case did they operate in any sort of opposition or were in a mood to challenge the might of the government. On the contrary, leading Unionist stalwarts were enjoying extensive perks as a result of generous British patronage. The best example of the Unionist Party's politically supportive attitude emerged when it openly and officially welcomed the Simon Commission[56] to Punjab. Even after Lala Lajpat Rai had been seriously injured in the agitation while opposing the Simon Commission the Unionists in the council opposed a resolution that demanded an inquiry into the assault on him (Lajpat Rai). The Unionist Party's stand with regard to the Simon Commission clearly underlined the view that the Unionists were merely pretending to adopt a politically confrontationist stand while raising various kinds of demands and administrative amendments but in reality were in no mood to oppose the government.

TABLE 2.2: PARTY POSITION IN PUNJAB LEGISLATIVE COUNCIL, 1930

Party	No. of seats won
Unionist Party	37
Nationalist Progressive Party	20
Independent and Others	14
Total	71

SOURCE: Yadav, *Elections*, p. 67; also *The Tribune*, 12 September 1930.

Elections to the 1930 Punjab Legislative Council were subdued and lack-lustre. The Nationalist Progressive Party led by Raja Narender Nath was the only important political organization apart from the Unionists in the field of contestants. The lack of interest in the proceedings of the election is apparent from the fact that of the total of 71 seats in the Council, 38 were returned unopposed.[57]

The formation of the new council once again saw the emergence of a predominantly feudal character. The Unionist Party which had from its very inception been faction-ridden witnessed an open conflict between different factions of the party for the post of a minister.[58] The Ahmad Yar Khan Daultana group was opposed to Shahab-ud-din's continuance in the cabinet, the group was instead supporting the claim of Firoz Khan Noon. The dispute disgusted and saddened Fazl-i-Husain who remarked that 'personal squables have hurt me more than anything else in recent years'.[59] The choice for this post was finally left to the governor, who chose Firoz Khan Noon and Sikander Hayat Khan[60] from the Unionist Party, Sardar Joginder Singh (non party) and Gokul Chand Narang of the Nationalist Progressive Party.[61] Once again Fazl-i-Husain was upset by the exclusion of Chhotu Ram and remarked 'that Government is caring more for peace than principle. . . . This policy has retarded the development of parties.'[62] Of all the influential Unionists, Chhotu Ram alone belonged to an ordinary peasant family, a fact that gave him a remarkable understanding of ground level problems which he used to outstanding effect in raising issues with the government. It was this fact which repeatedly made him somewhat unpopular among the British bureaucracy.

The 1930 Legislative Council and the ministry that followed also saw the emergence of a formidable alternative power centre in the Unionist Party. Sikander Hayat emerged as an important claimant to the top position in the party, backed fully by the network of his *biradari*, the Hayats of 'Wah'. The growing influence of Sikander Hayat weakened in proportion the hold of Fazl-i-Husain. A disheartened Fazl-i-Husain later remarked that 'Punjab affairs are all topsy turvey, some people have been too selfish and personal . . . the effect of this on Hindu and Sikh members of the party is bad . . .'.[63] Of Sikander Hayat in particular, he was sharply critical: 'Sikander has neither the power nor the inclination to produce unanimity and is not likely to sink his . . . differences for . . . personal advancement . . . is better than others because . . . his actions are less outrageous than the other two.'[64]

The term of the fourth council also coincided with the economic depression that had engulfed the world at the time. In Punjab, the effects of depression were the worst for the middle and small agriculturists. The fall in agricultural prices greatly increased the burden of debt, leading to more sale and mortgage of land.[65] For leaders like Chhotu Ram, the plight of the peasantry provided an added opportunity to pressurise the government into granting financial relief.

On 11 May 1931, Chhotu Ram made a memorable speech[66] in the council while moving a resolution to grant a special remission of land revenue and *abiana* for the year 1931, leading to the passage of the motion. On the persistent pleas of Chhotu Ram in particular in the three years 1930-3, the government allowed the remission of Rs. 265 lakhs in land revenue and irrigation tax in addition to the Rs. 200 lakhs remitted under existing rules of damage to crops.[67] The south-eastern districts of Punjab on his pursuance received an additional remission for about Rs. 20 lakhs in the Rabi season of 1934.[68]

As in the previous councils, the Unionists pleaded for more grants in rural education and female education, frequently opposing the sharp reduction in the education budget of 1932-3, and having it restored the following year.[69] The growth of primary education and the number of schools in rural areas can partly be credited to the

Unionist members' effort in this direction. The number of such schools showed a remarkable increase to 2300 in 1936 from a mere 153 in 1922-4.[70]

But the most important legislative measure undertaken by the council on the initiative of the Unionists, mainly Chhotu Ram was the passage of the Punjab Relief of Indebtedness Bill.[71] As a result of the combined effects of the depression years and bad crops, the debt on the Punjab peasantry had reached Rs. 92 per head in 1934, being by far the highest in the country.[72] According to provisions of the Act, interest on the loan amount was to be lowered. In no case was the amount of interest to exceed the principal amount. The Act provided for the introduction of the rule of *Dandupat* by which a creditor could not take more interest than the principal amount. The Act also provided that temporarily alienated land of the debtors could not be auctioned for recovery, nor could a debtor be arrested for non-payment. Besides, the word agriculturist under the Act was to include all landlords, labour and owner-tenants.[73] While this important Bill was sponsored by the government, it was strongly supported by the Unionists. Once again the speech of Chhotu Ram in defence of the Bill was widely acclaimed and made a deep impression on the members. In a way Chhotu Ram alone gave to the Unionists, a soul of consideration towards the poverty-stricken and debt-ridden peasantry: '. . . it is intended to benefit those teeming millions who are strangers to two square meals a day. It is the man behind the plough who will benefit by this legislation.'[74] Chhotu Ram strongly criticized the moneylenders and other opponents while defending the Bill in the Council.[75] The Bill was passed on 30 November 1934.

Another measure initiated to provide protection to debtors was the Debtors Protection Act, 1936[76] which in fact was a supplement to the above Relief of Indebtedness Act of 1934. This Act too was strongly defended by Chhotu Ram in particular and opposed mainly by leaders of the urban business community, particularly M.L. Puri. This Act provided that ancestral property owned by the successor of a debtor could not be liable for execution of a decree for a debt of the owner's predecessor. The Act also stated that sufficient property was to be left in the ownership of a debtor so that his family could subsist and in no case was alienation of land as a result of the execution of a debt decree to exceed 20 years. The most thoughtful provision in the new Act was its provision that crops, cattle, trees were exempted from the execution of a decree. In the history of providing relief to the peasantry from debt, this Act was undoubtedly a major milestone. In the framing of its provisions and in their defence Chhotu Ram revealed his outstanding legal acumen, oratory and above all his genuine concern for the peasantry.

In the context of industrial development, the Unionist members, mainly Chhotu Ram emphasized on the government the need to develop agriculture-based industry.[77] The main thrust was on small scale rural industry so as to decrease the pressure on agricultural land.[78] During the term, Unionist members also raised in the council many other important issues like inclusion of Scheduled Castes in the provision of Debt Conciliation Boards, jobs for youth from agricultural communities, reduction in land revenue and preventing import of foodgrain so that the Punjab farmers as a whole could benefit from good prices.

The true political character of the system that operated in Punjab during the term of the four Legislative Councils, 1920, 1923, 1926 and 1930 reflected remarkably well the unsoundness and duality of the system known as 'dyarchy'. From the Unionist Party's point of view, it could be said that they were never really in power nor out of it. A number of proposals put forward by Unionist members were implemented by the government, but the Unionists also quite often functioned as the main opposition in the council. The catalystic role of this opposition was usually performed by Chhotu Ram from amongst the Unionists. In many ways Chhotu Ram was a kind of conscience keeper of the party and never let pass an opportunity to point out flaws in the British administrative system.

Even though not much needs to be seen in these voting patterns but of the total of 345 votes caste against the government by members of the council in 1931-2, the Unionist members had cast 200 of them.[79] Similarly in 1932-3 of the total of 283 votes cast in the council against the government 255 were cast by the Unionist members.[80] In the same year, of the total of six defeats faced by the government in the council the Unionists were responsible for three of them.[81] In

1933-4 of the total 96 votes cast against the government in the council, the Unionist members cast 51 of them.[82] In 1933-4 three defeats were experienced by the government, the Unionists were responsible for all the three.[83] However at the same time all the anti-government votes apart, most of the Unionist members in all the four councils were critically dependent for their political influence and economic well-being on government patronage.

From its origin in 1923 up to 1936 the Unionist Party made substantial progress. Some of its policies were perhaps responsible for this, but considerable assistance was provided to the Unionists not only by the British administration in Punjab but also by the fact that the other political parties in Punjab were engulfed in problems which enabled the Unionist Party to have a clear ground. Some important factors that contributed to the growing popularity and strength of the Unionist Party between 1923-36, need to be briefly explained.

The success or failure of any political party is greatly dependent on the people whom it chooses to focus its attention. When Fazl-i-Husain chose to create his political edifice on the Muslims of rural Punjab in particular and adorn it with representative elements of non-Muslim communities he was in fact only taking the safest and the most obvious road. To strengthen his grip over the Muslim population of rural Punjab he was able to get hold of the traditional leaders among the Muslims, the landowners, *pirs, sajjada nishins* and others who formed a sort of patron-client mechanism with their followers for the benefit of the Unionists.

That the Unionists did not initially employ religious idioms to build their support base was again a decision dictated by ground realities. With just about 51 per cent population being Muslim, it was essential to garnish support from other communities. This compulsion rooted in Punjab's demographic character led to the projection of an economic policy which was attractive to powerful and influential people of all rural communities, the basic common bond being government patronage. This helped the Muslim Unionist leaders to bring under their influence traditional Hindu rural leadership especially of the region which is now Haryana on to one political platform alongside the Muslims. In this exercise the Unionist leaders were successful particularly because of the inclination among the peasantry to believe that notwithstanding differences based on reasons of faith, those associated with tilling of the soil did have something extra in common. The appeal by leaders like Chhotu Ram to the peasantry for political support cutting across community and caste lines had a kind of moral and rational strength emerging from the fact that the peasant had similar sociocultural roots and had much in common because of the similarity of economic compulsions.[84] It was a result-oriented prescription prepared after a sound understanding of Punjab's political character.

The Unionist leaders foresightfully built the foundation of their party on the neglected rural majority who formed almost 80 per cent of the population. Even among the rural people the Unionists chose the peasantry for special attention. The landowning peasant because of his economic clout played a major role in rural politics, being the foundation of the village economy. The decision to protect and project the cause of Punjab's rural population on the basis of economic development and growth was thus a calculated political exercise having little chance of failure particularly when the right to franchise was linked to property and social status. The level of success achieved by the Unionist Party was significantly linked to the restrictive nature of the political process which allowed only elite elements of similar social and economic background to emerge. The politics that was practised was restricted to an exclusive club supported by an electorate only marginally lower in hierarchy.

Another factor to which the Unionist success was significantly linked was that the Congress in Punjab 'wore a different shade', and was like a poor country-cousin as compared to its sister organization in other parts of India. Prior to 1929 (Lahore Session) it was predominantly an urban middle-class based party. Even though the Provincial Committee of the Congress had been founded as early as 1886 and the party had district and primary branches throughout the region, yet its influence was minimal.[85] In rural Punjab the Muslim population was totally averse to the Congress and even in the urban areas, the Muslim professional classes shunned it to such an extent that only 49 Muslims were included in the 1893 Indian

National Congress Session at Lahore in a 581 strong Punjab delegation. Only very briefly during the Khilafat movement was the Congress able to win over appreciable Muslim support in the region.

Like the Muslim rural peasantry, the Hindus too generally remained clear of the Congress because of its identification with the moneylenders' interests.[86] Somehow the Congress had conveyed the impression to the Hindu and Muslim cultivators that it did not have their interest at heart. For example, when the Congress leaders of Punjab came out against the Alienation of Land Act (1901), they failed to realize that even with all its shortcomings the Act was considered by a majority of the peasantry as being beneficial to their interests. The ambiguous stand of the Congress placed it in a situation where even the business classes felt let down by the indecisive policy of the Party.[87] The early boost derived by the Hindu Mahasabha was partly a result of its policy of opposing the Alienation of Land Act.[88] In doing so the Hindu Mahasabha was able to wean away a large section of Hindus who would normally have supported the Congress.

The Congress on the whole was also unable to adopt a clear and assertive policy on agrarian matters in the province. Whenever agricultural legislations came to the fore, the Congress found itself in trouble, unable to balance its need for rural support with its existing support in urban areas and the protection required by its urban supporters. While in the United Provinces for example, the party exploited the conditions of the depressed agricultural sections to undermine the landlord supporting parties, in Punjab the Congress remained effectively cut off from the countryside.[89] As a result, it failed to make any inroads into the rural support of the Unionist Party. The Congress also seems to have weakened its position in Punjab when it decided not to contest the Legislative Council elections as part of a broader national policy on the directions of the All India Congress Committee as it lost the initiative particularly to those groups of urban Hindus who argued that their community's interests must be defended in the legislature, at any cost. Included amongst these were leading Arya-Samajists, Gokul Chand Narang, Ruchi Ram Sahni and Gulshan Rai. In Punjab, the political scene had became more a fight between urban and rural areas; rooted in varying economic perspectives the Congress was simply unable to decide on which side of the fence it actually belonged, in the process losing ground on both sides.

The difficulties of the Congress were further aggravated by internal factionalism. The bitter rivalry between the Arya Samaj and the Brahmo Samaj spilled over into it. The Arya faction led by Lala Lajpat Rai competed with Harkishan Lal's Brahmo group for political control of the party. While the national leadership of the Congress was spearheading the fight for freedom from British rule, in Punjab which was in many ways a cornerstone, the party leaders projected a total lack of objectivity. As a result while the conservatives flocked to the Hindu Mahasabha, radicals shifted to the Nau Jawan Bharat Sabha. Until Lala Lajpat Rai's death in 1928, the gap between the Hindu Mahasabha and Congress remained narrow. Thereafter, it widened as Congress leaders such as Duni Chand and Satyapal became vocal in their criticism of the Hindu Mahasabha's communal politics. The dispute rumbled on within the Congress as Lajpat Rai's associate Gopi Chand Bhargava[90] fought a running battle with Satyapal[91] in the ensuing years.

The Lahore Session of the Congress followed some time later by the Civil Disobedience, revitalized the party to some extent.[92] Yet the Congress in Punjab was no match for the political opportunism of the Unionist leaders. Fazl-i-Husain in particular, effectively organized Muslim opinion against Civil Disobedience. On the whole, most Unionist leaders both as a policy and individually strongly supported the government against the Congress-led disobedience movement in Punjab. However, once again Chhotu Ram differed from the party line and opposed a Bill which was supposed to check the Congress agitation against the government.[93] His opposition to the Bill was on the ground that popular rights and individual freedom would be greatly curtailed by provisions of the Bill.[94] Otherwise Chhotu Ram too assisted the government against the disobedience movement in the south-eastern districts of Punjab, a region where he had widespread influence. The Congress influence in Punjab was mainly curtailed by a masterly mix of collaborative politics followed by the Unionists. This policy often exposed the party to mass ridicule but also became the main factor for its growing popularity in that it was an instrument for securing benefit from the government, an essential step for economic advantage.

The Muslim League in Punjab was for most of the period under review only a party of leaders with practically no cadre support.[95] Even the annual sessions of the Punjab Muslim League were mere formalities with poor attendance[96] and utter confusion.[97] As such up to about 1937 the Muslim League could not pose any challenge to the Unionists.[98] In fact in 1936 Fazl-i-Husain had even warned Jinnah not to meddle in Punjab affairs. An angry Jinnah had retorted, 'Fazli thinks he carries Punjab in his pocket. . . . I am going to smash Fazli.'[99] But Jinnah's words obviously lacked political strength, which left him helpless in Punjab throughout the 1930s.

Initially even at the all-India level Muslim politics revolved to some extent around Fazl-i-Husain.[100] This was mainly because of Fazl-i-Husain's contribution in the Communal Awards of 1932.[101] The Award considerably improved the electoral position of the Muslims in Bengal and Punjab. In Punjab for example, the Muslims were allotted 51 per cent seats in the Assembly the Hindus were allotted 27 per cent and the Sikhs 18 per cent. Fazl-i-Husain's role in the sanctioning of the Communal Awards being significant had caused much disillusionment among non-Muslim members of the Unionist Party. Chhotu Ram, for example, took a bold and independent stand against the Award. He strongly criticised both Fazl-i-Husain and Firoz Khan Noon on the issue, saying the Award was against all norms of justice and caused great harm to the political interest of the Hindus.[102] But among the Muslims Fazl-i-Husain gained good political mileage.

Besides the Congress and the Muslim League, the other important political parties in Punjab during the period were the, Kisan Sabha, The Akali Dal, the Hindu Mahasabha and the Majlis-i-Ahrar-i-Islam. The Kisan Sabha attempted to identify itself with the rural poor, calling for extensive reforms in rural taxation and the landholding system. Behind the Unionist Party, it rightfully saw the colonial state propping up the inequalities in Punjabi society. The Kisan Sabha gained a political boost from the economic crisis which came along with the economic depression years of 1930-1. It successfully extended its support in the Jullundur, Amritsar, Sheikhupura and Gujrat districts.[103] It was also able to lead a successful campaign in Hissar in April 1930 against the payment of rents in kind to landowners.[104] Soon afterwards, the Unionists noticing the growing influence of the Kisan Sabha made a strong representations to the Governor to provide relief. Their advice was accepted and the land revenue demand for the 1931 Rabi crop was reduced by 50 per cent. Several other similar remissions were made until 1933. These primitive steps initiated by the government restricted the Kisan Sabha's advance. The Unionists further deflected the cultivators' wrath from the large landowners and the British by blaming the moneylenders for the prevailing distress. The Kisan Sabha, as a result, remained to make little headway except in some Sikh villages of central Punjab.

The Akali Dal also had following the Gurudwara Reforms Movement, become a power to reckon with. In 1925, the Shiromani Gurudwara Prabandhak Committee got complete control of the Gurudwaras.[105] This not only gave the Akalis considerable economic power but also patronage, particularly among the rural Sikhs. The lack of a united resolve inhibited the political growth of the Akalis to a considerable extent. The lesser militants among the Sikh middle class, especially some Jat Sikhs formed their own organization in 1930s, the Khalsa National Party. Sunder Singh Majithia was their main leader. His main intention and ambition remained it appears, a berth in the ministry,[106] which materialized when the Unionists won him over to their side. As a result, a good section of the Sikh peasantry and even the urban middle class began supporting the Unionists on most issues particularly those that related to rural development.

The Majlis-i-Ahrar-i-Islam was founded in 1931 by Chaudhry Afzal Haq. Its nucleus consisted of urban middle class Muslims some of whom were former Congress men and had been associated with the Punjab Khilafat Committee. Its leadership was primarily religious.[107] The Ahrars rose to prominence in the confrontation between the Hindu Maharaja of Kashmir and his Muslim subjects. The Punjab's proximity to the Dogra kingdom and its large Kashmiri community aroused intense feelings among the Muslims about the dispute. The direct action organized by the Ahrars in Kashmir paid great dividends in the form of popularity even in Punjab. They would have won far more political mileage, had it not been for their lack of patience and discipline. Their efforts to win over the religious elements that supported the Unionists failed because they could not build trust among the *sajjada nishins* and other rural religious leaders. Besides their lukewarm attitude to communally flared matters like the Shahidganj Mosque dispute (Lahore, 1935),[108] made them lose considerable support among urban Muslims.

The Hindu Mahasabha was a heterogeneous group of leaders professing different social and religious views, generally belonging to the urban areas. But what was common among them was a desire to safeguard 'Hindu interests'.[109] Lala Lajpat Rai's part association with the organization gave it considerable influence. He exhorted the Hindu electorate to 'elect genuine nationalists, true patriots, and firm Hindus who will not compromise or yield to endanger the Hindu community'.[110] After Lala Lajpat Rai's death, the party lost ground and became ineffective and faction-ridden. As such, like other primarily urban parties the Hindu Mahasabha too could not contain or restrain the Unionist Party from proceeding forward and building upon its political base.

Faced by weak political opponents, the Unionist Party made fair and early political progress. The Unionists made efforts, somewhat pretentious no doubt, to serve and protect the interests of those who formed its social and political base which had been chosen with great care. Besides, they appeared to be secular in their approach to problems of the day and generally kept away from controversial issues. The secular attitude of the Unionist leaders was considerably facilitated by their political appeals which usually stressed the common features of Punjab's rural society rather than the differences. Similarity in cultural ethos, the binding of economic compulsions that grew from activities associated with agriculture provided to the efforts of the Unionist leaders a kind of moral backing. They formed a superficial opposition to the government and opportunistically managed to serve and keep the government in good humour. Hence barring a few occasions, the Unionists on the whole received consistent support from the government.

The very nature of 'dyarchy' was such that the weaker partner or rather dependent partner could be treated with contempt and be kept in or out of power at will, a fact which the British never overlooked themselves, or let the Unionists forget. As a result, during the period 1923-36 the Unionists as a political party were never really in power or out of it. They were neither the opposition nor the government. Yet the peculiar character of the system was such that it permitted the Unionists to influence most political events. Without doubt, they were the most important political organization in Punjab during the period and were destined to influence the destiny of the province in the future.

NOTES

1. Also see Talbot, *Khizr Tiwana*, p. 58.
2. Malik Sir Firoz Khan Noon (1892-1970) was a close friend and political associate of Fazl-i-Husain. He was among the more influential of Muslim elite in Punjab and remained with the Unionist Party from its inception only to drift away and breaking completely just before the 1946 elections, when like a large number of other important Muslim figures he too jumped on to the Muslim League 'bandwagon'. He remained member of the Punjab Legislative Council from 1921-36, India's High Commissioner in London from 1936-41. In 1941 he joined the Viceroy's Executive Council, but resigned in 1945 to campaign for the Muslim League and the cause of Partition. After the formation of Pakistan, he was member of the Punjab Legislative Assembly, 1953-8, Constituent Assembly of Pakistan, 1947-58, governor, East Bengal, 1950-3, chief minister of Punjab, 1953-5, foreign minister of Pakistan, 1956-7 and prime minister for a short while in 1958. See his *From Memory*. He was perhaps the first to present a broad political programme of the Unionist Party. See article by him, 'The Punjab National Unionist Party', *The Tribune*, 30 July 1924.
3. As Chhotu Ram started playing an important role in the decision-making process of the Unionist Party, his paper the *Jat Gazette* (Rohtak) assumed the role of a kind of policy and programme announcement forum. See for example issue of 20 April 1927, p. 3.
4. Ullah Khan, *A History of Education in Punjab*, vol. 1 (Lahore, 1937), pp. 100, 117, 119.
5. Ibid.
6. Ibid.
7. Azim Husain, *Mian Sir Fazl-i-Husain: A Political Biography*, p. 137.
8. Ibid., p. 141.
9. *PLCD*, vol. IX, 23 October 1926, pp. 1769-74.
10. Azim Husain, *Mian Sir Fazl-i-Husain: A Political Biography*, p. 139.
11. The problem of peasant debt in Punjab was of a critical nature. For example while only one out of fifty of British India's inhabitants lived in Punjab,

yet the province's population supported one out of five of British India's moneylenders. In 1934, for example the per capita debt in Punjab was calculated by the government at Rs. 92 per head, whereas in Assam it was Rs. 31, in U.P. Rs. 36, in Bengal Rs. 56. See *PLCD*, vol. XXV, 26 October 1934, pp. 335, 678, 837.

12. *The Tribune*, 12 January 1939.
13. Ibid., 24 September 1939; also *The Punjab Legislative Assembly Debates* vol. XV, 24 January 1941, p. 270 (hereafter *PLAD*). It is estimated that in 1921 the urban tax payer paid Rs. 2.16 as tax per head on an average, whereas the rural tax payer paid Rs. 5.1 per head. See B.B. Mishra, *Administrative History of India, 1934-1947* (Bombay, 1970), p. 404.
14. Darling, *Punjab Peasant*, pp. 18-20:
15. *PLCD*, vol. VII, 18 November 1924, p. 507.
16. *The Tribune*, 7 February 1925.
17. Ibid., 8 April 1926.
18. Ibid., 7 February 1925.
19. *PLCD*, vol. IX, 7 July 1926, p. 1506.
20. Ibid., p. 1544.
21. Azim Husain, *Mian Sir Fazl-i-Husain: A Political Biography*, p. 146.
22. *Jat Gazette*, 20 November 1925, p. 7.
23. For details see Y.P. Bajaj, 'Genesis of the Bhakra Dam Scheme' (1914-48). *Punjab Past and Present*, vol. XI, I April 1977.
24. American experts came to India in November 1927. See ibid., also, *Jat Gazette*, 29 April 1927, p.5.
25. See Y.P. Bajaj, 'Sir Chhotu Ram', p. 173.
26. *PLCD*, Vol. X, 15 March 1927, pp. 455 and 459.
27. Ibid., 12 March 1942, pp. 185 and 255.
28. Though much of the work in this direction was done by the 1937 Unionist government under the '*Mandi* Act', a modest beginning was made in 1924.
29. It was estimated so that the farmer in reality got only about 9 annas for every rupee worth of produce he sold in the market, the rest was pocketed by the commission agent on account of various service charges.
30. *PLAD*, Vol. VIII, 24 September 1939. The Bill was vetoed notwithstanding the fact that later a government-conducted inquiry had found that 49 per cent of weights and 69 per cent of scales which were used by grain merchants to purchase grain were fraudulently incorrect. See *Report Punjab Provincial Banking Enquiry Committee, 1929-30*, vol. I, pp. 219-20.
31. *PLCD*, vol. IX, February 1926.
32. I. Talbot, 'Muslim Political Mobilization in Rural Punjab, 1937-46', in Peter Robb (ed.), *Rural India Land Power and Society Under British Rule* (London, 1983), pp. 245-73.
33. *The Tribune*, 24 October 1926.
34. Ibid., 3 November 1926.

35. Ibid.
36. Ibid., 11 November 1926.
37. Ibid., 8 November 1926.
38. Ibid., 4 August 1924.
39. Sir Joginder Singh (1877-1946) was from the family of the Rasulpuria Chiefs (Amritsar dist.). He remained minister (Agriculture) from 1926-37. He also served as home minister of the Patiala State and was a member of the Viceroy's Executive Council from 1942-6.
40. Sir Manohar Lal (1879-1949), like Joginder Singh was chosen by Governor Haily as minister (Education) in 1926 to represent the Hindu community. He was elected to the Legislative Council and in 1937 to the Assembly from the University Constituency. He was minister from 1926-30 and again from 1937-46. In the Punjab Legislative Assembly Elections of 1946 he was defeated by Gopi Chand Bhargawa.
41. Interview with Ch. Hardwari Lal, 20 December 1995.
42. Waheed Ahmad (ed.), *Diary and Notes of Mian Fazl-i-Husain*, entry of 17 July 1935.
43. *The Tribune*, 8 April 1927.
44. *PLCD*, vol. X, 24 November 1927, p. 1145. In this debate there is sufficient proof to show how keen some of the Unionist legislators were to improve the availability of education. For example, members offered even to 'run schools under trees', but wanted the government to acknowledge and accept the need for more schools.
45. *PLCD*, vol. XV, 7 March 1930, p. 320.
46. Chhotu Ram in fact said in a speech that for boys from distant and unconnected rural areas hoping to get admission into the Medical College at Amritsar was difficult if not impossible. This he said was particularly the case with south-east Punjab (now Haryana), see *PLCD*, vol. X, 18 November 1927, p. 742. In the speech he goes on to explain the problems confronted by youth in rural areas when they aspire for higher education.
47. *PLCD*, vol. XI, 2 February 1928, p. 64. Proposals initiated by Unionists to focus attention of higher education on rural areas were often opposed by important public figures essentially on the ground of the urban rural divide, see *Jat Gazette*, 1 June 1927, p. 8.
48. *PLCD*, vol. X, 23 November 1927.
49. *Jat Gazette*, 1 June 1927, p. 8.
50. *PLCD*, vol. XI, 22 February 1928, pp. 96-7.
51. *Jat Gazette*, 25 May 1927, p. 5.
52. In 1926-7 the Punjab government made a contribution of Rs. 85.73 lakhs, to the Central Exchequer. See *PLCD*, vol. XII, 4 March 1929, p. 628, Direct contribution by the provinces to the Centre was stopped in 1928, but indirectly it continued. See, *Report Indian Statutory Commission, 1929-30*, vol. X (Lahore, 1930), p. 845.

53. *PLCD*, vol. XI, 7 May 1928, p. 969.
54. Azim Husain, *Fazl-i-Husain*, p. 148.
55. *PLCD*, vol. XII, 25 February 1929, p. 381.
56. Ibid., vol. XVIII, 26 February 1931, p. 69.
57. Noon, *From Memory*, p. 113.
58. *Civil & Military Gazette*, 3 September 1930.
59. Husain, *Fazl-i-Husain*, p. 268.
60. Waheed, Ahmad (ed.), *Diary and Notes of Mian Fazl-i-Husain*, p. 102, letter from Fazl-i- Husain to Chhotu Ram (13 October 1930).
61. Sikander Hayat Khan (1892-1942), was after Fazl-i-Husain the second more important among leaders of the Unionist Party. He became Premier of Punjab with the introduction of provincial antonomy (by the Act of 1935) and remained so until his premature death in 1942. He belonged to one of the most important landowning families of west Punjab, 'Hayats of Wah' (then in Attock Dist. now in Rawalpindi). He was elected to the Punjab Legislative Council from the Landholders Constituency in 1921 (later unseated), 1923, 1926 and then to the Punjab Legislative Assembly in 1937. He also had a short period as deputy governor of the Reserve Bank of India. See Lajpat Rai Nair, *Sikander Hayat Khan: The Soldier Statesman of the Punjab* (Lahore, 1943).
62. Gokul Chand Narang (1878-1969) was a member of the 1923, 1926 and 1930 Punjab Legislative Councils and also the 1937 Punjab Legislative Assembly.
63. Waheed Ahmad (ed.), *Diary and Notes of Mian Fazl-i-Husain*, p. 32.
64. Ibid., p. 29.
65. Azim Husain, *Mian Sir Fazl-i-Husain: A Political Biography*, p. 271.
66. See, for example, Hari Singh, *Agrarian Scene in British Punjab*, vol. I (New Delhi, 1983) p. 121.
67. In the speech referred to here Chhotu Ram gave one of his most eloquent performances in the legislature. To drive his point forcefully he projected the peasantry of Punjab as the 'roots of the tree . . ., injuring or ignoring the roots', he said 'would surely kill the (Punjab) tree', see *PLCD*, vol. XIX, 11 May 1931, pp. 370-90.
68. Ibid., vol. XXIII, 2 March 1933, p. 655.
69. Ibid., vol. XXIV, 1 March 1934, p. 386.
70. Ibid., vol. XXVI, 25 February 1935, p. 93.
71. *Annual Report on the Progress of Education in Punjab, 1935-6*, p. 41.
72. *The Punjab Government Gazette 1931*, Part 1, p. 657.
73. *PLCD*, vol. XXV, 28 June 1934, p. 379.
74. *The Indian Annual Register*, vol. I, 1934, pp. 214-16.
75. *PLCD*, vol. XXIV, 28 June 1934, p. 326.
76. Ibid.
77. Ibid., vol. XXVII, 1935, pp. 1135-42.

78. Ibid., vol. XXIII, 11 April 1933, p. 1019.
79. Ibid., p. 53.
80. *Report of the Administration of Punjab, 1931*, p. 32.
81. Ibid., 1932-3, p. 22.
82. Ibid., p. 23.
83. Ibid., 1933-4, p. 19.
84. Interview, Rai Sahib Narsing Das of Village Keorak (dist. Kaithal), 18 November 1995.
85. *Report of the Administration of Punjab, 1933-4*, p. 19.
86. See S.P. Shukla, *India's Freedom Struggle and the Role of Haryana* (New Delhi, 1985), p. 43.
87. Azim Husain, *Mian Sir Fazl-i-Husain: A Political Biography*, p. 77.
88. Ibid.
89. See Duni Chand, *Ulster of India: An Analysis of The Punjab Problem* (Lahore, 1936), p. 2.
90. The lack of direction, foresight, internal strife, etc., in the Punjab Congress was among the more important causes for the rise of the Unionist Party and greatly worried its national level leaders. Jawahar Lal Nehru in a letter to Gopi Chand Bhargava [5 March 1937, A.I.C.C. File No. B-17(i), p. 119 (NMML)] expressed disgust at the Party's functioning in Punjab and admitted the fact that Congressmen in Punjab had for some peculiar and self-seeking reasons confined themselves to cities, in the process ignoring the rural areas and majority of the population.
91. Gopi Chand Bhargava (1899-1966) was among the prominent Congress leaders in Punjab during the period. He was elected to the 1926 Punjab Legislative Council, but resigned when the Nehru Report was not accepted by the government. He was again elected to the Punjab Legislative Assembly in 1937 from the same seat (Lahore Urban) but resigned in 1939, this time in line with the Congress policy of protesting against the British war policy in India. In the 1946 Assembly elections he was returned from the University seat. Bhargava was chief minister of Punjab 1947-9, education minister 1949, for a short period chief minister again in 1950. During 1958-63 he remained finance minister of Punjab.
92. Satyapal (1884-1954) was another prominent Congress leader during the period and remained a consistent rival of the better known and Nehru supported Bhargava. He remained a member of the Punjab Legislative Assembly from Amritsar city (General) seat (1938-41). He wrote a book (co-authored with Prabodh Chandra), *Sixty Years of Congress: India Lost, India Regained* (Lahore, 1946).
93. *The Tribune*, 12 November 1929.
94. *PLCD*, vol. XXII, 4 March 1932, p. 203.
95. Ibid.
96. Nur Ahmad, *Martial Law*, p. 100.

97. Ibid.
98. Ibid.
99. Ibid., also M. Isphani, *Quaid-i-Azam: As I Knew Him* (Karachi, 1976), p. 20.
100. Azim Husain, *Mian Sir Fazl-i-Husain: A Political Biography*, pp. 394-6.
101. See Anil Seal and Ayesha Jalal, 'Alternative to Partition: Muslim Politics Between the Wars', *Modern Asian Studies*, 15 March 1981, p. 432.
102. Ibid.
103. *The Tribune*, 22 August 1932, also, 25 November 1932.
104. For detail of the Communist movement and its politics in Punjab in relation to the Unionist Party see Bhagwan Josh, *The Communist Movement in the Punjab 1926-47* (Delhi, 1979), p. 105.
105. Ibid.
106. For facets of Sikh political agenda during a major part of the Unionist party's period in Punjab see K.L. Tuteja, *Sikh Politics, 1920-40* (Kurukshetra, 1984), in this case p. 122.
107. Azim Husain, *Mian Sir Fazl-i-Husain: A Political Biography*, p. 156.
108. W.C. Smith, *Modern Islam in India* (London, 1946), pp. 270-2.
109. *The Tribune*, 24 July 1935.
110. See V.C. Joshi (ed.), *Lala Lajpat Rai, Speeches and Writings*, vol. II (Delhi, 1965), pp. 316-22.

CHAPTER 3

Elections of 1937: Unionists Form Government

THE GOVERNMENT of India Act, 1935 was an important milestone in the constitutional history of India. The Act provided for the replacement of 'dyarchy' with supposed 'provincial autonomy'. The Punjab Legislative Council was not only renamed as the Punjab Legislative Assembly but its composition was altered significantly. The new body was to have no official or nominated members. The concept of joint ministerial responsibility to the Assembly was introduced. The Act was significant also because it increased considerably the number of people who were enfranchised. About 24 per cent of the adult population of Punjab was enrolled for the Legislative Assembly electoral process.[1] In actual terms, however, this 24 per cent constituted just about 12 per cent of the total population of the province.[2] With landowners comprising almost 60 per cent of the new electorate and non-agriculturalist, still not permitted to stand from rural constituencies, it meant that loyalist supporters would continue to dominate all important posts and public life as a whole.[3] The average number of voters for each of the 175 constituencies of the new Legislative Assembly of Punjab was to be about 16,000, as compared to 33,000 in Madras, 18,600 in Bombay, 33,000 in U.P., 32,000 in Bengal, 20,000 in Bihar and 18,600 in Central Provinces.[4] Table 3.1 shows the distribution of the constituencies into various categories for the Punjab Legislative Assembly as provided for by the new Act.

The bifurcation of seats into rural and urban groups with 138 seats out of the 175 being allocated to rural areas was based on the proportion of rural population but the decision was also and perhaps more pointedly in line with the British policy of sustaining goodwill

TABLE 3.1: PUNJAB LEGISLATIVE ASSEMBLY CONSTITUENCIES, 1937

Constituencies	Urban	Rural	Total
General	8	34	42
Mohammadans	9	75	84
Sikhs	2	29	31
Special	—	—	18
Total	19	138	175

SOURCE: Yadav, *Elections*, p. 16.

in rural Punjab. An important change was made in the policy of demarcating constituencies; they now came to tally with Tehsil boundaries, which in turn were usually based on tribal dominance patterns. Thus, a Tehsil was frequently dominated by one tribe. The policy also ensured that politics continued to revolve around tribal affiliations rather than religon.[5] More specifically, the new electoral process was what the rural elite of Punjab had been waiting for. In any case it suited sections of the elite inclined towards politics.

As the prospect of being elected to power increased, so did the internal dissension and intrigue within the Unionist Party, so much so that the founder of the party Fazl-i-Husain was keen to stay away from Punjab politics. Though he said his failing health had influenced his decision, it seems his disinclination towards active politics in Punjab may also have been due to the fact that there was within the Unionist Party a group of formidable leaders who were opposed to him. Sikander Hayat, Muzaffar Khan[6] and Ahmad Yar Khan Daultana[7] were the main leaders of this group. They also had the sympathy and support of some Hindu and Sikh leaders who considered Fazl-i-Husain excessively and unduly biased towards the Muslim community. In comparison Sikander Hayat was not only considered more liberal, but also had a large number of influential non-Muslim political friends, including Raja Narender Nath and Sunder Singh Majithia. Some of these leaders considered supporting Sikander Hayat a more convenient and preferable political strategy also because Sikander's base among the Muslim elite was thought to be restricted. In any case, it was felt that under no circumstances would he have received the support of the powerful Noon-Tiwana faction within the Unionist Party. This assumption was based on the fact that close family relations existed between Fazl-i-Husain and Firoz Khan Noon (Fazli's daughter was married to Noon's younger brother).[8] Keeping in mind the internal dissension within the party, the non-Muslim leaders thought and with some basis that Sikander's position was more fluid and he would in all probability require their support more critically, thus making him more amenable to pressures. At one stage it was even rumoured in the 'political lanes' of Lahore that Sikander Hayat and Raja Narender Nath were toying with the idea of floating a separate political party, independent of the Unionists.[9]

Fazl-i-Husain, however, was prevailed upon by friends like Agha Khan III, Chaudhri Shahab-ud-din and Mir Maqbool Mahmood to remain in active politics.[10] The imminent crisis of division within the party was tided over, it seems, mainly because Sikander Hayat had realized that Fazl-i-Husain was critically ill. In November 1935, for example, Fazl-i-Husain's doctor informed him (Fazli) that Muzaffar Khan had enquired from him about his (Fazli's) health.[11] The tension between Fazl-i-Husain and Sikander Hayat eased somewhat also when Firoz Khan Noon agreed at Fazl-i-Husain's suggestion to distance himself from politics in Punjab and join as a member of the Council of the Secretary of State for India in London. As a result Sikander felt assured that he would be able to succeed Fazl-i-Husain as Premier whenever the opportunity arose and perhaps would not need to seek the support of non-Muslim members of the Unionist Party, at least not as desperately as would otherwise have been necessary. In December 1935, Sikander Hayat met Fazl-i-Husain to sort out differences and misunderstandings.[12] The meeting helped to tide over the immediate crisis but beyond that achieved little else.

Fazl-i-Husain summoned a meeting of the Executive Board of the All India Muslim Conference in Delhi in February 1936. The Agha Khan presided over the meeting. Fazl-i-Husain formally announced his intention to reconstitute and reorganize the Unionist Party. His proposals were well approved. The essence of his new scheme was published in a pamphlet and released during the conference. He suggested that communal conflict was not religious but economic and political in nature and that major communities were essentially in a race to secure and grasp economic and political advantage. With this in mind he proposed that the three major communities should forget caste, class and creed, and form a party based on 'liberal and socialistic programmes' and work for the 'upliftment of backward people and areas'.[13] This document served as a policy statement and became the principal agenda for the 1937 elections to the state assembly and initiated the Unionist Party's preparation for the polls.

To begin with, an elaborate blue print for redesignating the party was drawn up in which details relating to the organization, functioning, aims, objectives and work of the party were provided.[14] The party was redesignated as the Punjab Unionist Party or Ittihad Party.[15] A five-tier system was adopted at the organizational level.[16]

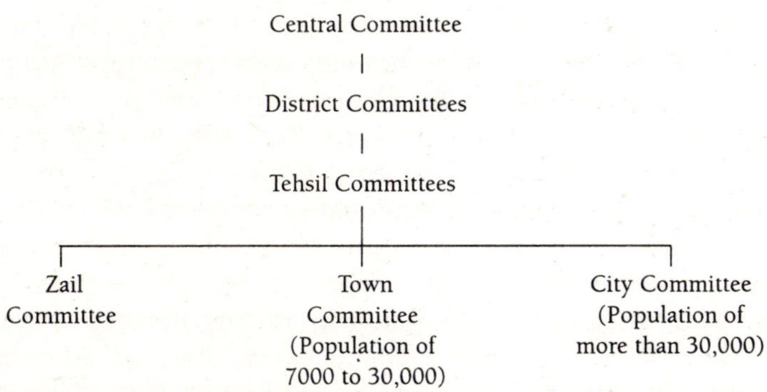

The central committee had its headquarters at 14-C Davis Road, Lahore. It comprised two members nominated from each Tehsil and city committees, all the sitting and retired members of the central and provincial legislatures and other eminent persons (whose total number was not to exceed thirty).[17] These members were to elect every three years the office-bearers of the central committee, namely, one president not more than five vice-presidents, seven general secretaries one of whom was also to be party treasurer. The rest of the members were to form the executive committees.[18]

At the district level the committees were composed of two members from each Tehsil, city and village committees.[19] Five members from different organizations, like labour groups, etc., were also included. The office-bearers included a president, one or more vice-presidents, one secretary and an assistant secretary. A treasurer was also to be elected every three years.[20] The Tehsil committees comprised two members from each Zail committee.[21] The Zail committees constituted on similar lines had one member from each village. The city committees were formed on identical lines, with members included from wards and *mohallas*. The office-bearers of these committees were elected for three years.[22]

The village and small town committees stood at the lowest rung of the organizational hierarchy and could enroll any person as a member, provided he was above 21 years of age and had faith in the aims and objectives of the party and also paid some nominal fee into the party funds.[23]

Though great care was taken to give the party a democratic form, in essence for a party so completely dominated by feudal practices such committees, etc., were meaningless. The Unionist Party was never a political party in the contemporary sense. For the feudal lords who constituted a major section of the party the whole exercise was merely a means to grab more power and secure some credibility for the sustaining of a political and social system which was inherently alien to democratic attitudes and practices. In any case, there is no information on the people who manned the lower levels of the Unionist Party's organizational structure, if, that in they were manned at all. The central committee comprised Fazl-i-Husain as President, Chhotu Ram was one of the Vice-Presidents, Ahmad Yar Khan Daultana was one of the General Secretaries. Sardar Habibullah, Maulvi Ghulam Mohyuddin and Syed Afzal Ali Hasni were Organizing Secretaries, the Nawab of Mamdot[24] was Treasurer and Mian Maqbool Mahmood[25] Drafting and Propaganda Secretary. Begum Jahan Ara Shah Nawaz was appointed Office Secretary. A sum of Rs. 50,000 was collected for party work and Rs. 10,000 each was contributed by the Nawab of Kalabag, Syed Maatab Ali and Sardar Muhammad Nawaz Khan. Fazl-i-Husain, Zafarulla Khan, Nawab Allaha Bakhash, Nawab of Mamdot, Sir Chhotu Ram, Malik Umar Hayat Khan Tiwana, Ahmad Yar Khan Daultana, Ch. Shahabuddin all contributed Rs. 3000 each.[26] The Agha Khan also promised a sum of Rs. 20,000 of which he sent Rs. 10,000 in June 1936.[27]

An election office was set up at Lahore, special emphasis was laid on publicity through the press, with notes being prepared and supplied to newspapers and periodicals to enable favourable coverage for the party. Certain newspapers like *Eastern Times* (Lahore) provided good coverage to the party.

The election manifesto prepared mainly by Sir Chhotu Ram focussed on issues like: (a) attainment of dominion status by 'constitutional' means at an early practicable date; (b) the securing of an honorable status for Indians living overseas; (c) the establishment of 'provincial autonomy in Punjab; (d) economic criteria as the basis for forming political parties; (e) equal facility and opportunity for all, with special consideration for backward classes and rural areas.[28] The manifesto also said that the problems of the provinces were primarily economic and therefore required attention mainly in that direction with 90 per cent of the population depending on agriculture or related occupations. An average Punjabi, the manifesto point out, irrespective of being urban or rural or an agriculturist or non-agriculturist, had an average income which was less than the expenditure on food and clothes by the government on a prisoner in the state jails.[29]

The manifesto also raised the point that 80 per cent of all landed property owned by the peasantry was involved in debt hypothecation. In real terms the debt on the peasant was 40 times more than the land revenue. The interest charges alone, it was pointed out, were 10 times the land revenue. Unemployment, the manifesto stated, was rampant, where government services could at best absorb only 3 out of 1000 people seeking employment. It demanded more jobs in the government as well as the private sector.[30] It mentioned that the rich were getting richer and if the gulf between the rich and the poor increased, no government could permanently protect the rich. Therefore, it said, it was in the interest of the rich to help in the lessening of poverty if not removing it altogether.[31]

The Unionist Party also pledged to stand by the 1901 Alienation of Land Act, treating it as a pro-peasant measure. The party advocated a policy of 'limited liability socialism', and mentioned the need for agrarian reforms. As was so common of Unionist Party policy statements here too there was a significant contradiction. The talk of agrarian reforms by a party whose principal components were among the largest landholding owners of Punjab was obviously meaningless talk.[32] Essentially the political philosophy of the Unionist as reflected in the manifesto was a mixture of paradoxes and inherent contradictions, and in a way the document represented the true political character of the Unionist Party.

The Unionist leaders were fully conscious of the fact that the politics of Punjab was controlled and influenced in a profound manner by factors like caste, religion and regionalism. Therefore the party leaders strove to reconcile influential people on a platform where no single idealogy was important, essentially the whole exercise was an effort towards self-aggrandisement. Specific efforts were made by Unionist workers to retain the goodwill of the leading *pirs* and other traditional socioreligious leaders. A large number of such *pirs* including those of Taunsa, Golara, Makkad, Jalalpur, Alipur, the *sajjada nishins* of the Chisti Shrine of Mahar Sharif, the *dargah* of Mouniuddin Chisti (Ajmer) and Nizamuddin Aulia (Delhi) were brought under Unionist Party influence.[33] Most of them agreed to provide tacit support to the party, some like the *pirs* of Makkad, Multan, Shergarh and Sheikh Jiwana even joined the party.[34]

Likewise the party leadership made efforts to sustain the goodwill of the leading and influential landlord families. A large number of such families were actively retained or introduced into the Unionist plan for the elections. Some such families were, the Quizilbash's of Lahore, Chattha's of Gujranwala, Hayat's and Shamsabad Awan's of Wah, the Tiwana's, Noon's, Qureshis, Pircha's of Mianwali, the Giliani's, Daultana's, Gardezi's of Multan, the Gurmani's and Dastri's of Muzaffargarh.[35]

Besides bringing into the Unionist network their large network of *biradaris*, these feudal lords were able to influence the smaller peasants and the tenants on their estates in favour of the Unionists. The ability of the large landowners to influence the small peasant was a result of economic compulsions which were typical of feudal societies like Punjab. Most of the small peasants and tenants were not even voters, but they formed by sheer number the critical element which the British were keen to isolate from the influence of nationalist parties like the Congress. The vast crowds that came to listen to Unionist leaders mainly consisted of this deprived section.

It is one of the numerous multi-dimensional ironies of Punjab's feudal political system that the deprived peasantry sought succor, help and guidance from the very people who in the first place were the cause of their pitiful condition.

The Unionists were also able to manage considerable support from the non-Muslim peasant communities of Punjab. In Haryana or the south-east Punjab region for example this support was gathered mainly by the efforts of Sir Chhotu Ram, who was held in high esteem among agricultural communities particularly the Hindu Jats. In addition to the kind of support secured by the Unionist Party to follow its opportunistic politics, it was also able to gather the goodwill of the British administrative system particularly of the system that effectively mattered in rural Punjab, the *patwaris*, *lambardars*, etc.,[36] as also the lower level officials of the police department.

The other important and politically active Muslim organizations in Punjab like the Muslim League, Ittehad-i-Millat and the Ahrar's were also in the race for support from important opinion-making sections of Punjab's Muslim society, like the *biradari* leaders, the *pirs*, influential landowners, etc. Initially these parties made little impact on them because the Unionist Party was considered by such people as a more reliable medium to preserve and protect their interests. But more importantly, most of the people who constituted the Unionist Party or were sympathetically inclined towards it were in some way or the other indebted to the government and were always on the lookout for patronage. People dependent on government goodwill obviously had no other option than to support the Unionist Party, which itself frequently, acted as an extension of the British administrative system. It appears that any one on the lookout for advantage from the government was expected to be sympathetic towards the Unionists.

In the period 1936-7 the Indian National Congress in Punjab was in a state of confusion and drift. This was mainly due to its indifferent and often negative attitude to various pro-rural legislative measures initiated by the Unionist leaders in the previous Legislative Councils. The Congress had failed to draw popular support in rural Punjab. Its non-committal stand vis-a-vis the moneylending legislations in particular made it lose considerable following both among urban Hindu business classes and the rural peasantry. This happened because the Congress could not put forth a convincing policy for either of the two sections. While the business classes felt that the Congress adopted a policy not sufficiently strong to oppose the Unionist proposals, the rural peasantry at the same time held it responsible for being lukewarm towards measures which were introduced to help the rural areas. Essentially the Congress was in a no-win position.

Fazl-i-Husain, however, made efforts to reach an electoral understanding with the Congress. He carried out talks with the Congress leadership through Bhulabhai Desai at the national level and at the provincial level through his friend Raizada Hans Raj, asking Congressmen 'to make common cause with us'.[37] The Congress remained unimpressed by the appeal of the Unionist Party considering the Unionists unacceptable, mainly because the Unionists were representing a system which the Congress was morally bound to oppose and had been opposing all along the politics and policy of collaborative rule. Of course there are opinions which suggest that, 'had the Congress accepted the Unionist offer at this juncture, India's history would have taken a different turn'.[38] The basis of this view was that a Congress-Unionist alliance in Punjab might have prevented the Muslim League from reaching an unassailable position which it did in the 1940s. There does seem substance in the suggestion that a Congress-Unionist alliance in 1937 could by far-reaching implications have prevented the partition of Punjab a decade later. But to this we will get back later.

The political position of the Muslim League in Punjab on the eve of the election was worse than that of the Congress. Ispahani, a close associate of Jinnah writes that the Muslim League 'had not of course fifty coppers in its coffers'.[39] There was no office: 'The President and Secretary both honorary, carried their offices in their respective portmanteaus.'[40] The Muslim League made efforts to reach some sort of understanding for electoral objectives with the Unionist Party. Jinnah even offered Fazl-i-Husain the Presidentship of the All India Muslim League (Bombay Session, January 1936), saying:

> I feel that at this moment no one can give a better lead to the Muslims of India than yourself. We want a man of your callibre and experience, and nobody can well, at this critical moment, as far as I can see, perform that

duty and render that service to the community as you would be able to do.[41]

But so confident was Fazl-i-Husain of his own strength, as well perhaps of the weakness of the League that he twice rejected Jinnah's proposal for an electoral understanding, first in January 1936 and then again in April 1936.[42] For the Muslim League it was a serious initial setback. Jinnah spelt out the consequences of Fazli's rejection of his hand of friendship and cooperation: 'Your refusal', he said, 'will be the greatest misfortune and terrible disappointment.'[43] But Fazl-i-Husain was a master political tactician and had correctly anticipated the consequences of an understanding between his party and the Muslim League. Having played an important role in securing the numerous advantages for the Muslim community which were included in the Act of 1935, he was satisfied with what had been provided as electoral safeguards for the Muslim community and thereafter did not want to take the Muslims away from the national mainstream:

> Joining hands with the Muslim League meant as already noted, taking the Muslims away from the mainstream and losing the chance of forming ministry. I shall be in a position to field only 86 Muslim members from the Muslim constituencies. My communal propaganda for my candidates would have strong reaction among the Hindus and Sikhs and Chhotu Ram's position will be compromised and weakened in his area and this way shall be instrumental in defeating a group which has been supporting me for 12 years. Then 86 is not a majority in the House of 175, how would we be able to form the ministry.[44]

Fazl-i-Husain had correctly concluded that joining hands with a weak and disjointed Punjab Muslim League would prove of little benefit to the Unionist Party. It was with this in mind that he advised Jinnah to leave Punjab alone and let Muslims of India solve their problems as per local conditions, further suggesting that after the elections some arrangements at the all-India level could possibly be worked out.[45] However, Jinnah would have none of it and said 'Fazli thinks he carries the Punjab in his pocket. I am going to smash Fazli.'[46] A disgusted Jinnah further remarked, 'I shall never come to Punjab again.'[47] Yet he went on to make another attempt after the death of Fazli, and the formation of a new ministry in 1937.

The serious political differences between the two leading

politicians was mainly with regard to the ground realities of the political situations in Punjab. Both Jinnah and Fazl-i-Husain were in their own manner aspiring to build and sustain their political influence by projecting themselves as leaders of the Muslim community. While Jinnah wanted to use the Unionists to build a Muslim League base in Punjab, Fazl-i-Husain wanted to keep the Unionist Muslims of Punjab isolated from Muslim politics at the national level so as to sustain his political clout in Punjab. Jinnah wanted to proceed purely on the Muslim card, where as Fazl-i-Husain knew that to form a ministry in Punjab it was essential to take a section of Hindus and Sikhs along.[48] For Jinnah, the Muslim support of Punjab was sufficient, for Fazli the support of the Hindus and Sikhs too was important.

The Sikhs of Punjab were divided among the Unionists, the Khalsa National Party, the Akali Dal and the Congress. The Khalsa National Party was represented by Sir Sunder Singh Majithia and Sir Jogender Singh. The Khalsa National Party like the Unionists followed a political policy of opportunism and collaboration. The small section of Sikh population that composed the party were generally big landlords or rich businessmen. The Congress and the Akalis attracted the common Sikhs, as both the parties represented the nationalist opinion of the community.[49]

The sudden death of Fazl-i-Husain on 9 July 1936 was an important setback to the Unionist Party. His death altered the political scene of Punjab and also left the field open for Sikander Hayat and to a lesser extent Chhotu Ram. Chhotu Ram had by now come to represent to a considerable extent in the Unionist Party, its secular image, and by 1936 he was not only the main political representative of south-east Punjab and the non-Muslim section in the Unionist Party but he enjoyed widespread support even among Muslim leaders. But the most important fallout of Fazl-i-Husain's death was that the doors of Punjab fell open for the politics of Jinnah. With Fazli gone, Jinnah's claim to the leadership of the Muslims of Punjab got a boost. In any case after Fazl-i-Husain, Punjab did not have a Muslim leader who could claim as much standing at the all-India level as Fazl-i-Husain had done.

Fazli had predicted just before his death that his party would bag 80 Muslim, 15 Rural Hindu, 15 Sikh and 4 Landholder seats. The opposition, he said, would win about 10 Muslim seats mainly of the Ahrars and some urban Muslims, 5 Congress, 15 Sikhs and 21 Urban Hindu seats.[50] This prediction was to later prove fairly correct, once again indicating the masterly understanding that Fazl-i-Husain had of the complex and unpredictable politics of Punjab.

The election was keenly contested by various parties which put up a total of 7775 candidates. The Unionist Party put up candidates in 107 of the 175 constituencies.[51] Chhotu Ram led the Unionist election compaign. By far the best public orator in Punjab, be captivated audiences in his simple but hard-hitting speeches and represented the common man's association with the party. Chhotu Ram usually started his political speeches by emphasizing common values, culture, and the bond of poverty. Rai Sahib Anant Ram explained how within a few minutes of his (Chhotu Ram's) coming to the stage there would be 'pin-drop' silence in the meeting and for many days after such meetings Chhotu Ram's words would continue to travel across the villages of the region giving the whole process almost a 'godly' guise.[52] Leading Congress stalwarts like Jawaharlal Nehru,[53] Sarojini Naidu and Vallabhbhai Patel, toured different parts of Punjab and explained the Congress creed of freedom and self-respect. The Hindu Mahasabha had Raja Narender Nath and Rao Balbir Singh as its main spokesmen. They sought votes on the basis of protecting the rights of the Hindu community.[54] Master Tara Singh was the main attraction of the election campaign of the Akalis who had aligned for the election with the Congress.[55] The Muslim League was represented in its election effort by Mohammad Ali Jinnah, Raja Ghazanfar Ali Khan and Malik Barkat Ali. Electioneering for the Ahrars was conducted mainly by Mir Abdul Qayyam,[56] Muhammad Abdur Rahman Khan, Maulana Mazhar Ali Azhar, and Khwaja Ghulam Husain.[57] For the urban-based Ittehad-i-Millat, Sheikh Muhammad Alam and Khalid Latif Gauba led the election campaign.

The fact that the franchise was extremely restricted and the manner in which the seats had been demarcated somehow did not dampen the expectancy and excitement that is usually associated with elections. Lorries, *tongas*, etc., were used to bring voters to booths. Some scattered election clashes took place, mainly involving the supporters of the Ahrars and the Majlis-i-Ittehad-i-Millat. The better reported of these clashes was in Lahore at the women's polling booth where police had to be called to separate some *burqa*-clad female voters.[58] Surprisingly, despite the excitement and enthusiasm the turnout was low, just over a third of those entitled actually cast their votes.[59] This general indifference partly reflected the futility of creating an electoral system comprising exclusively of the privileged and elite section of society. As pointed out by Talbot, money power played a big role, some Unionist leaders were returned unopposed because the rivals were paid off.[60]

The declaration of results started on 1 February 1937. There were no major upsets, in fact the percentage of votes polled by different parties and even the voting trend in general was in line with what the government had expected. These expectations were based on the complex division of constituencies and other rules that governed the election. In rural Muslim areas, for example, the Unionists secured about 70 per cent of votes that were cast, whereas in the urban areas they got just about 25 per cent votes. The voting trend underlined the predominantly rural character of the Unionist Party. In the Muslim women constituencies the Unionist Party secured around 32 per cent of votes polled. In the Hindu rural constituencies they polled about 34 per cent of votes. The rural Hindu votes were secured mainly in the south-east Punjab where Chhotu Ram was the chief vote catcher for the Unionist Party. In sharp contrast the Unionists did not even contest any of the eight seats reserved for urban Hindus. This fact alone shows how clearly the urban and rural divide had come to be established. In the rural Sikh constituencies the Party managed just about 2 per cent of the votes.[61] The poor performance of the Unionist Party in rural central Punjab was mainly due to the hold of the Akalis, particularly over the Jat Sikh peasantry. But among the large landholders of the Sikhs the Unionists did well securing about 47 per cent votes in the Sikh Landholders' constituencies.[62]

The Unionists as had been expected performed best in the rural Muslim constituencies winning seventy-three of the total seventy-five seats. In the towns, however, they could secure only one of the nine Muslim seats. Among the Hindus the Unionists' support in the Hindu Jat belt of the Ambala Division, the area that today forms

Haryana, was widespread and is testified by the fact they captured all but one of the rural Hindu seats.[63] Regionwise, the Unionist Party's greatest success was achieved in the Canal colony constituencies of west Punjab, the grainery of today's Pakistan, in which its candidates had been members of the leading *biradaris* or had the support of the region's influential *pirs*.[64]

The most remarkable feature of the election was the highly compartmentalized manner of vote seeking and vote casting. *Biradari*, caste and religious belonging were the predominant factors that influenced the election process. This retrograde and communalized nature of the election is underlined by the fact that apart from the Congress and the Unionists all other important parties appealed exclusively to specific religious communities only. For example, the Khalsa National Party and the Akali Dal contested only on Sikh seats, winning 12 and 11 seats respectively of the 33 exclusive Sikh seats.[65] The Hindu Election Board, for example, won 15 seats, of these only one was from a General Urban constituency.[66]

The Unionist Party's success could best be attributed to the feudal character of Punjab's political system. The role of the so-called 'natural leaders', a term coined by the British to address the colonial intermediaries, was all important in the Unionist Party's success. The restrictive nature of the electoral process as contained in the Act of 1935 and above all the uniquely opportunistic composition of most of the political parties that participated in the elections contributed in their own way to the Party's success. The level of success actually achieved by the Unionists was well beyond expectations particularly of important parties like the Congress. Even though the exercise to analyse the failure or success of a party in an election in which only one-fourth of the eligible adult population constitutes the electoral college appears at first instance to be meaningless, however some important causes for the Unionist Party's success could perhaps be underlined. At the outset it seems that the effort of some of the leading Unionist leaders who had been actively involved in various legislative measures and development schemes which were aimed towards benefiting the peasantry appear to have yielded results. Specific references could be made in this context to the efforts made by leaders like Chhotu Ram to emancipate the peasantry from the cycle of debt.[67] Even though the Unionist Party under the scheme of 'dyarchy' was never really in power, nor even functioned as a political organization with mass support yet some of its actions and proposals left a good impact particularly among rural inhabitants. The party had surely struck a sentimental chord among the peasantry.

The second and more important reason that explains the Unionist Party's success was the fact that there was no worthwhile opposition. The Congress, the main party in opposition was overidden by internal dissension, a situation that made it contest only 32 of the 170 Indian seats in the Assembly.[68] There were two main groups among the Congressmen in Punjab, one of Satyapal and the other of Gopi Chand Bhargava. Both did their utmost to discredit the other. Leaders of the Satyapal group included Abdul Ghani, K.N. Sehgal, Shano Devi, etc., while the Bhargava group was led by Seth Sudershan and Verender.[69] The Congress party's internal rivalry had seriously spilled over into the election campaign. The Amritsar and Lyallpur Congress Committees, for example, actively opposed the candidates approved for their constituencies by the Provincial Parliamentary Board.[70] Satyapal journeyed to Karachi to address Congress election meetings to avoid having to do any electioneering in Lahore on behalf of Gopichand Bhargava.[71]

The internal rivalry of the Congress of course was not unique to the party, it was in fact more in evidence among the Unionists. But important was the Congress party's total lack of political and policy decisiveness which repeatedly emerged whenever important legislative measures were discussed in Punjab, in or outside the Legislative Councils. Often the party's stand on measures directed to benefit rural Punjab was either negative or neutral, particularly on important legislative enactments like the ones aimed at curtailing the burden of debt and creating provisions to keep a check on moneylenders. Because of this totally inexplicable negative and indifferent attitude, the party could not make any worthwhile impact in rural Punjab. The Unionist Party easily outwitted the Congress, realizing and acting well in time in the belief that the feudal political structure of Punjab politics necessitated an approach to the voters through the rural elite. This fact is best substantiated by the case of Mian Iftikhar-ud-din who was elected from the Kasur seat on Congress ticket by defeating the veteran Unionist, Khan Bahadur

Sardar Habibullah Khan. Mian Iftikhar-ud-din had somehow manipulated the support of the Arian kinship network for himself. This was one of the few cases where the Unionists had failed to secure the support of the local *biradari* or of the local *sajjada nishin*.[72] Having been totally outmaneuvered by the Unionist Party in rural Punjab, in the towns the Congress faced formidable opposition from the Hindu Election Board which was supported both by the Sanatanists and some Arya Samajis.

The elite of the majority community, the Muslims were almost totally under Unionist influence. The support of the third major community in Punjab, the Sikhs was scattered, but the main concentration of the Sikh peasantry, particularly the Jat Sikhs was with the Akalis. The large landowning Sikh families supported the Unionist, essentially a common bond of political and economic opportunism. The manner in which Punjab was successfully isolated from the winds of change which Congress policies had created all over India is a reflection of the deep nexus between the Unionist Party and the colonial administration. This single fact alone contributed immensely to the Unionist success in Punjab.

The impressive success of the Unionists in 1937 was not a chance development. Talbot suggests that the manner in which the Unionists dominated Punjabi politics in fact 'demonstrates that parties devoted to intercommunal political accommodation can achieve a large degree of success even in plural societies which are marked by a high degree of ethnic and communal hostility'.[73] To understand the Unionist phenomena it is also important to realize that because of the highly restricted franchise a great majority of the population was apolitical and as Talbot points out, 'deferentially integrated into a patron-client relationship'.[74] A considerable measure of Unionist success was also the result of Chhotu Ram's rural-based political philosophy. 'Being a peasant is in itself a community', he would often say, 'how can there be communities within communities'.[75]

The 1937 Legislative Elections were an important milestone in Punjab's political history. The elections were conducted under the new Government of India Act, 1935 which introduced the so-called provincial autonomy in the province. The electoral college was an improvement on the Act of 1919, yet it gave the right to vote to just about 24 per cent of the agewise eligible voters of the province. Each of Punjab's 175 constituencies was composed of about 16,000 voters. The demarcation of constituencies was complex, essentially oriented towards giving benefit to the privileged and elite sections of society, making the Legislative Assembly that was constituted on the culmination of this election a widely representative organization of the elite of Punjab, having little to do with the masses. The whole exercise appeared to give a boost to tribal attitudes and politics essentially maintaining the existing power structure which had time and again proven its loyalty to the colonial state.

The election results also highlighted the level to which Punjab's society had been compartmentalized on the basis of *biradaris*, castes, and religious segments. Votes were sought on purely personalized and subjective consideration totally devoid of programmes and policies. This natural trend was facilitated by the manner in which constituencies were created, Hindu, Muslim, Sikh, Urban, Rural, etc. But more significantly,while demarcating constituencies,care was in fact taken to further institutionalize the tribal leadership structure.

The Unionist Party's outstanding victory had been predicted by Fazl-i-Husain, but came as a surprise to most. The victory was mainly due to the fact that no worthwhile opposition to the Unionists could emerge because the main opposition, the Congress was ridden with dissension among the top leaders. Besides the indecisiveness of the Congress on important matters of policy, like rural development and peasant debt prevented it from securing the assured support of any section of society, rural or urban. The extensive support secured by the Unionists in rural Punjab both among the Hindu and Muslim peasantry was the main reason for their victory. The election results also highlighted the fact that apart from the Congress, the Unionists were the only other political party which could claim to have secured ballot support cutting across community lines. The number of seats won by the party in the predominantly Hindu area of south-east Punjab as well as the massive support received in the predominantly Muslim areas of west Punjab serves to substantiate this view. The only section of the electoral college where the Unionists drew no response in fact did not even put up candidates were the urban Hindu seats. The opposition to the Unionist Party in the urban areas in a way and quite in proportion reflected the support the party secured in the rural areas. The politics of urban against rural yielded good results for the Unionist Party. The outstanding victory of the party was in many ways a feather in the cap of the British bureaucracy of Punjab, which ensured the election of the very people who suited the colonial edifice the most. The success also hinged on the remarkable tact with which Punjab was isolated from Congress influence. This could never have been achieved by the Unionists alone. Yet with all the flaws that were inherent in the electoral system, it was a step forward. It gave to the people of Punjab the first taste of 'restricted democracy'.

NOTES

1. See K.C. Yadav, *Elections in Punjab* (Delhi, 1987), p. 19.
2. Ibid.
3. Also see Talbot, *Khizr Tiwana*, p. 61.
4. Yadav, *Elections*, op. cit., p. 19.
5. Talbot, *Khizr Tiwana*, p. 58. In a way this policy perhaps unintendedly kept communalization of politics away from rural Punjab. While tribal politics did keep the people isolated from the wind of real politik, yet it served a good purpose by keeping people together on grounds of economic improvement.
6. Nawab Muzaffar Khan (1879-1951) was closely related to Sikander Hayat Khan (his son was married to Sikander's daughter). On Sikander Hayat's death, it was he who vacated the Attock seat to enable Sikander Hayat's son Shaukat Hayat to be elected to the Assembly. His son Mazhar Ali (the one married to Sikander's daughter) rose to high positons in the Pakistan media, being editor of *The Pakistan Times* and *Dawn*.
7. Ahmad Yar Khan Daultana (1896-1940) was elected to the 1921, and the 1926 Punjab Legislative Councils, and also to the 1937 Legislative Assembly. His book *Leaves from a Unionist Diary* (Lahore, 1949), provides an interesting insight into the party.
8. At times it was political alliances that emerged from matrimonial relations, sometimes it was the other way round, matrimonial alliances developed among political colleagues. The two major factions in the Unionist Party were often a mixture of both, providing an ideal example of the functioning of feudal politics. In this case Fazl-i-Husain's daughter was married to Firoze Khan Noon's younger brother. See Nur Ahmad, *Martial Law*, pp. 124-5 and 180.
9. *The Civil & Military Gazette*, 23 June 1936.

10. Azim Husain, *Mian Sir Fazl-i-Husain: A Political Biography*, p. 302, refers to a number of influential well wishers who were keen that Fazl-i-Husain should not quit active politics. For example, Agha Khan. Ch. Shahabuddin wrote 'without you the Muslims will be no where . . . you must lead the Muslims as long as you can . . .' (p. 30, letter of 4 August 1935). Mir Maqbool Mahmood wrote 'you are the . . . leader . . . we all respect' (letter of 25 July 1935).
11. The assumption that the faction strife between the Sikander and Fazl-i-Husain groups got somewhat subdued after it became clear that Fazl-i-Husain was critically ill seems fairly probable. For this see Nur Ahmad, *Martial Law*, p. 127.
12. Ibid.
13. Azim Husain, *Fazl-i-Husain*, p. 304.
14. *The Constitution, Aims and Objectives of the Unionist Party* (Urdu) (Lahore, 1936), was published on the eve of the 1937 Legislative Assembly elections, in the form of a samll booklet. The document was the first and only such document published by the party. It was to serve the purpose of a election manifesto, a broad outline of organizational hierarchy, policies, programmes, objectives, etc. But essentially and more importantly it was an effort by the Unionist to follow the democratic tradition wherein political parties are expected to make policy statement to seek support from the electorate.
15. The Punjab Unionist Party was also known as the Ittihad Party, but in common and more usual practise it came always to be known as the Zamindara League Party or simply as the Zamindara Party. For reference to Ittihad Party see ibid., p. 1.
16. Ibid., p. 2.
17. Ibid., pp. 3-4.
18. Ibid.
19. Ibid.
20. Ibid., pp. 4-5.
21. Ibid.
22. Ibid.
23. It was 2 paise per rupee for those paying Rs. 10 or more as land revenue, one anna per rupee for those paying income or Hasiyat Tax. The various committees at different levels were empowered to grant relaxation from fee payment in special and needy cases, see ibid., p. 6.
24. Nawab Shah Nawaj Khan of Mamdot (1883-1942) was one of the largest landholding owners of Punjab. He was a close friend and political confident of Sikander Hayat and also enjoyed good relations with Mohammad Ali by virtue of which he became the first president of the reorganized Punjab Muslim League (after the Sikander-Jinnah Pact, 1937). He was elected to the Punjab Legislative Assembly for the first time in

1937. His vast financial resources enabled him to play a crucial role in the Unionist Party particularly in matters of financial support.

25. Mian Maqbool Mahmood (d. 1942) was a close relation of Sikander Hayat, his two sisters were married to Sikander Hayat. In 1923 and 1926 elections he was elected to the Punjab Legislative Council from the Amritsar rural constituency and in 1937 from Amritsar.
26. Azim Husain, *Mian Sir Fazl-i-Husain: A Political Biography*, p. 340.
27. Agha Khan took back the amount (telegraphically) when he learnt of Fazl-i-Husains' death in July 1936, see ibid.
28. *The Constitution, Aims and Objectives of the Unionist Party*, pp. 15-18.
29. Ibid.
30. Ibid.
31. Ibid.
32. Ibid.
33. For detail see Waheed Ahmad, *Letters of Mian Fazl-i-Husain*, p. 592; also Talbot, *Punjab and the Raj*, p. 109.
34. The support provided by such leaders is well explained by D. Gilmartin, 'Religious Leaderships and the Pakistan Movement in Punjab', *Journal of Modern Asian Studies*, 13, 3 (1979) pp. 493-500.
35. Also see Craig Baxter, 'The Peoples Party Versus The Punjab Feudalists', *Journal of Asian and African Studies*, vol. VIII: 3 and 4 (July-October 1973). p. 168.
36. See I. Talbot, 'Muslim Political Mobilization in Rural Punjab, 1937-46', in Peter Robb (ed.), *Rural India Land Power and Society Under British Rule* (London, 1983), pp. 244-273.
37. Imran Ali, *Punjab Politics in the Decade Before Partition* (Lahore, 1974), p. 75.
38. See for example K.C. Yadav, 'The Partition of India: A Study of Muslim Politics in Punjab 1849-1947', *Punjab Past and Present*, vol. XVIII-I, April 1983, p. 125.
39. M.A.H. Isphani, *Quad-i-Azam*, p. 20.
40. Ibid.
41. Imran Ali, *Punjab Politics*, p. 75.
42. Yadav, op. cit., 'Partition of India', op. cit., p. 125.
43. Imran Ali, *Punjab Politics*, p. 75.
44. Azim Husain, *Mian Sir Fazl-i-Husain: A Political Biography*, pp. 339-40.
45. Ibid.
46. Ibid.
47. Ibid.
48. Muhammad Ashraf, *Letters of Iqbal to Jinnah* (Lahore, 1956), p. 10.
49. K.L. Tuteja, *Sikh Politics*, p. 176.
50. Azim Husain, *Mian Sir Fazl-i-Husain: A Political Biography*, p. 342.
51. *The Tribune*, 2 February 1937.

52. Being an M.L.A. of the party from 1937-46, he was usually present in most of the meetings addressed by Chhotu Ram.
53 *The Tribune*, 17 January 1937.
54. Ibid., 10 January 1937.
55. K.L. Tuteja, *Sikh Politics*, p. 176.
56. *The Tribune*, 24 May 1937.
57. Nur Ahmad, *Martial Law*, p. 184.
58. Home Pol. (FR), 2nd half of January 1937 (18 January).
59. Yadav, *Elections*, pp. 84-7.
60. Talbot, *Khizr Tiwana*, p. 67.
61. Ibid.
62. Ibid.
63. Ibid.
64. Talbot, *Punjab and the Raj*, p. 114.
65. *Indian Annual Register*, vol. II, 1938, p. 223.
66. Yadav, *Elections*, p. 84.
67. See Y.P. Bajaj, 'Unionist Politics and The General Elections of 1936-37: An Analysis', *Proceedings Punjab History Conference* (20th Session, March 1986), p. 374.
68. Y.P. Bajaj and Naresh Inder Singh, 'Congress Politics on the Eve of 1936-37 General Elections to the Punjab Assembly', *Proceedings Punjab History Conference* (19th Session, March 1985), p. 429.
69. Ibid.
70. Home Pol. (FR), 2nd half of November 1936 (18 November).
71. Ibid., 2nd half of December 1936.
72. Talbot, *Punjab and the Raj*, p. 110.
73. I. Talbot, 'Back to the Future? The Punjab Unionist Model of Consociational Democracy for Contemporary India and Pakistan', *International Journal of Punjab Studies*, vol. 3, No.1, 1996, p. 67.
74. Ibid., p. 71.
75. Rai Sahib Anant Ram (M.L.A., Unionist Party, 1937-46) Interview, 30 January 1988.

CHAPTER 4

The Unionists and Provincial Autonomy

THE PUNJAB Legislative Assembly elected in the winter of 1936 assembled for its first session on 16 April 1937. Sir Sikander Hayat was chosen by the Unionist Party as its leader in the Assembly and although the Unionists had sufficient strength to form the ministry on their own, Sikander Hayat opted to constitute a coalition ministry. The council of ministers so formed comprised Sir Sikander Hayat (Prime Minister), Sir Chhotu Ram (Development Minister), Malik Sir Khizr Hayat Khan Tiwana (Public Works Minister), Mian Sir Abdul Haye (Education Minister), Sir Manohar Lal (Finance Minister), Sir Sunder Singh Majithia (Revenue Minister).

In addition to the ministers, fifteen Parliamentary and Parliamentary Private Secretaries were also attached to different departments. The eight Parliamentary Secretaries were Mian Ahmad Yar Khan Daultana, Mir Maqbool Ahmad, Sardar Ujjal Singh, Begum Jahanara Shah Nawaz, Raja Ghazanfar Ali Khan, Ch. Tika Ram, Thakur Ripudaman Singh, and Sheikh Faiz Mohammad.[1] The Parliamentary Private Secretaries were, Syed Ahmad Alik Shah, Bhagat Hansraj, Sardar Jagjit Singh Mann, William Roberts, Ch. Sham Lal, Muhammad Faiz Ali Khan, Sardar Gopal Singh.[2] Chaudhary Sir Shahabuddin[3] was elected Speaker of the Assembly and Sardar Dasaundha Singh was elected Deputy Speaker.

The two non-Unionists in the ministry were Sir Manohar Lal and Sir Sunder Singh Majithia. Sir Manohar Lal had been elected as an independent but had later joined the Hindu Election Board and was a close associate of Raja Narender Nath. Sir Sunder Singh Majithia represented the Khalsa National Party. His appointment as minister was strongly opposed by the Akalis.[4] The decision to associate non-Unionist members with the ministry was based mainly on the consideration that both the Khalsa National Party and the Hindu Election Board were politically on the same platform as the Unionists, collaboratively loyal and in most cases beholden and dependent in some way or the other on the patronage of the British government.[5] The Khalsa National Party comprised mainly of big landlords and likewise members of the Hindu Election Board too were mostly the elite, Rai Bahadurs and the like.

The decision to include non-Unionists in the ministry was also politically expedient and was initiated by Sikander Hayat keeping in view the factional feuds in his party. The dissension in the Unionist Party was deeply embedded with roots going into the background of feudal support. The total lack of any ideological or principled bond among many Unionist legislators stands well reflected in the fact that in the 1937 election in 20 Muslim constituencies more than 2 Unionists fought against each other.[6] Even though there was no immediate and imminent danger to Sikander Hayat's ministry, he chose to play safe. By including non-Unionists in the ministry, in essence he sent a message to dissenters within the Unionist Party that he was not dependent solely on them. Sikander also understood well and was an able manipulator of *biradari* loyalties. The fact that the Hayat family did not always adhere to the customary cross-cousin marriage pattern, created a condition where he could trace family links to numerous leading Muslim families.

Sikander's relatives within the Punjab Legislative Assembly included Nawab Muzaffar Khan, Mir Maqbool Mahmood, Sheikh Muhammad Sadiq, Sheikh Sadiq Hasan, Ahmad Bakhash Khan, Pir Ashiq Husain, Mian Bashir Ahmad, Mian Iftikhar-ud-din, Nawab Shah Nawaz Khan and Begum Shah Nawaz.[7] They formed an impressive and influential block rivalled only by the Noon-Tiwana group from the Shahpur district.[8] The loyalty of the Noon-Tiwana group too was assured once Khizr Hayat Tiwana was included in the government as a cabinet minister.[9] The inclusion of the non-Unionists also enabled Sir Sikander Hayat to project himself as a secularist and as a representative of all the major communities in the State.[10] To further bolster this image of communal harmony the first of March was declared Communal Harmony Day and was also made a public holiday.[11]

Sir Sunder Singh Majithia with his feudal background and economic interests common with leaders of the Unionist Party was a natural ally and had no problem working in the Unionist ministry. But for Sir Manohar Lal it was not the same. A crisis of choice arose a number of times particularly when the Unionist Party pursued the debt relief legislations which targeted in most cases the section of trading classes represented by Sir Manohar Lal. Unionist Party programmes were essentially based on rural themes often creating an urban-rural divide, which must have frequently been embarrassing for Manohar Lal. Talbot shows the condescending assessment of some ministers by senior British functionaries. Abdul Haye was once described by Governor Glancy, as 'scarcely a very satisfactory member of the team'. Of Sardar Dasaundha Singh he remarked 'his intentions are good, but his mental calibre is regretably low'.[12]

Sikander Hayat handled the situation quite well as a result of which 110 of the 175 members in the Assembly supported him on most occasions.[13] By April 1938 Governor Emerson had come to believe that Sikander Hayat had become indispensable to the Unionist Party's continued success, 'The ministers have come through the year very well', he wrote to the Viceroy in April 1938, 'success had depended very largely on the personality and popularity of the Premier. It would be difficult to replace him if for any reason he were not able to carry on.'[14]

On assumption of office, Sikander Hayat delivered what can be termed as an inaugural speech. He began by explaining his constraints and difficulties:[15]

> The Punjab Cabinet is under no delusion as to the nature and extent of the limitations and restrictions which the Government of India Act imposes on autonomy even in the provincial sphere. Nevertheless, in pursuance of the clearly expressed wish of the electorate, it has undertaken the task of running the administration and securing the utmost good out of the new constitution. . . .[5]

With regard to the main objectives of his government Sikander said:

> Lightening the burden of the peasantry, tackling the problem of unemployment, development and expansion of nation-building activities, uplifting backward classes, including our brethern of the scheduled castes and creating a more favourable atmosphere for the promotion of communal amity and goodwill are questions which have been a subject of universal comment not only in the Punjab, but throughout India. . . .In order to afford the requisite relief to the peasantry and to provide for the removal or even mitigation of unemployment and the intensification of nation-building activities, it would be necessary to explore fresh avenues and examine the existing sources of revenue with a view to augmenting our income to the extent which would enable us to take appreciable action in these very desirable directions without adding to the burden of the poorer classes.

The statement of Sikander Hayat was in a way a reiteration of the Unionist Party's policy of giving priority to rural development in Punjab. The difference now was that in the Legislative Councils under 'dyarchy' the Unionists were often helpless and even well meaning legislations fizzled out mainly due to opposition in the council as also because of the hurdles created by the government. However, with the introduction of 'provincial autonomy' the ministry formed by the Unionists had a comparatively more free hand to complete and pursue their earlier reforms. The problem of debt naturally attracted the highest priority, having since the inception of the party been the focal theme of its political programme.

In 1937 rural indebtedness in Punjab amounted to around Rs. 200 crore. The Punjab farmers paid back annually as interest alone on the above amount, four to five times the aggregate amount of land revenue and water charges.[16] Moneylending had grown second only to agriculture as the most important industry in the province. Punjab had one-tenth of the population of the British India but it supported one-fifth of its moneylenders.[17] The urgency and priority marked for the problem led the Unionist government to introduce its first legislative proposal in the Assembly, the Registration of Moneylenders Bill.[18] This Bill among other things, aimed at establishing an effective control on moneylending by making a compulsory provision for licences. It provided that a moneylender would not be helped by the courts of law to recover dues unless he was registered and licensed to carry on the trade of moneylending. The act provided that licences could be suspended on detection of malpractice and that during the period of suspension the moneylender would be unable to successfully sue for the recovery of his loans without the permission of the Deputy Commissioner. The Act was applicable to non-agriculturist and agriculturalist moneylenders alike. The fact that only 8232 people got themselves registered as required by the Act out of the estimated 55,000 moneylenders in Punjab shows that people involved in the trade had other methods and alternatives to recover their dues.[19]

The objectives and proposed provisions of the Bill evoked sharp opposing responses in the House.[20] The opposition to the Bill came mainly from the urban members led by Gokul Chand Narang. The opposition to the Bill was based on the plea that it did not have adequate provisions to protect the moneylenders against dishonest debtors for recovery of dues.[21] The Bill, its opponents said, would harm trade and industry in the province.[22] The Unionists defended the Bill, saying 'the need of the day was not protection of the moneylender but the peasant'.[23] Besides, the Unionists said, the intentions and provisions of the Bill were not to harm honest moneylenders but to restrict dishonest practices and regulate the business.[24] Quite in line with the politics of the time, the issue took the form of an urban-rural divide.

The role of the Congress as a party in the Assembly and out of it once again showed a total lack of direction. The party members could not support the Bill openly because they feared the loss of the support of the urban business class but at the same time could not oppose it for the fear of losing the already meagre support the Congress had among the peasantry.[25] While Congress members said that the Unionists were merely wanting to protect the big landlords, the Unionists accused the Congress of wanting to do the same for the moneylenders.[26] The embarrassing situations in which the Congress leaders often found themselves when faced with Unionist Party programmes that were proposed by big landlords but were supposed to benefit the peasantry, were of its own making. This was so, because the Congress failed to offer alternative programmes and in the process failed to win sympathy among the peasantry. The Registration of Moneylenders Bill came into effect from 15 June 1939.[27]

Another issue which had earlier been the point of heated debate in the Punjab Legislative Councils and had now been taken up in the Assembly by the Unionists was the question of mortgage of land. The Restitution of Mortgaged Land Bill 1938 was like the Registration of Moneylenders Bill introduced on priority. It provided for the termination of the mortgages of land contracted by members of the agricultural tribes before 1901. The Bill also provided that a mortgager who had received from the mortgaged land twice or more than twice the principal amount advanced, was not entitled to any further compensation.[28] The introduction of the Bill aroused much controversy and opposition both in the Assembly and outside. 'This is a step calculated to destroy the confidence of the people in the present government', declared Sir Gokul Chand Narang during the course of a debate. He further said: 'It may please a number of mortgagers to whom the land is to be restored, but there are at least fifty per cent of the people who look upon these gentlemen as usurpers.' Opposition to the Bill was also based on the tentative estimates that its provisions when implemented would benefit the Muslim community more than the Hindus and Sikhs. This assumption was later proved by Raja Narender Nath in an article in 1939 in which he said that due to provisions of the Bill about 2,00,000 Hindus and Sikhs had to return land to the original owners as compared to only 84,167 Muslims.[29] Of the total land returned by mortgagers to the original landowners agriculturist moneylenders returned only 5 per cent whereas non-agriculturist moneylenders had to return about 95 per cent.[30] There was widespread demand that the date for implementation of the Bill should not be with retrospective effect that is from 1901 but should be implemented with effect from 1938. This proposal was not accepted by the Unionists and the Bill was passed, however, in its original form by the Assembly on 21 July 1938.[31] About 7,56,131 acres of mortgaged lands were restored to their owners, in most cases without the payment of any compensation to the mortgagers. Sikander Hayat himself lost Rs. 5.5 lakhs and Khizr Hayat Tiwana lost about Rs. 1.5 lakhs. The total amount of mortgage money involved in these old mortgages was about Rs. 4,13,00,000, an amount on which debtors had been paying between Rs. 24 crores to Rs. 50 crores by way of interest every year.[32]

The provisions of the Restitution of Mortgaged Land Act continued to attract criticism for many years. This was mainly because of the date of its implementation and also because its provisions were written in a manner that essentially left out a large number of big landlords who had been involved in a serious manner in the business of moneylending. But there is little doubt in that the Act did give major relief to a vast number of ordinary peasants and as such was an important milestone in the history of agrarian legislations initiated by the Unionists.

Another major legislative measure initiated by the Unionists in the first year of coming to power was the Punjab Alienation of Land (II) Amendment Bill (Act X of 1938), popularly known as the *benami* Bill.[33] The need for such a Bill had arisen because non-agriculturists often indulged in fictitious transactions in respect of land transfers to avoid provisions of the Land Alienation Act. The *modus operandi* was that purchased and transferred land was registered in the names of trusted agriculturist friends. *Benami* transactions had in reality negated the very spirit of the effort to end indebtedness and prevent the sale of land from small peasants to moneylenders. The issue of *benami* transactions had been raised on many occasions for example by Pir Akbar Ali in 1933 in the Punjab Legislative Council.[34] This Bill was passed by the Assembly on 16 July 1938 and received the governor's assent on 23 February 1939. The main provisions of the Bill included the powers to detect illegal transactions and contained provisions to declare such transaction void with retrospective effect.[35] By March 1940, about 41,000[36] such *benami* transactions had been detected, the amount relating to these transactions was about Rs. 16 crore.[37] The Act could have proved even more beneficial but its effective implementation was greatly hampered because some of its provisions were not only challenged in the High Court but more importantly the basic infrastructure required for its stringent and effective implementation like revenue staff, records and manpower did not exist.[38] The main shortcoming of the Act however was the fact that it was applicable only to the pre-1901 period.[39] Once again the Unionist policy clearly suggested that most of its legislative measures were actually directed towards protecting the interests of big landholders. Between 1901 and 1938 it is estimated, for example, that two-third of the land alienated away from the small peasant was in favour of the large landowners.[40]

In 1938, the Unionists put forth another amendment to the Land Alienation Act 1901. It was termed as the Punjab Alienation of Land

(III) Amendment Bill, 1938. In common usage, however, it came to be called the Zamindar Sahukar Act.[41] The Bill was introduced by Sikander Hayat himself and made provisions to protect the agriculturist debtors from agriculturist moneylenders. To discourage underhand transactions the Act provided that even after a debtor had paid off his dues he could not alienate (transfer) his land in the name of his former creditor. The provisions of this Bill were important because some creditors were known to give debtors a clean chit to free themselves from provisions of the various laws and later on mutual understanding, had the lands transfered to their names. Under this Bill even for three years after a debtor was said to have paid off his dues he could not transfer his land in favour of his former creditor. The Bill received the governor's assent in September 1938.

The Punjab Agricultural Produce Markets Act 1939 (Act V, 1939) more popularly known as the Mandi Act[42] passed by the Assembly on 2 February 1939 was an extremely important milestone in the Unionist Party's policy and programme of attempting to restore the financial health of the agriculturists. The actual implementation of the Act was postponed due to widespread protests from affected quarters particularly the grain traders. It was the middlemen trading in agricultural commodities who were directly affected as the purpose of the Bill was essentially to regulate the market to ensure fair prices and judicious dealing by traders with the farmers. The use of unfair practices in the grain trade by the traders was a serious problem in the grain markets of Punjab. Commission agents often made illegal cuts in the farmer's produce.[43] It was estimated that 69 per cent of scales and 42 per cent of weights were fraudulently manipulated as a result of which the farmer got only, '9 $^1/_2$ annas for every rupee worth of grain he sold in the market'.[44]

The Act provided for creation of specified markets where only dealers who were registered with the government could deal in the trade of grain. In each such approved centre, Market Committees were formed. Of the 9 members of a Market Committee, 5 were to be farmers, 2 traders, 1 nominee of the government and 1 nominee of the weighmen.[45] The Act provided for a fine of up to Rs. 500 for violation of regulations as laid in the Act. Widespread agitations to oppose the implementation of the Act were organized by traders mainly in the cities. A non-agriculturist association was formed by Gokul Chand Narang and named 'The All Punjab Non-Agriculturists Association'. In July 1938, a *hartal* was organized by the Association in many Punjab towns and a provincial level conference was organized at Lyallpur.[46] From 15 to 21 August, a 'black week' was organized to protest against such legislative measures of the Unionist Party. Never before had Punjab been divided on rural against urban to such an extent. The tussle was viewed by most as a fight between the 'Banias and the farmers'.[47] The Act could be passed only in April 1941, and was implemented on 1 December 1941. The Act was, as time was to prove, a boon to the farming community, its benefits were beyond doubt. It remains to date the basis of the trade in produce sold by the peasantry and was surely a major milestone in legislation pointed to benefit the peasantry. Of all the legislative measures of the Unionist Party the *Mandi* Act had the most significant and widespread impact.

The Relief of Indebtedness [(Amendment) Act, 1940] provided that interest of above 7.5 per cent for secured debts and 12.5 per cent for unsecured debts would be treated as usury. However, this was not to apply to cooperative societies and banks. The Act also provided that no debtor could be imprisoned or arrested in execution of a decree for debt. Furthermore, milch and transport cattle and personal dwellings of the debtor were protected under provisions of the Act. The preparation of false documents by the creditors was made a criminal offence. The Act further provided that no decree or claim could be passed against an agriculturist debtor for any sum more than twice the original amount. This provision came to be commonly known as *Dandupat* and was made applicable to debts incurred even prior to 1934.[48]

The role of the Debt Conciliation Boards was also further streamlined by this Act. The Debt Conciliation Boards had earlier come into existence under the Punjab Relief of Indebtedness Act, 1935, with such Boards being set up in each district. The objective of the Boards was to settle debts amicably and fairly. The new Act, however, had provided that if creditors failed to appear before these Boards or prove by documents their claims, the case of the creditors against the debtors was to be discharged.[49] Besides, a provision in the Act added that if a creditor refused to accept the settlement decision of these Boards, he would not be able to claim any interest on the amount after the date of the decision of the Board.[50]

While these Boards provided much needed relief to the debt-ridden peasantry of Punjab at the same time, they also enabled evasive and dishonest debtors to avoid paying genuine and fair creditors.[51] The Act was an important legislative measure in the history of debt relief. Chhotu Ram as usual provided a lead in the forceful defence of its provisions.[52] Sohan Singh Josh was among the strong opponents saying that most provisions of the Act were aimed to benefit the big farmers.[53]

The legislative measures which were directed towards improving the condition of the agriculturists and of other rural people had on the whole gathered widespread support from various sections of rural society in Punjab. While some support was based on the merit of the legislations, some was derived from propaganda and a great deal as a sequel to the urban-rural divide that was commonly encouraged by the Unionists in particular.

The political rivals of the Unionist Party while opposing the pro-agriculturist legislative measures of the Unionists also sought to broaden their base of support in rural Punjab by attempting to enlist the support of peasants with marginal landholdings and of those involved in agriculture but having no land on an anti-landlord platform. This being the main objective, a *Kisan* Conference was organized in September 1938 at Layallpur, to coincide with the *Zamindara* Conference that was being organized by the Unionists in the same town.[54] However the response to the *Kisan* Conference was poor and failed to enlist the extent of the support that was expected from the peasantry with small-holdings. On the other hand the *Zamindara* Conference of the Unionist Party which was addressed among others by Sir Sikander Hayat and Sir Chhotu Ram attracted a massive crowd of over 1.5 lakh people.[55] The massive response received by the Unionist leaders comes out as perhaps the best example of cross-community politics of the party. But even more importantly the response proved the views of Unionist leaders like Chhotu Ram who had always stressed that the size of landholdings owned by different people as also communal differences got naturally diffused because of the elements of similarity like cultural and social values and problems that were related to the agricultural profession.

The political agenda of the Unionists, that those involved in agriculture were a class by themselves irrespective of which community they belonged to stood out successfully in the Lyallpur *Zamindara* Conference.[56]

The *Kisan* Conference organized mainly by the Congress and addressed among others by Jawaharlal Nehru could attract only about 15,000 people.[57] That a worthwhile and gainful opposition could not be built up against the agrarian legislations of the Unionist Party in spite of widespread publicity partly indicates quite significantly that majority of rural Punjab's populace accepted the Party's stand vis-a-vis the legislations. All over Punjab numerous meetings were organized in support of the Unionists with over 100 meetings being organized in Amritsar district alone.[58] A large number of farmers attended these meetings out of genuine enthusiasm. Chhotu Ram was always the star attraction at these meetings which were held across the length and breadth of the state.[59]

During the period (1937-46) the Unionist government also pursued the consolidation of small and scattered landholdings. The ownership of land in scattered units entailed numerous problems for the farmers making such holdings economically unviable. The consolidation of landholdings had an extremely encouraging impact on agricultural production as well as reduction in actual costs. This work was initially assigned to the Cooperative Department, later the Revenue Department was also associated with it.

The development of new irrigation infrastructure and improvement in the existing one was also given priority by the Unionist

TABLE 4.1: PROGRESS OF LAND HOLDING CONSOLIDATION

Year	Area consolidated (*in Acres*)	Expenditure incurred (*in Rupees*)
1937-8	1,50,784	2,84,281
1939-40	2,16,644	4,33,754
1942-3	2,27,305	4,31,910
1945-6	2,69,112	4,53,712

SOURCE: *Punjab Govt. Gazette* (Extraordinary), 8 March 1945, p. 33.

government. The Haveli Canal Project was completed at a cost of Rs. 3.63 crores and provided irrigation to an area of about 50,000 acres.[60] The Thal Project (started in May 1939) on its completion provided irrigation to 10 lakh acres in Mianwali, Muzaffargarh and Shahpur districts.[61] The Western Yamuna Canal System was further extended and by September 1940, it was providing irrigation to about 4.2 lakh acres of land in what is today the Haryana region.[62] Chhotu Ram was perhaps the single most important person who galvanised a new movement for growth in irrigation facility. Y.P. Bajaj has presented an exhaustive review of the large number of irrigation schemes initiated and developed by the Unionist Party.[63]

Other small but important irrigation projects included an experimental scheme of 20 tubewells to irrigate 1000 acres near Lahore, some modifications were made to Tajewala Headworks on the river Yamuna, for Ambala and Karnal districts and a project was also started to control the waters of the Beas in Hoshiarpur district.[64] Table 4.2 shows the growth in the irrigation facility in Punjab during the years that the Unionists were in power in Punjab.

Another important feature of development aimed mainly at rural Punjab was in the field of veterinary service. It was mainly due to the Unionist government's effort that by 1945-6 there were 371 veterinary hospitals and 506 dispensaries in Punjab,[65] with a budget of Rs. 20.05 lakhs in 1945.[66] A small but important step for encouraging the growth of veterinary science was the offering of a half-fee concession by the Punjab Veterinary College at Lahore to students opting for the veterinary course.

The impact of agricultural developmental policies in rural Punjab during the 'provincial autonomy' years however was not directly

TABLE 4.2: GROWTH IN AREA UNDER IRRIGATION

Year	Area irrigated in lakhs of acres
1932-3	105
1936-7	119
1937-8	123
1941-2	131
1945-6	143

SOURCE: *Five Years of Provincial Autonomy in the Punjab* (Lahore, 1942, Govt. Publication), p. 61.

reflected in the increase in food-grain production, even though the budget head of agriculture showed an increase of 197 per cent in the years 1937-46.[67] The main reason for this it seems was that World War II was at its peak in the years when the developmental work should actually have started yielding expected results. The conditions of war, however, disturbed the economy and disrupted the economic activity in Punjab as it did all over the world. But more importantly the compulsions of war influenced government policy which in turn proved to be dispiriting for the growth of agriculture. For example, during the War years compulsory requisition of grain at unreasonably low prices had a discouraging effect on the farmers. Even the policy of importing wheat from Australia and cotton from Egypt, for example, contributed in creating a condition where prices remained low.[68] Other factors that prevented growth in food grain production were backward and obsolete techniques of farming,[69] outdated implements, shortage of good manure, fragmentation of holdings and above all shortage of adequate and timely funds.[70]

Numerous infrastructural developmental measures were initiated and encouraged during the 'provincial autonomy' years by the Unionist government. In the public health sphere, for example, efforts were made to provide clean drinking water to a number of villages. From a mere Rs. 10.37 lakhs in 1937 the public health budget went upto Rs. 36.06 lakhs in 1945-6.[71] As a result by 1945-6 there were about 500 drinking water supply schemes in Punjab as compared to not even one before 1937.[72]

TABLE 4.3: PRODUCTION OF IMPORTANT FOOD GRAINS IN PUNJAB, 1942-6

(in thousand tons)

Foodgrain	1942-3	1944-5	1945-6
Wheat	1241.1	1189.2	1152.6
Gram	673.6	519.0	730.4
Barley	170.4	125.3	105.3
Paddy	195.8	182.5	159.3
Maize	295.8	335.2	297.1

SOURCE: *Agricultural Statistics of Punjab 1939-49* (Simla, 1950, Govt. Publication), p. 1.

Similarly the expenditure of the health department also showed a sharp increase from Rs. 16.34 lakhs to Rs. 2,822 lakhs in 1945.[73] This enabled hitherto ignored areas to secure funds, for example the number of clinics for leprosy patients had increased from 106 in 1937 to 211 in 1945.[74] Similarly the number of centres for maternity and child welfare went up to 280 sub-centres in 1945 from 89 sub-centres in 1937.[75] Special schemes for metalling of roads, maternity hospitals, dispensaries, child centres, sanitation lessons, etc., were launched on a large scale.[76] In 1942 a Peasants' Welfare Fund was started to provide financial assistance to peasants with very small holdings and families of soldiers.[77] Similarly about Rs. 55 lakhs was provided in 1944 for opening cooperative stores in rural market towns and also to improve road conditions, etc.[78]

Financial aid was also provided in the form of *taccavi*, in times of natural disaster like famines, hail storms, etc. Sikander Hayat, for example, visited Hissar following the Hissar famine. Free fodder for milch cattle was provided, costing about Rs. 19 lakhs,[79] in addition revenue and water rates too were remitted. Loss due to 'hail storm' in 1937 (*Rabi*) was compensated with about Rs. 44 lakhs.[80] Remission of revenue, and *taccavi* remained a common feature throughout the period 1937-46. Sikander Hayat said in 1942 (Budget speech) that in the preceding five years his government had remitted *abiana* mainly due to the Unionist Party's efforts, as a result of which the peasant of Punjab paid the lowest land revenue in the country.[81]

The Unionist government's work with regard to local self-governing institutions also merits some mention. The passage of the Punjab Village Panchayat Act, 1939 was an important initiative. Later a separate Panchayat Department was created.[82] The Punjab Village Panchayat Act considerably broadened the functional scope of the Panchayats by bringing under their control all such criminal cases in which the punishment on the event of conviction was not supposed to exceed one year in normal cases. In matters of civil litigation the Panchayats were also empowered to try cases upto a value of Rs. 200 which could be extended by the government to Rs. 500 under special circumstances. The administrative functions of the Panchayats had also been broadened so as to include the level of taxes on select items which were previously under the competence of the Legislative Assembly. The Act was implemented in 12,000 of Punjab's 36,000 villages significantly contributing to the develop-ment of local government. The utility of the Act is well illustrated by the fact that in 1946 alone, for example, the concerned Panchayats in Punjab entertained and decided 27,715 criminal and 32,345 civil suits, in which decisions of these Panchayats were reversed only in 327 cases.[83] The operating objectivity of the Panchayats and their acceptance as instruments of justice and decision-making reached a high peak during the period. This fact stands even more underlined when we consider that by 1945-6 Punjab was on the verge of flaring up into flames because of communal strife.

Like in the field of rural local self-government the Unionist government also did some useful work in the field of education. The Punjab Primary Education Act was passed in January 1941. It provided for free and compulsory education for children in the age group of 6-12 years.[84] A special scheme was also started in 1938, under which one special school was started in every Tehsil of the province.[85] The special features of these schools were that they possessed relatively modern equipment and educational appliances with a curriculum which included the teaching of agriculture on an attached farm. The schools also functioned as model schools for teachers and students of neighbouring regions.

Efforts were also made during the Unionist period to make teaching and instructions more effective and attractive. Syllabi were revised and emphasis was given to vernacular education. For spreading vernacular education, 400 teachers were specially recruited and trained.[86] Education for girls showed a marked progress during the years. In 1937, for example, Punjab had 1,67,858 school going girls, by 1945 this figure had gone upto 2,33,290, showing an increase of over 34 per cent.[87] This stands out as a major contribution of the Unionist government, though in terms of the total population it was just the beginning but it was a positive step.

A scheme to encourage education among backward tribes was also started with the opening of 42 such schools for boys and girls.[88] Primary education in particular made good progress during the years 1937-46. For example, in 1937 only 25 per cent of the 52 per cent of the children enrolled could reach class IV, whereas by 1946 about

53 per cent of the enrolled children managed to enter class IV.[89] In 1937 there were 7,641 primary schools in Punjab, this figure had risen to 8,375 in 1942 and to 9,763 in 1946.[90] The figures become even more significant when we realize that there was a severe crunch of resources and finance during the war years 1939-45.

In industry the Unionist government gave emphasis to cottage and rural-based industry. In many ways Sir Chhotu Ram represented the planning and policy face of the Unionist Party.[91] Y.P. Bajaj has discussed in detail a long list of Unionist contributions in the field of industry mainly in relation to Chhotu Ram. The Punjab State Aid to Industries (Amendment) Act was passed in 1939. The main objectives of the Act were to encourage cottage and rural industry. A scheme of subsidies was started,[92] and an amount of Rs. 1,50,000 was also provided for industrial research.[93] Special attention was given to small scale industry like toilet goods, starch, oil extraction, rope and nivar making, carpentry, pottery, tailoring and even sericulture.[94] To give a boost to the weaving and hosiery industries special incentive schemes of rewarding weavers were started.[95] A few cooperatives were also set up to assist selected industry for the sale of goods.

The Unionist Party leadership, however, betrayed, on various occasions an attitude which appeared to be anti-labour. For example, Chhotu Ram opposed the Minimum Rate of Wages Bill, introduced in the Assembly by Gopi Chand Bhargava on 2 January 1938 and again by Giani Kartar Singh on 23 November 1939.[96] Chhotu Ram's opposition to the Bill as pointed out by Bajaj was based on two ideas, namely that industry in Punjab was far too weak to withstand provisions of the proposed Bill and that extensive staff would be required to enforce the provision which the government appeared in no position to provide.[97] On similar grounds some Unionists opposed a bill introduced by Sheikh Muhammad Alam on 22 January 1939, which proposed to regulate working hours of employed labour. This Bill, the Punjab Hours of Work Bill had proposed a 40-hour per week of work.[98] Likewise the Unionists also opposed the Printing Press Control Bill, introduced by Sohan Singh Josh on 26 October 1939.[99] This Bill had proposed to give security of service to workers in printing presses which were not covered by the Factory Act because more often they employed less than twenty people. Sir

Chhotu Ram was among the principle speakers who opposed these labour oriented Bills, on the floor of the Assembly. Essentially his basic argument was that industry in Punjab was in an infant and unsure stage and would not be able to survive the labour protective measures that were contained in the Bills.[100]

The opposition of Chhotu Ram to some of the labour favouring legislative proposals whatever his reason was obviously retrograde. The Unionist Party, however, showed some change for the better when it came up with the Trade Employees Act of 1940.[101] The Act was similar to the like which was already implemented in Bombay. Basically it provided for, (i) four paid holidays a month; (ii) not more than 11 hours of work a day and not more than 40 hours a week; (iii) no employee could be dismissed without a month's notice; (iv) children less than 14 years of age were not to be employed in industrial establishments.[102]

The Unionist government (1937-46) maintained a bias towards rural Punjab in matters of allocation of funds and pursuance of development schemes. This policy enabled them to establish considerable goodwill among the masses in rural areas. The support and widespread acceptance of the Unionist government is best reflected in the peasantry's response to the 'golden agrarian laws', in particular and also in the fact that no worthwhile opposition could be built against the Unionist Party programmes during the years that it ruled Punjab. The party's policy of working to improve the quality of rural life, to decrease the burden of rural debt was not only a basic political strategy but also a political compulsion that enabled it to stay afloat. The result the pro-rural policy yielded were in fact expected of it.

The Unionist government provided funds and administrative support for better sanitation, water supply, medical relief, rural health, roads, night schools, intermediate colleges, more primary and high schools. The cooperative and local self-government departments, agriculture, consolidation of land holdings, veterinary services, irrigation, etc., were all given increased financial support.

It is difficult to overlook the fact that its collaborative politics and isolation from the national political mainstream notwithstanding, the Unionist Party was able to retain for most of the period it was in power the goodwill of the rural masses of Punjab. The period from 1937 to 1946, but more effectively only up to Chhotu Ram's death in January 1945, is correctly known in rural Punjab as the period of the 'golden laws'. Even today the old timers remember with nostalgia the 'revolutionary' enactments of new laws for the improvement of life in rural Punjab, for emancipation of the peasantry from debt, for more protection against exploitation by traders, etc. Collaboration with colonial rule or no collaboration the fact remains that the very names of Unionist leaders like Chhotu Ram and Sikander Hayat were enough to assemble lakhs of ordinary peasants in any part of Punjab particularly so in the eastern and south-eastern districts. The differences in response to the conference organized simultaneously by the Congress and Unionists in Lyallpur in 1938 is a good example. While just about 15,000 people came to the Congress-organized conference to listen to Jawaharlal Nehru, approximately 1.5 lakh people turned up to participate in the Unionist-organized conference addressed by Chhotu Ram and Sikander Hayat.

NOTES

1. *The Tribune*, 7 March 1937.
2. Ibid.
3. Chaudhry Sir Shahabuddin (d.1946) belonged to Sialkot district and was a successful lawyer in the Lahore High Court. He was a member of the Central Legislative Assembly, 1921-3; Punjab Legislative Council 1923-36; and the Punjab Legislative Assembly 1937-46. In the council he remained president from 1923 to 1936 and was speaker in the new Assembly up to his death in 1946. See Craig Baxter, 'The Peoples Party Versus The Punjab Feudalists', *Journal of Asian and African Studies*, vol. VIII: 3 and 4 (1973), pp. 166-89.
4. *The Tribune*, 7 March 1939.
5. Penderel Moon, *Divide and Quit* (London, 1961), p. 32.
6. See Yadav, *Elections*, p. 88.
7. See C. Baxter, 'The People's Party Versus the Punjab Feudalists', p. 171; also Talbot, *Punjab and the Raj*, p. 115.
8. Talbot, *Punjab and the Raj*, p. 115.
9. Ibid.
10. *The Tribune*, 15 October 1938; also ibid.
11. Talbot, *Khizr Tiwana*, p. 77.

12. Ibid., p. 71.
13. *Five Years of Provincial Autonomy in the Punjab,* p. 14.
14. Home Political (FR), 1st half April 1938, cited in Talbot, *Punjab and the Raj*, p. 116.
15. *Five Years of Provincial Autonomy in the Punjab*, p. 14, also *The Tribune*, 2 April 1937.
16. D.C. Verma, 'Provincial Autonomy in the Punjab, April 1937-October 1939', *Indian Journal of Political Science*, vol. I (1940), p. 457.
17. Calvert, *Wealth and Welfare*, p. 367.
18. *Punjab Government Gazette* (Extraordinary), 2 September 1939, pp. 111-14.
19. *PLAD*, vol. V, 1938, pp. 228-30.
20. Ibid., pp. 978-89.
21. Ibid.
22. Ibid.
23. Ibid.
24. Ibid.
25. Ibid., pp. 983-9.
26. Ibid.
27. *Punjab Govt. Gazette,* Part I, 9 June 1939.
28. *PLAD*, vol. V, 1938, pp. 228-30.
29. See Raja Narender Nath, 'The Punjab Agrarian Laws and their Economic and Constitutional Bearings', *Modern Review*, 65 (1939), p. 30.
30. Ibid.
31. *Punjab Govt. Gazette* (Extraordinary), 6 July 1938, p. 115.
32. Raja Narender Nath, 'The Punjab Agrarian Laws', op. cit., p. 30.
33. *Punjab Govt. Gazette* (Extraordinary), 17 July 1939, p. 119.
34. N.N. Mitra, *Indian Annual Register*, vol. II, 1938, p. 228.
35. Ibid.
36. Prem Chaudhary, *Punjab Politics and the Role of Sir Chhotu Ram* (Delhi, 1984), p. 274.
37. *PLAD*, vol. XII, 5 March 1940, p. 3.
38. Prem Chaudhary, *Punjab Politics and the Role of Sir Chhotu Ram*, p. 278.
39. Ibid.
40. Ibid.
41. N.N. Mitra (ed.), *Indian Annual Register*, vol. II, 1938, p. 196.
42. Ibid.
43. *Punjab Govt. Gazette* (Extraordinary), 1 May 1939.
44. *Jat Gazette,* 23 November 1938. This meant a peasant received about half of the worth for every Rupee of produce he sold. At that time a Rupee was of '16 Annas'.
45. N.N. Mitra (ed.), *Indian Annual Register*, vol. II, 1938, p. 229.
46. *PLAD*, vol. VII, 19 January 1939, p. 594.
47. Talbot, *Punjab and the Raj*, p. 120.

48. *The Hindustan Times*, 2 May 1941.
49. *Punjab Govt. Gazette* (Extraordinary), 5 October 1940.
50. Ibid.
51. *PLAD*, vol. XII, 12 April 1940, pp. 50-3; also *Punjab Govt. Gazette* (Extraordinary), 5 October 1940.
52. Ibid.
53. *Report on the Working of Debt Conciliation Boards in Punjab* (Lahore, 1940), p. 1.
54. *PLAD*, vol. XII, 8 April 1940, p. 283.
55. Ibid.
56. Interview, Rai Sahib Anant Ram (Unionist Party MLA, 1937-46), 28 January 1988.
57. Home Political (FR), 1st half September 1938, cited in Talbot, *Punjab and the Raj*, p. 119.
58. Ibid.
59. Ibid.
60. *The Tribune*, 31 August 1938; also Talbot, *Punjab and the Raj*, p. 119.
61. See Pardaman Singh (ed.), *Chhotu Ram in the Eyes of His Contemporaries* (New Delhi, 1992).
62. *PLAD*, vol. XII, 6 March 1940, p 132.
63. Ibid., vol. XI, 1 January 1940, p. 557; also vol. XIX, 12 March 1942, p. 185.
64. *Jat Gazette*, 8 August 1943, p. 5.
65. Y.P. Bajaj, 'Sir Chhotu Ram and His Work' (unpublished Ph.D. thesis), pp. 166-87.
66. *Five Years of Provincial Autonomy*, pp. 552-3.
67. *PLAD*, vol. XXII, 10 March 1944, pp. 490-3.
68. *Punjab Budgets*, with detailed estimates, 1944-5, cited in Bajaj, 'Sir Chhotu Ram and His Work . . .', p. 114.
69. *Punjab Govt. Gazette* (Supplement), vol. II, 1945, p. 28.
70. *Jat Gazette*, 20 October 1943, also 16 June 1943, p. 1.
71. See B.S. Saini, *Social and Economic History of Punjab*, pp. 171-81.
72. Raj Pal, 'Agricultural Production in Haryana 1900-1966' (unpublished Ph.D. thesis, Kurukshetra University, 1996), has shown in a remarkable manner how various policies of the government influenced the production of food grain in south-east Punjab (today Haryana).
73. See *Punjab Budgets*, with detailed estimates for 1936-7 and 1945-6.
74. *Five Years of Provincial Autonomy*, p. 39; also Bajaj, 'Sir Chhotu Ram and His Work . . .', p. 243.
75. N.N. Mitra, *Indian Annual Register*, 1945, p. 237.
76. *Five Years of Provincial Autonomy*, pp. 36-8.
77. Ibid.
78. *PLAD*, vol. I, XXIV, 5 March 1945.

79. Ibid., vol. XVIII, 12 February 1942, p. 506.
80. Ibid., vol. XXII, 10 March 1944, p. 405.
81. Ibid., vol. VI, 12 November 1938, p. 148.
82. *Eighteen Months of Provincial Autonomy*, p. 13.
83. *PLAD*, vol. XIX, 10 March 1942, p. 220.
84. Bajaj, 'Land Revenue Reforms of The Unionist Party', *Punjab Past and Present*, vol. X-II, October 1976, p. 355.
85. *PLAD*, vol. XII, 6 March 1940, pp. 135-6.
86. *Annual Report on the Working of the Panchayats in Punjab*, 1945-46, p. 2.
87. *Five Years of Provincial Autonomy*, p. 30.
88. Ibid.
88. Ibid, p. 31.
90. Ibid., p. 32.
91. Ibid., p. 28.
92. Ibid.
93. *Annual Report on the Progress of Education*, 1945-6, p. 37.
94. Bajaj, 'Sir Chhotu Ram and His Work . . .', pp. 188-218.
95. *PLAD*, vol. X, 27 October 1939, p. 231; also see Bajaj, 'Sir Chhotu Ram and His Work . . .', pp. 188-218.
96. Ibid.
97. *Five Years of Provincial Autonomy*, p. 57.
98. *PLAD*, vol. IV, 25 March 1939, p. 26.
99. Ibid. vol. II, 21 January 1938, p. 702 and vol. X, 23 November 1939, pp. 901-10.
100. Bajaj, 'Chhotu Ram', pp. 203-4.
101. *PLAD*, vol. X, 26 October 1939, p. 719.
102. Ibid., p. 157.

CHAPTER 5

Politics and Political Relations

THE POLITICAL tradition of the Unionist Party was deeply embedded in the politics of vested class interest. The politics of the party was in fact significantly influenced by the feudal background of a large majority of its leaders. The collaborative nature and the frequently contradictory policy towards other political parties for example, reflected its opportunitic character. This political opportunism was partly responsible for the fact that the party found it difficult and nearly impossible to withstand the onslaught of its political opponents once the people of Punjab were confronted with an 'issue'-based political agenda. So fickle was its basis of support that even a far weaker tide than that which was created by the demand for Pakistan could have dislodged it. Yet quite paradoxically the concept of Unionist politics did not disappear with it and has in fact persisted as we shall see later in regions that formed pre-partition Punjab.

The common economic interests of the feudal elite apart, the most significant feature that bound together the Unionist Party legislators and its other leaders was the existence of some association or obligation on their part towards the colonial establishment. Perhaps there was not even a single important Unionist leader who was not in some form or the other indebted to the British for assistance or favour. This remarkable ability of the British to create support and loyalty among the influential elite of Punjab's society went a long way in deciding the course and colour of politics the province would adopt.

A majority of Unionist Party legislators and other influential leaders were owners of large landed estates, but even among them some owned exceptionally large estates. The Hayats, Tiwanas and Noons for example, were three such families, and were also pillars of the Unionist Party. The Hayat family was popularly known as the Hayats of Wah (Attock District).[1] Sardar Sir Sikander Hayat Khan, who became the Premier of Punjab in 1937, was the most famous scion of the family. Sikander's father Nawab Muhammad Hayat Khan started the family's tradition of loyal service to the British. He served as General Nicholson's aide-de-camp when Nicholson was Deputy Commissioner of Peshawar. He was by the side of Nicholson when the latter was fatally wounded in the recapture of Delhi in 1857.[2] He rose rapidly in the British administrative hierarchy for outstanding loyalty, from a 'thanedar' in 1858 to an assistant commissioner in 1872. In 1896 he was made divisional judge and in 1899, (two years before his death), he was given the title of Nawab.[3] Sikander had five brothers. The eldest, Sardar Aslam Hayat Khan retired as Additional District Magistrate, and the second Masud Hayat Khan, rose to become Quarter Master General in the Patiala State forces.[4] The third, Abdul, was in the Indian Police Service, he had played an important role in detecting the Ghaddar conspiracy leaders.[5] In 1928 he was made Nawab, for services rendered to the police department.[6] Sikander himself was the first Indian to command a company of the British Indian Army in active service.[7] He played an active role in recruiting men on behalf of the colonial government for being sent to Europe to take part in the First World War and was also an honorary magistrate. The youngest of the Sikander brothers was Nawab Muhammad Hayat Khan, who was member of the District Board and President of the Hassanabdal town committee. Sikander had five sons Shaukat, Azamt, Rizatt, Issat and Ghairat.[8] Of these the eldest passed out from the IMA in 1937 and played an active political role in pre- and post-Partition Punjab. After his father's death (1942) he became the focal point of dissent against his father's successor Khizr Hayat in Unionist politics and later played a crucially important role in building the political prospects of the Muslim League in Punjab. A large number of other close and distant relations of Sikander served the British government in Punjab on various important positions.[9] Sikander, the main Unionist leader after Fazl-i-Husain was thus ideally placed to play an important role in Punjab politics with his well spread out network of close relations in important positions, high social status and vast landed estates.

Like the Hayats, the Tiwanas too, had a history of devoted and loyal service to the British. The most famous of the Tiwanas was Khizr Hayat who became Premier after Sikander in 1942. But his grandfather Malik Sahib Khan had also played an important role in suppressing the 1857 Revolt in Jhelum under the command of Col. Cooper. He later accompanied General Napier in the central India campaigns to suppress the Revolt.[10] His son Umar Hayat Khan Tiwana (Khizar's father) followed in his father's footsteps of unquestioned loyalty to the government. He was among the six Muslims to represent his community at Queen Victoria's Diamond Jubilee celebrations. He held various important positions in the army, being the first Indian to be chosen as a Herald for King George's Coronation Durbar.[11] He was made a major-general and appointed aide-de-camp to King George. Khizr Hayat Khan graduated from Aitchinson College and served in the army for some time. He first joined Sikander's ministry in 1937 as minister for Public Works. Many of Khizr's cousins were provincial darbaries, zaildars, jagirdars, etc.

The third family that influenced the politics of Punjab and of the Unionist Party were the Noons. Like the Hayats and Tiwanas they too had a long history of loyalty to the British and were also the owners of large land estates. Sir Firoz Khan Noon was the most famous member of the family. He remained a minister in Punjab for eight years.[12] In 1936 he was appointed India's high commissioner to England. Firoz Khan's father Muhammad Hayat Khan Noon retired as commissioner in 1931 and from then until his death he remained a member of the Council of States. His brothers too like most of the other members of the clan were well placed in military and civil services.

There were many other families some of whom owned even larger land estates than the Hayats and Tiwanas and were equally influential in their regions in Unionist politics. Among such families for example, were the Chathas of Gujranwala, the Gurumanis of Muzaffargarh, the Sials of Jhang and the Mamdots of Firozepur. The close knit character of politically influential families and the manner in which they dominated the politics of their respective regions and of Punjab becomes obvious from the fact that in the elections of 1920, 1923, 1926 and 1930, of the 21 seats reserved for Muslim landowners only 51 different persons were elected: 4 were elected in all the four elections, 7 were elected thrice and 13 twice.[13]

Like the well-established feudal families of Punjab the *pirs* and *sajjada nishins* were important constituents of the Unionist Party and were instrumental in influencing the course of its politics and policies. Some important supporters of the party for example, were the *pir* of Taunsa, *pir* of Golara, *pir* of Makhad, *pir* of Jalalpur, *pir* of Alipur, *pir* of Pakpattan, the Gilani and Qureshi *pir* of Multan, the *sajjada nishin* of the Chishti Shrine of Mahar Sharif (Bhawalpur State), the *sajjada nashin* of the Dargah of Hazrat Khwaja Mouddin Chishti (Ajmer), and the *sajjada nishin* of the *Dargah* of Nizamuddin Aulia (Delhi). Most had widespread religious influence and at the same time were also big landlords,[14] a combination strong enough itself to bring the masses under complete subjugation and political control.

The other important political constituent of the Unionist Party were the *biradari* leaders. They were responsible for the party's image of opportunism, contradictory political stands and total lack of a principle and ideological orientation. Support or opposition, loyalty or disloyalty of such members to the party was governed by parameters which were almost always dominated by non-political issues and self-seeking plans. It is not surprising that important decisions were invariably influenced by *biradari* loyalty and the *biradari* network. Sikander Hayat, for example, and later his son Shaukat were better known as leaders of the Hayat *biradari*. Even though Chhotu Ram was a merited leader of the peasantry, yet he was and to this day remains better known as a leader of the Jats. Caste politics, as Louis Dumont suggested,[15] has always been known to assert at the cost of politicoeconomic politics. Unionist politics in its naked form was essentially caste and *biradari* politics.

The Unionist Party's political tradition was also considerably influenced by a small but very powerful class of privileged people, the Nawabs, Khan Bahadurs, CIEs and the retired and serving senior Indian officials of the British bureaucratic and military system. As the system of recruitment for Indians to good government jobs gave emphasis to family background, most of those who joined pivotal services usually had land or other sound financial resources, but even those that did not were frequently given large land grants, a routine practise in the Raj to acknowledge loyalty of Indians to the colonial rulers.

Unionist Party politics and political relations both appeared to be representative of a society compartmentalized on the basis of traditional and feudal values and attitudes. In many ways the political character of the Unionist Party was an extension of Punjab society itself and as such its political relations must be studied within the context of the peculiar and unprecedented political conditions that British rule had created in Punjab.

During his lifetime Fazl-i-Husain had remained the guiding force of his party's relations with other political organizations as also with the British, often overshadowing the political affairs of the Muslim community in Punjab. As a result of the fact that in the 1930s Fazl-i-Husain was able to retain the political focus on himself and his party, the All India Muslim League could manage only a nominal political presence in Punjab.[16] It had few workers, no office, practically no resources.[17] The 1931 session of the Muslim League, for example, presented a picture of confusion, disorder and insignificant attendance.[18] The fact that the Muslim League could manage to win only two seats out of 175 in the 1937 elections to the Assembly was also not a coincidence but in fact only pointed to its rootless presence in the region.[19]

In the death of Fazl-i-Husain (1936), not only did the Unionist Party lose its leader but the Muslim community was deprived of a person who had been guiding its political destiny for some time. A definite political vacuum had appeared. It was this vacant slot in the Muslim politics of Punjab that Mohammad Ali Jinnah rushed to fill. Sikander Hayat the new leader of the Unionist Party was smaller in political stature than his predecessor Fazl-i-Husain, perhaps even less resourceful. In essence this meant that he was far more amenable to political pulls and pressures. As for Jinnah, Punjab was not only to be the cornerstone of the 'two nation' theory,[20] he may have had in mind, but in any case it was also politically the most important

Muslim majority province in the country. Notwithstanding the significance of Punjab in Muslim politics, the Punjab Muslim League was overshadowed by its embarrassing political performance in the 1937 elections to the Punjab Legislative Assembly. This important setback had initiated serious and widespread introspection within the League leadership both at the provincial and at the national levels.

The Muslim League's approach towards the Unionist Party after 1937 and more specifically towards its Muslim constituents came to be influenced by the urgent desire to establish a consequential political presence in Punjab, mainly because it was understood that the Muslim League's non-functional condition would derail the plans that Jinnah had in mind. It seems that the Muslim League supremo had come to consider the fortunes of his party in Punjab as a kind of springboard for his own political future. Jinnah's first step towards strengthening the Muslim League in Punjab thereafter appeared in the form of the Sikander-Jinnah Pact (15-18 October 1937).[21] Sikander Hayat was invited by Jinnah to attend the Muslim League Conference at Lucknow. Jinnah's invitation to Sikander was an important departure from the known stand of the Punjab Muslim League towards the Unionist Party. For the Unionists too the invitation from Jinnah must have come as a surprise. Isphani, a close associate of Jinnah provides two main reasons to explain the circumstances that led to this political meeting.[22] In fact the acceptance of the invitation by Sikander Hayat itself raised many an eyebrow.

Isphani has attempted to explain this sudden and unexpected political development by suggesting that Sikander Hayat accepted the invitation of Jinnah because he was unnerved by the growth in popularity of the Congress following its mass contact programme after 1937. The Congress as we know had formed a government in eleven provinces in the country after the elections. In Punjab too during the post-election years the Congress showed a marked improvement in its popular appeal mainly as a result of its mass contact programme. Yet Isphani's suggestion, that the Congress had recovered enough ground within a few months of the elections to challenge the existence of the Unionist government seems somewhat far-fetched and scarcely credible as also pointed out by Talbot.[23]

The second reason provided by Isphani to explain Sikander Hayat's agreeing to associate in a political understanding with Jinnah is that Muslim public opinion had undergone a marked swing in favour of the Muslim League in Punjab soon after the elections. Isphani has suggested that Sikander Hayat by signing the agreement with Jinnah showed respect to the change in the political inclination of the Muslim community towards the Muslim League in Punjab. This suggestion too, seems off the mark simply because there was no important development during the period that could have possibly indicated the change being suggested in favour of the Muslim League so soon after it had been dramatically routed. In the intervening months that is between the elections and the 'Sikander-Jinnah' Pact, nothing of any political significance is noticed either in favour or against the Unionist Party or the Muslim League so as to have altered the situation to such an extent that Sikander should be so unnerved.

Imran Ali,[24] explains the genesis of the Sikander-Jinnah meeting saying that influential Unionist leaders including Shah Nawaj Khan Mamdot had prevailed upon Sikander Hayat. He believes Sikander Hayat was made to understand that a division of the Unionist Party was imminent if Sikander ignored the overtures of the Muslim League.[25] Imran Ali further suggests that a section of the faction-ridden Unionist Party saw the Muslim League as 'an open door', welcoming desertion. Intrigue and division were embedded in the Unionist Party with its whole edifice standing on feudal support. It was this feudal and opportunistic character of the Unionist Party that seemed to provide sufficient basis to assume that the Muslim League could have achieved considerable success in initiating desertions from the Unionist Party. But quite at the same time the type of politics practised by the Unionist Party should remind us of the fact that big landlords in colonial countries depending greatly on government patronage for political and economic influence have been known to desert only in favour of greener pastures. With complete and meaningful support of the British it must be remembered that the Unionist Party in 1937 was surely a better option for the opportunistic politicians of the time. Whatever the Unionist Party achieved in terms of development of Punjab was essentially in the period 1937-42. It needs hardly be stressed that this was possible only because the Party's government enjoyed the support and confidence of the British administrators.

A politically more feasible reason for Sikander Hayat's accepting the invitation of Jinnah may have been the fact that during September and October 1937 there was a marked increase in communal tension and related riots in scattered pockets of Punjab.[26] The Shahid Ganj mosque issue, for example, had been raked up by extremist Muslim groups.[27] Sikander Hayat by joining the political dialogue with Jinnah was perhaps hoping to diffuse and control such people. He hoped to achieve this by conveying the point that he was as much concerned with the welfare of the Muslim as his rivals claimed and that he was not totally averse to joining hands with the Muslim League for causes that could prove beneficial to the Muslims of Punjab.

Khizr Hayat, the man who succeeded Sikander as the Premier too has put forth the view that before proceeding to Lucknow Sikander Hayat had consultations with important personal friends including Sir Henry Craik with whom Sikander had also served in the Provincial Executive Council. Sir Craik supported the idea of Sikander Hayat entering a dialogue with Jinnah which would mean from the British government's point of view, strengthening the resolve of Jinnah in the fight against the Congress. This explanation of Khizr Hayat appears more acceptable mainly because it was believed that the revival of the Muslim League's influence in the Punjab would not only sustain British influence in the province but would also counter the increasing influence of the Congress all over the country. In any case, there is little doubt in that the Sikander-Jinnah pact provided a much needed respite to the Muslim League in Punjab. In a way it was the starting point of the League's renewed effort to bring the Muslims of Punjab under its unchallenged influence.

Chhotu Ram had disapproved and expressed strong reservation to Sikander Hayat with regard to participating in the proposed talks with the Muslim League, at one stage he even threatened to resign from the party. Chhotu Ram relented only after Sikander vowed on the Holy Koran that he would not sacrifice the Unionist Party's interest to the Muslim League. This assurance of the premier averted a major crisis in the Unionist Party. The agreement was signed on 13 October 1937 and announced the next day amidst great rejoicing and shouts of '*Allah-o-Akbar*'.[28] The main points accepted were:

(i) That on his return to Punjab, Sikander Hayat will convene a special meeting of his party, of people who are not members of the Muslim League already, to sign the creed and join it. As such they will be subject to rules and regulations of the Central Parliamentary Board of the All India Muslim League. This will not affect the continuance of the present coalition of the Unionist Party in Punjab.

(ii) That in future elections and bye-elections for the legislature after the adoption of this arrangement the group constituting the present Unionist Party will jointly support candidates put up by their respective groups.

(iii) That the Muslim members of the legislature who are elected on, or accept, the League ticket, will constitute the Muslim League Party within the legislature. It shall be open to the Muslim League Party so formed, to maintain or enter into a coalition or alliance with any other party consistent with the fundamental principles of the policy and programme of the League. Such alliances may be evolved before or after the elections. The existing combination shall maintain its present name, the Unionist Party.[29]

The net result of Sikander's acceptance of the agreement with Jinnah was that Jinnah and the Muslim League significantly benefited from the agreement. The agreement had far-reaching implications not only within the context of the Unionist-Muslim League relations but also for the overall future of politics in the Punjab. 'Sikander saved Muslim India by coming to the League session and by infusing life into the organization. His association with the Muslim League at this crucial hour in the fate of Muslim India is an event in history.'[30]

The content and objectives of the agreement were vague,[31] overlapping and confusing. In a way the agreement also reflected the complex and inherently contradictory nature of politics that people of Punjab were accustomed to and accepted with no hesitation. The confusion in the political circles that the agreement created may also have been what the signatories had actually wanted. Essentially the event proved to be for the Muslim League and Jinnah the turning point in their rise to power in Punjab. Henceforth Jinnah was always in a position to maintain an effective influence on the politics of Punjab that was beginning to revolve around him.

From Sikander Hayat and his Party's point of view the visit to

Lucknow proved to be the beginning of the end. The agreement not only opened the gates of the Unionist Party to Muslim League interference but facilitated the damage that was done to its multi-community if not secular image. The political benefits derived by the Muslim League were on the other hand proportionately significant. The battered Punjab Muslim League not only received a renewed and emboldened lease of life but soon after October 1937 we see Jinnah's true political and manipulative genius beginning to emerge. Jinnah wrote to Barkat Ali 'once a Unionist Muslim accepts the League and its creed, he ceases to be anything but a Leaguer'.[32]

The fact that Sikander Hayat, by associating with Jinnah had committed a political mistake stands underlined by the reactions of his allies particularly the non-Muslim constituents of the Unionist Party. Chhotu Ram in particular was extremely upset.[33] Sikander Hayat soon realized the folly of his action in that it had annoyed an important section of the party. Chhotu Ram, however, appears to have been pacified by Sikander's assurance to him 'that Jinnah was in his pocket'.[34] As things happened the point appears to be that Punjab had been handed over to Jinnah on a platter by the Unionist Premier himself.

It was Jinnah's political astuteness that had made him seek an agreement with the Unionists. Notwithstanding his dislike for most of the Unionists he remained conscious that the Unionists had done well in Punjab, even when they had practically no grass-root support. After the agreement he showered lavish praise on Sikander Hayat and even requested him to preside over the Sholapur Session of the All India Muslim League (May 1939).[35] But all along, Jinnah was in reality working to a plan. The Unionist Party had no relevance in his scheme of things. In any case Jinnah was also aware that Sikander Hayat was under pressure to break the agreement and obviously with the agreement itself under threat, Jinnah could not have depended on it for too long.

Realizing well enough that the agreement with the Unionists would soon become meaningless, Jinnah turned his attention to the Muslim masses of Punjab. The political introspection among the League leaders of Punjab that followed the Party's rout (1937) made them realize that the support of the middle class alone could never be enough to capture power. There was no political significance of the middle class if it was unable to operate as a catalyst of the masses. Henceforth Jinnah directed his party to shed their urban image and fan out into the countryside.

With the very basis of the Sikander-Jinnah agreement having been under dispute and totally unacceptable to non-Muslim sections of the Unionist party, Sikander Hayat's position became difficult. The understanding came under doubt from the very first time it was put to test, the initial strains of discord being the hesitation among the Unionist legislators in formally joining the Muslim League.[36] The relations between Sikander Hayat and important Punjab Muslim League leaders like, Mohammad Iqbal had never been cordial. Likewise Sikander's relations with Malik Barkat Ali, Ghulam Rasul too were far from cordial. The distrust and hostility between influential leaders from both parties particularly leaders of the provincial level, made the agreement even more difficult to implement. Many Unionist leaders including some influential Muslims were seriously apprehensive of the agreement and had doubts about the earnestness of the Muslim League. For example Ahmad Yar Khan Daultana, a close associate of Sikander wrote to Jinnah:

> Everyone assured Sir Sikander that they would obey his orders and join the League when so desired, but they all expressed their alarm and anxiety over the present state of affairs in the Provincial League. They were not prepared to trust their funds in the hand of Mr. Ghulam Rasul or to acknowledge the present office-bearers of the Provincial League with the exception of Dr. Sir Mohammad Iqbal as their leader or representative . . . I request you in the interests of the Muslims of the Punjab to be very careful of what the old Leaguers write to you. It is impossible for us to carry on with people like Ghulam Rasul.[37]

Likewise, Jinnah too was under pressure from his old confidantes like Barkat Ali to assertively curtail the influence of Sikander Hayat and other leaders of the Unionist Party in Punjab. Jinnah, however, acted on the understanding that for the time being he really had no option but to permit Sikander Hayat to guide League affairs in Panjab. At the Calcutta Session of the Muslim League (April 1938), Jinnah gave Sikander Hayat a free hand to reorganize the Punjab Muslim League. Mohammad Iqbal who had been critically ill for some time was replaced as President of the Punjab Muslim League by Shah Nawaz Khan Mamdot.[38] Shah Nawaz Khan was more acceptable to the Unionists primarily because like most leading Unionists he too was a feudal lord, being among the largest land owners of Punjab.

Among the first actions of Sikander Hayat on return to Punjab was that he took Jinnah in confidence and dissolved the original body of the Punjab Muslim League.[39] In the new set-up, of the 35 Organizing Committee members, only 4 were hard-core Muslim Leaguers, the rest were either Unionists or had a 'soft corner' for the Unionist Party. The members were Sir Mohammad Iqbal (President of the old Punjab Muslim League), Nawab Shah Nawaz Khan Mamdot (Unionist), Maulana Zafar Ali Khan, Editor, *Zamindar* (Muslim League), Khalifa Shujaddin (Muslim League), Ghulam Rasul Khan (Secretary of the old Punjab Muslim League), Pir Tajuddin (Muslim League), Malik Zaman Mehdi Khan (Deputy President old Muslim League), Nawab Sadat Ali Khan (Muslim League), Sheikh Sadiq Hasan (Unionist), Mian Abdul Azia (Muslim League), Malik Barkat Ali (Muslim League), Pir Ashiq Husain (Unionist), Khan Murtaza Ahmed Khan, Editor, *Ehsan* (Muslim League), Sir Sikander Hayat Khan (Unionist), Nawab Khizr Hayat Khan Tiwana (Unionist), Mian Abdul Haye (Unionist), Ahmad Yar Khan Daultana (Unionist), Syed Afzal Ali Hasan (Unionist), Mir Maqbool Mahmood (Unionist), Syed Amjad Ali (Unionist), Raja Fateh Khan (Unionist), Sir Mohammad Hayat Khan Noon (Unionist), Sheikh Faiz Mohammad (Unionist) and Maulvi Ghulam Mohy-ud-din (Unionist).

There was considerable resentment among the old Muslim League members as a result of the political reorganization initiated by Sikander Hayat, but at this stage Jinnah did not waver in his support to Sikander. The final moment of triumph for Sikander came when the Punjab Muslim League as proposed and constituted by Sikander was affiliated to the All India Muslim League body in spite of strong opposition from the old members of the Punjab Muslim League. Mian Nurullah from (Lyallpur), even issued a press statement asking Jinnah to take action against the Punjab Muslim League led by Unionists meaning Sikander Hayat and his group:[40]

> Thanks to the policy pursued by the High Command of the Muslim League the Unionist Party has become the complete master of the (Punjab) Muslim League.... So far the Muslim League headquarters do not seem to be realising

the peril to which their policy of vaccilation and drift pursued during the past two years has exposed the organization in the Punjab. . . . I would appeal to Mr. Jinnah in the interests of the League to see that a living Muslim League organization is established in the Punjab. The Muslim League under the leadership of the Premier is merely a creature of the Unionist Party, packed by Honorary Magistrates and Sub-Registrars. . . . Their allegiance is first and last to the Unionist Party in power and they can any day flout Mr. Jinnah on the Central Body.[41]

During the course of time that the Sikander-Jinnah Pact lasted, Sikander showed occasional flashes of political assertiveness. When Malik Barkat Ali, a hard-core League member, for example, attempted to rake up the Shahidganj Mosque issue so as to embarrass and weaken the secular character of the Unionist ministry, Sikander acted promptly. He threatened to resign from the Assembly if Barkat Ali's provocative Bill on the issue was not turned down.[42] Sikander's tough stand earned him widespread support all over the state, even the Viceroy agreed that Sikander Hayat had handled the situation well.[43] Jawaharlal Nehru too appreciated Sikander's tough secular stand on the sensitive issue.[44] The Hindu Mahasabha also praised the manner in which Sikander contained the explosive potential of the dispute.[45]

The Sikander-Jinnah Pact worked or rather was forced to last for about two years.[46] It had never been an easy relationship, the actual breaking point came up on the question of support to the British war effort (World War II). While Sikander Hayat was for whole-hearted support to the British in the war, Jinnah had reservations based on the argument that the government had not acceded to some of his demands particularly pertaining to Muslim representation in the central government.[47] Sikander's stand for supporting the British in the war was clear and without conditions, he therefore rejected Jinnah's point of view outright.

The disturbed partnership had other causes of irritation as well. For example, Sikander took a tough stand against some Muslim League members in the Legislative Assembly,[48] when they sought to condemn his government for the death of a few Khaksars while they were participating in a religious procession. The most important issue of a break between Jinnah and Sikander, however, was the Pakistan Resolution, approved by the historic Muslim League Session of Lahore (1940).[49] The days that preceded and followed the League conference proved a severe test for Sikander Hayat. With the passing of the Pakistan Resolution, Jinnah had finally succeeded in putting Sikander Hayat and other Unionists like him on the defensive. In fact, with Pakistan being the agenda of the Session, it acquired the significance of a major turning point in the political history of Punjab. Essentially, the Pakistan Resolution Session greatly restricted the political options that were henceforth available to the Muslims of Punjab.

The turning point in Sikander Hayat's political fortunes was partly of his own making. It was he who had provided Jinnah the initial opportunity of gaining control over the Muslims of Punjab but more importantly his frequently contradictory and vaccilating stand on important political matters and policy only served to further confuse his party legislators and supporters. However, to the premier's credit it needs to be mentioned that he had never been in favour of the two nation theory. He had believed 'Pakistan would mean massacre',[50] and was in fact in favour of a federation within India in which the provinces would enjoy power and autonomy. In any case he was also aware that if he supported Jinnah on the separate state resolution the non-Muslim Unionists would almost certainly desert the party. The next best option for him was a sort of half way measure falling between his old stand and the Muslim League's demand of a separate autonomous state.[51] What Sikander Hayat therefore suggested as a solution was somewhat of a face saving formula:

— each province be a sovereign state;
— the sovereign states be vested with unlimited powers, except insofar as subjects like defence, communication, foreign affairs were concerned, which were to be controlled by a central body;
— the central body have power to control only subjects contained at number-II as an agent of the sovereign states.[52]

The proposal put forth by Sikander Hayat to reach an amicable point of understanding vis-a-vis the Muslim League's Pakistan Resolution should in the normal course have been acceptable to the Muslim League mainly because the proposal if accepted would have given to the Muslims of Punjab a more assertive say in the province's politics. All along Sikander Hayat had remained conscious of how the non-Muslims in his party would react to his proposals. He was aware of the strong feelings on the Pakistan Resolution among non-Muslims of his party as reflected particularly by Chhotu Ram: 'Can not for one day . . . be associated with a political party, the Muslim members of which are committed expressly or by implication by the ideal of Pakistan.'[53] Sikander had wishfully believed that his proposals would satisfy both the Hindu and Muslim constituents of his party thereby ensuring not only communal harmony but the smooth continuance of the ministry. His proposal was, however, not accepted by the Muslim League Session. The proposal that was finally approved by the Muslim League left little scope for pacifying the non-Muslim members of the Unionist Party or for diluting the negative impact that was inevitable from the Resolution. Henceforth the Unionist Party in its original form and the Muslim League in its new role were incompatible.

> It is the considered view of the session . . . that no constitutional plan would be workable in this country or acceptable to the Muslim League unless it is designed on the following basic principles i.e. geographically continuous units be demarcated into regions which should be so constituted with such territorial readjustment as may be necessary. That the areas in which the Muslims are numerically in a majority as in the North West and Eastern zones of India should be grouped to be constituted with territorial readjustment as may be necessary, to constitute independent states in which the constituent units shall be autonomous of sovereignty.[54]

The weak and indecisive handling of the situation by the Unionist leadership was partly responsible for the crisis in which the party found itself following the Pakistan Resolution. The issue raised by the Muslim League in the form of demanding an autonomous Muslim majority state was thoughtfully and quite correctly based on the belief that it would generally be difficult for any Muslim whether in the Punjab or eastern India to oppose the proposal. Implicit acceptance of the Muslim League's programme would in fact be acceptance of the League itself. Sikander and his Muslim associates in the Unionist Party were truly outmaneuvered as they could neither support nor oppose the Pakistan Resolution. In his effort to please both the diehard Muslim League supporters in his party as well as the non-Muslim Unionists, the premier had in fact become suspect in the eyes of both.

In March 1941, Jinnah sought a clarification from Sikander Hayat of his stand on the issue.[55] But in an assertive and changed tone, Sikander Hayat for the first time came out openly and categorically against the proposal of Pakistan: 'If Pakistan means Muslim *Raj*, he would have nothing to do with it. He wanted a *Raj* in which every community would be a partner.'[56]

On 10 March 1941 Sikander Hayat made a famous statement in the Punjab Legislative Assembly which clarified his position on the Pakistan Resolution and gave to Jinnah an answer for which he was not prepared.

> If partition of the country is what Pakistan means I will have nothing to do with it. Let us join hands in order to preserve and maintain peace and harmony within the province, and unite with the rest of India to face with courage and confidence the danger from without. And let us above all show to the rest of India that we in the Punjab stand united and will not brook any interference from whatever quarter it may be attempted. Then, and only then, we will be able to tell meddling busy-bodies from outside, hands off the Punjab.[57]

A little later he again said in the Punjab Legislative Assembly, 'we do not ask for the freedom where there may be Muslim Raj here and Hindu Raj there'.[58] Sikander Hayat's stand on the Pakistan Resolution was strongly resented by Jinnah.[59] Relations between the two soured to such an extent that Sikander even offered to resign from the League Working Committee, saying that differences on the Pakistan issue with Jinnah were irreconcilable.[60] But on persuasion and advise by his British friends he decided not to aggravate the situation.[61] The British it appears were keen to avoid a division and weakening of the Muslim League at this stage[62] because they believed that it would strengthen the Congress and cause more problems for the British government in India. In a sudden and remarkable reversal of political commitment, Sikander Hayat mellowed down and submitted to the dictates of the separatist demand. Henceforth his attitude remained conciliatory, no longer remaining a diehard opponent of the concept and demand of Pakistan. At the Lyallpur Muslim League Conference (November 1941) Sikander Hayat openly stated and accepted Jinnah as his leader and also as that of all the Muslims in India:[63] 'I have acknowledged (Jinnah) as my Quaid-i-Azam and . . . follow his instructions right or wrong.'[64]

The differences between the two did not completely disappear however. Sikander Hayat was nominated by the government to the National Defence Council (for his support in the war effort). However, Jinnah was annoyed keeping in view the League's policy of not supporting the British in the war[65] Jinnah was of the view that Sikander Hayat should not have accepted the nomination. Keeping in view Jinnah's reaction to the nomination the British government explained that Sikander apart from being a Muslim was also premier of Punjab, the capacity in which his nomination to the National Defence Council was made. Jinnah, however, refused to accept the explanation and maintained that Sikander Hayat's nomination was from the Muslim community and must be treated as such.[66] Believing this to be the correct position Jinnah was of the view that neither should Sikander Hayat have accepted it nor should the British have made the nomination without approval from him.

Sikander Hayat went to Bombay to explain his position to Jinnah. Once again he buckled in under the pressure of Jinnah and resigned from the Defence Council. The reason given by him for doing so, was obviously, only an excuse.[67] 'It would have been an act of treachery to Punjab if I had not resigned.'[68] In sharp contrast, while going to Bombay he had said: 'he would resign from the League but not give up his seat in the Defence Council.[69]

Sikander Hayat's resignation from the National Defence Council attracted much criticism. The incident once again exposed the inherent contradictions and complexities that governed the Unionist Party's relation with the Muslim League. Just as compromise and reconciliation with Jinnah with regard to the National Defence Council nomination had barely been accepted, Sikander Hayat's pact with Baldev Singh (15 June 1942)[70] provided another cause for rupture and misunderstanding. Jinnah was once again furious, because for him the Sikhs in Punjab had been the main hurdle in the Muslim League's demand for a separate Muslim state. He was of the view that a government in which the Muslims were a major constituent should not have reached an agreement with the Sikhs independent of him.

The deterioration in relations between the two prominent Muslim leaders and their parties in a way also reflect the rapidly changing political scene in Punjab. From the point of view of the Muslim population of Punjab it was only a matter of time after the Pakistan

Resolution that the Unionist Party lost its relevance. In any case by 1942, Jinnah had established a firm hold in Punjab. Sikander Hayat and his party were perhaps no longer of any use in the Muslim League's scheme of things. Sikander was finally removed from the All India Muslim League in July 1942.[71] Sikander had finally reconciled his incompatibility with the incorrigible League 'dictator'. By temperament the two men were poles apart. Ideologically as we have already seen they had fundamental differences on issues like supporting the British in the World War, the demand for Pakistan, the future constitution and even communal problems. Realizing that reconciliation was not possible, Sikander Hayat tried to settle scores with Jinnah, as Fazli had done in 1935-6. Chhotu Ram appears to have played an important role in preparing him to confront Jinnah. However, Sikander's untimely death on 26 December 1942 gave Jinnah a free hand to play his political cards in Punjab. It was the turning point in Punjab politics particularly for its Muslim constituents.

The Punjab premier's death was a tragic blow for the Unionist Party. Apart from Chhotu Ram, the party now had no other leader of experience and stature. But Chhotu Ram being a Hindu was aware that his election as premier could have led to desertion by some Muslim members in favour of the Muslim League. The premier, Chhotu Ram was convinced, had to be a Muslim.[72] In any case the Muslim League had already protested against the possibility of appointing a Hindu as premier.[73] Therefore, Chhotu Ram himself led other influential Unionist legislators in proposing the name of Khizr Hayat Khan Tiwana as the new premier. His candidature had the support of the governor of Punjab and the Viceroy.[74] Khizr Hayat was elected unopposed, on 23 January 1943.[75] Shaukat Hayat (Sikander's son) filled the vacancy caused by the death of Sikander Hayat in the ministry.

Khizr was young, perhaps more resolute but lacked the shrewd political experience of his predecessor.[76] His youth and cautious and conservative approach were politically unsuitable for the troubled Punjab of 1943. His task was all the more difficult because besides Chhotu Ram the old guard of the party had over the years passed away. During his lifetime Sikander Hayat had been well advised by leaders like Mir Maqbool Ahmad and Ahmad Yar Khan

Daultana. Khizr on the other hand had only Allah Baksh Khan (his uncle) from among important and senior Muslim Unionists to advise him. Therefore, increasingly he began to rely and quite rightly so on the sane, mature and resolute advice of Chhotu Ram. But this in itself led to accusations made against him of being soft and more inclined towards the non-Muslim section of the Unionist Party. Allegations on these lines continued to be fuelled up to the very end (1947) when Khizr Hayat ultimately resigned from the leadership of the Unionist-led coalition government in the province.

Much had changed in Punjab since the days of the Zamindara Conference (Lyallpur 1938) organized by the Unionists, when Hindus and Muslim peasantry turned up in vast numbers to listen to Sikander Hayat and Chhotu Ram. It was now projected by the Muslim League propaganda machine that Chhotu Ram was merely a cover created by Hindu leaders of Punjab in their effort to deprive the Muslims of political influence. Nothing could have been farther from the truth. But Punjab's politics had gradually drifted to a stage where political ambitions had made leaders transgress into seeking religious support. The initial hesitation and inhibition of doing so had now given way to a diehard resolve of using religious propaganda for political ends. The Muslim League had put Punjab well on the path to being politically divided in an unprecedented manner on community lines. It was not surprising, therefore, that a large number of Muslim Unionists began to fall under the influence of the Muslim League's communally divisive propaganda. There were even rumours in Lahore that the Unionist Party might split on the question of Hindus having excessive say in the affairs of the Unionist Party. However, tactful handling proved the rumours false and 69 Unionist Muslim legislators were gathered specially for the purpose of providing assurance and support to Khizr Hayat.[77]

In his anxiety to placate the Sikander-Daultana faction, Khizr Hayat had accommodated Sikander's son Shaukat Hayat Khan in his cabinet. Politically the decision was essentially expedient, yet it proved to be Khizr's undoing. The personal rivalry between the two notwithstanding Shaukat Hayat soon become a catalyst for dissenters within the Unionist Party, particularly for those who were inclined to drift towards the Muslim League. By August 1943 relations between Shaukat Hayat and Khizr had reached a state of no return.[78]

The Unionist Party as we have already seen had never really been a homogeneous one. But following the death of Sikander Hayat intrigue and internal feud within the party fuelled by dissenters assumed alarming dimensions. It is from about the inclusion of Shaukat Hayat in the Punjab ministry that the actual change in political fortunes of both the Muslim League and the Unionist Party begins. Shaukat Hayat represented an aggressive and ambitious group of sons of feudal lords. His close associates at the time were Mumtaz Daultana the son of Ahmad Yar Khan Daultana and Iftikhar Husain Mamdot the son of Shah Nawaz Khan Mamdot. Ironically while their fathers had been close friends and were among the founding members of the Unionist Party, the sons had taken on themselves the role of derailing it. Shaukat and Mumtaz had correctly gauged the changed political environment and correctly concluded that the wind of successful political fortune in Punjab had begun to flow in favour of the Muslim League. Through the ages it was this remarkable ability of the feudal clans of Punjab that found them always on the winning side. This ability to predict greener pastures was an important reason for the continued influence of the feudal lords in the politics of Punjab, particularly in rural areas. The capacity of the Unionist Party to fight internal dissension was always suspect but after the passage of the Pakistan Resolution the party stood defenceless against internal strife. Even if Shaukat Hayat and friends had not created problems the Unionist Party was well on its way downwards and in spite of the advantages derived from pro-rural legislations and other similar measures, the party had considerably weakened.[79]

As such, in its efforts to effect desertion among Unionist Muslim legislators the Muslim League drew considerable help from families which had earlier built and supported the Unionist, but after the younger generation had taken over the role of their fathers such families chose to support the Muslim League. The political relations between the two, the Unionists and the Muslim League were precariously balanced by vested and temporary short term interests, so much so that the rise of one was proportionately dependent on the decline of the other. While this is true of most political activity and relations, the intensity of the rivalry between the two was based on the fact that the growth of the Muslim League could take place only if the Muslims who supported the Unionist Party transferred their support to the Muslim League. For the League's strength and Jinnah's political stature in Punjab it was totally imperative that the Muslim population of the province should give its undivided loyalty to the league. In this sense the Unionist Party was for the League a serious hurdle and therefore weakening it was the only way to build its own (League's) strength.

Just at about the time that the Muslim League had begun to achieve success in eroding Unionist influence from the rural Muslim masses came the announcement by Sir Stafford Cripps that states might at some later stage even have the option of separating from the Indian Union. The time and nature of this announcement gave to politics of Punjab a new dimension and greatly benefited the Muslim League in its exercise of demanding the separate state of Pakistan and gathering support for it.[80] The most remarkable implication of the untimely intervention of Sir Stafford Cripps was that Jinnah came to understand and project it as a concealed acceptance by the British of his two nation theory. The British policy of depending on the Muslim League in fact encouraging it to offset the pressure of the Congress particularly its Quit India Movement, surcharged the Muslim League in its fight against the Unionists in Punjab. In less than five years, that is from 1937 to 1942, Jinnah had in a masterly manner considerably derailed the Unionist Party and brought a section of the Muslim community of Punjab under the Muslim League influence.

With every passing day after the adoption of the Pakistan Resolution the Muslim League moved one step closer to its goal of a separate home land for Muslims. For example, 23 March 1943, was celebrated as Pakistan Day and a 'Muslim League Week' was organized in Punjab from 12 April 1943 to 18 April 1943. Essentially political efforts of the League concentrated on strengthening the orgariizational structure, enrolling members, opening branches, collecting funds.[81] Having done so, Jinnah took the next step of squarely challenging those Muslim leaders who were inclined towards the Unionist Party and were still beyond the influence of the Muslim League.

The opportunities for Jinnah to rake up a controversy with the Unionist Party were easily forthcoming. The most convenient were the operational rules that governed Jinnah's political understanding with Sikander Hayat. After Sikander Hayat's death this struggle continued against Khizr Hayat and Chhotu Ram. From the very outset, as we have already seen, many Unionist legislators had never wholeheartedly accepted the Sikander-Jinnah Pact. This fact was a cause of great worry for Muslim League leaders. Jinnah, for example, viewed the Ministry in Punjab as that of the Muslim League.[82] The substance of his argument was based on the terms provided in the Sikander-Jinnah Pact. Khizr Hayat, however, did not accept this version and said he and his Unionist colleagues in the legislature, both the Muslims and non-Muslims would remain bound by the creed of the Unionist Party.[83]

Jinnah's first attempt to browbeat the dissenting Unionist Party legislators into submission (March 1944) was effectively blunted by Chhotu Ram who stood his ground and refuted Jinnah's version and his interpretation of the Sikander-Jinnah Pact. Chhotu Ram maintained that the ministry and party were governed by the policy and programmes of the Unionist Party and the Muslim League was merely transgressing into Unionist affairs.[84] An infuriated Jinnah vowed to finish Chhotu Ram's power.[85] Chhotu Ram, however, emerged a hero and was widely praised in leading media versions.[86]

Khizr Hayat unfortunately appeared less resolute and determined than the great Unionist 'war-horse' Chhotu Ram. Khizr's approach, as Talbot[87] has suggested, was perhaps influenced by the fact that he seemed to consider politics not as a profession but as a kind of hobby. The view of Talbot that he lacked personal ambition of the power and perks of office in fact explains a lot about Khizr's basic approach to politics and the Muslim League. There is evidence to suggest that Khizr Hayat may possibly have succumbed to Jinnah's rehtoric and threats[88] but did not do so because he was encouraged to maintain the identity of the Unionist Party by the British at least till the time that the War with Japan was on.[89] But it also appears that what Khizr valued most at this stage was the support and opinion of Chhotu Ram who vehemently opposed Jinnah both for his two-nation theory as also his unwarranted interference in Unionist Party affairs. Khizr Hayat was also well supported by leading nationalist newspapers. *The Hindustan Times*, for example, praised the Unionist Party as 'the hope of Indian nation builders'.[90]

Jinnah made a second attempt to browbeat the Unionist Party leaders in the talks with Khizr Hayat in April 1944 in Lahore. The talks eventually broke down on 27 April.[91] Jinnah had put forward the following terms:

(i) Every member of the Muslim League Party in the Punjab Assembly should declare that he owes allegiance solely to the Muslim League Party in the Assembly and not to the Unionist or any other party;
(ii) The present label of the coalition, namely the Unionist Party should be dropped;
(iii) The name of the proposed coalition should be the Muslim League Coalition Party.

Khizr Hayat refused to accept these terms even though he stood committed to supporting Jinnah on issues that exclusively involved the Muslim community. However, he insisted that disunity among communities would be dangerous and may lead to communal violence, something that needed to be avoided.[92] The 'dye was cast' when Khizr refused to respond to a call of explanation from Jinnah,[93] following which Khizr Hayat was expelled[94] from the Muslim League, of which he was assumed to have become a member as per the clauses of the Sikander-Jinnah Pact. The differences between the two increased dramatically with Jinnah, as Talbot points out, refering to Khizr as a 'traitor'.[95]

That Jinnah's influence had grown considerably during the period is reflected in the large number of influential Unionists who revolted against Khizr Hayat in favour of the Muslim League at Jinnah's behest. By the end of 1944 the Muslim League Assembly Party had grown to 27 from just 2 in 1937.[96] These included Shaukat Hayat, Begum Shah Nawaz and the Nawab of Mamdot. During the course of all this confusion Khizr Hayat was able to manipulate the dismissal of Shaukat Hayat from the Ministry to preempt Shaukat Hayat from resigning.[97] The reason provided for the action was misuse of position and charges of corruption. Mir Maqbool Mahmood and Ahmad Yar Khan Daultana also resigned as Parliamentary Secretaries. The action proved to have far-reaching implications as it further increased the division between the group led by Khizr Hayat and that of the 'Khattars' led by Shaukat Hayat. But it was in fact a logical culmination of the political developments and strife between the two.[98] No longer could Khizr Hayat have effectively operated the Unionist Party with Shaukat Hayat as a minister.

Khizr's assertive rebuff to Jinnah was a setback to the Muslim League. Jinnah's 'efforts for a shortcut to power by an attempt to browbeat Khizr were premature . . . the method tried was by no means the wisest of political maneuvers, the weight behind it lacked sting and authority', writes Imran Ali.[99] Quite obviously the League supremo had failed to make a judicious assessment and 'displayed lack of understanding of politics in Punjab'.[100] In the process Jinnah lost some political influence not only in Punjab but also at the all India level. Soon after these setbacks in Punjab, Khizr Hayat claimed membership of the Viceroy's Executive Council for a Muslim of his nomination from Punjab. The political implication of the claim was that Khizr Hayat did not accept the Muslim League as the sole representative of the Muslims in India.[101] This was in sharp contrast to Jinnah's view that he personally and the Muslim League alone represented the political will of the Muslims in India.

Relations between the Muslim League and the Unionist Party henceforth deteriorated rapidly to a state of open hostility. Jinnah, wanted to 'kill' the very word Unionist and 'attend the "Party's funeral"'.[102] The Unionist Party as we shall see in the next chapter scarcely stood a chance in the fast changing political scene. Khizr Hayat attempted to keep his party afloat but the measures adopted no longer seemed relevant and in any case the Unionist Party had never equipped itself for a struggle based on religious lines and that too with an organization like the Muslim League.

After having been unsettled by Jinnah Khizr Hayat attempted to stabilize the situation. He appointed two new Muslim ministers, Sir Mohammad Jamal Khan Leghari and Nawab Ashiq Husain, both of whom came from the Multan Division.[103] Sir Mohammad Jamal Khan Leghari was an important tribal leader with large landholdings in the Dera Ghazi Khan District. Nawab Ashiq Husain was a member of the leading Qureshi *pir* family of Multan. He was the son-in-law of Sir Liaqat Hayat Khan (Sir Sikander Hayat's elder brother) and leader of its 'Khattar' faction. In December 1944, the 'Khattar' faction comprised about one-third of the Muslim section of the Punjab

Legislative Assembly.[104] This seemed a wise move even though it did not prove to be quite as fruitful as expected. Many of the MLAs who Khizr had hoped to rope in by the exercise later joined the mass desertion from the Unionist Party in favour of the Muslim League. The nucleus of desertion and dissent developed around Shaukat Hayat and formed a well-knit group of 23 MLAs. By the end of 1944 the Muslim League had shaken the foundations of the Unionist Party. Even though the Unionist Party did win some local body elections in 1944,[105] its vertical division initiated the process of its ultimate rout.

While reviewing the political relations of the Unionist Party with the Indian National Congress it is important to remember that the founding and leading stalwarts of the Unionist Party both Sir Fazl-i-Husain and Sir Chhotu Ram started their political careers as Congressmen. Fazl-i-Husain had joined the Congress in 1905. In 1920 he was president of the Punjab Provincial Congress.[106] Earlier in 1901 and again in 1914 he was engaged by the revolutionary nationalist Bhai Parmanand to defend him in cases of sedition.[107] While addressing a conference of the Provincial Congress in 1917 Fazl-i-Husain had remarked that the British Government of India was 'too wooden, too iron, too inelastic to be of any use, . . . The evil system' he said, 'converts an irresponsible servant into an insolvent master'.[108]

Sir Chhotu Ram had joined the Congress in 1916 and remained President of the District unit of the party from 1917-20.[109] Like a large number of other important Congress leaders both Chhotu Ram[110] and Fazl-i-Husain[111] parted company with the Congress because of differences with regard to the Non-Cooperation Movement. Chhotu Ram's exit from the Congress was an important turning point in his career. His parting of ways with the Congress was unfortunate both for him as also for the Congress. He was a sensitive leader who remained perturbed by the political and economic paradoxes which British rule presented in India particularly in Punjab. The most remarkable trait of his character was that even at the peak of his political power he could never disassociate himself from his humble roots. In a letter which was part of a series of letters exchanged with H. Harcourt, ICS in 1924 on the nature of the Non-Cooperation Movement, for example, Chhotu Ram wrote:

> whatever the temporary checks and setbacks within the movement may suffer, Non-Cooperation has come to stay. It will reassert itself over and over again . . . as long as the causes which gave it birth continue to exist. An active rebellion is a tangible thing and can be met by brute force. But non-cooperation is an elusive ghost which your (British) guns, bayonets cannot touch.[112]

While replying to another letter from Harcourt in January 1924 on the true nature of the British rule in India and how the system of repression operated, Chhotu Ram wrote:

> This [government's] ridiculuous position is due to the fact that the government is in essence a despotic government. While it seeks to make itself out to be popular and representative . . . the government is neither sufficiently generous to concede legitimate demands nor sufficiently wicked to put down opposition by ruthless repression. . . . The result is that in practice it flouts public opinion, in theory it seeks to respect it. . . .[113]

Chhotu Ram's perception of British rule importantly points to the need of assessing the Unionist Party's relations with the Congress not merely in terms of a 'collaborator'. This is so because the Unionist Party had within its rank a fair number of leaders like Chhotu Ram whose nationalist credentials were beyond doubt. In any case most of these leaders like Chhotu Ram did not view the Unionist Party as being a collaborator of the British. In reality the choice of parties in such cases was also influenced usually by individual and personal considerations rather than principles and policies. For example, Chhotu Ram's appreciation of the Congress ideals and objectives is fairly evident but at the same time he thought very lowly of some Congressmen. His dislike for some Congress leaders of Punjab in particular was often extreme. He thought of them as 'capitalists' and even 'cowards'.[114] This is not surprising because Jawaharlal Nehru himself had stated that the 'Congress in Punjab meant only a few persons in the cities quarreling continuously.'[115]

The Congress in Punjab was conspicuously out of step as compared to branches of the organization in other parts of the country. Being essentially an urban party,[116] it evaded peasant problems and issues, often taking ridiculously opposing and contradictory stands on legislative proposals which favoured rural society. The basis of this thoughtless approach of the Punjab Congress leadership was the fear of losing sympathy and support among influential urban people. This double-faced policy of the Congress in Punjab cost the party dearly not only in the elections of 1937 but also in terms of mass appeal and influence particularly when Punjab was confronted with the prospect of its partition.

A study of political relations between the Congress and the Unionist Party in Punjab must also keep in mind the fundamental differences that existed in the nature, character and objectives of both the parties. Even while the Congress could not quite control developments in Punjab it *did* represent India's fight for freedom whereas the Unionist Party represented a success story that was supported by the British political policy of constructing, in colonial societies, a loyal and collaborative system of support.

The Unionist-Congress relations were also influenced by the fact that the British, being 'British' wanted to legitimize even the oppressive nature of their colonial rule. The Unionist Party for the British in Punjab was an instrument which gave their rule credibility, an element of acceptance. The Congress on the other hand remained the principal opposition to British rule, a factor that substantially reflected itself by implication in the character of the Unionist Party and its relations with the Congress. The Unionist Party's relations with the Congress can therefore said to have been remote controlled by British administrators.

The bitterness and hatred that came to symbolize Unionist-Congress relations in Punjab was based both on principles as well as on individual relations. The Unionist government was responsible, even if indirectly, for the oppression let loose on Congress workers. Nehru called the Unionist government 'reactionary'.[117] Even on the floor of the Assembly the Unionist government was frequently attacked for its ruthless silencing of the opposition particularly from Congress leaders.[118] A good example of it was the manner in which dissent was silenced with regard to the difference of opinion on the question of supporting the British involvement in World War II. The anti-war propaganda by Congress workers was suppressed with repeated pleas being made by Unionist members in the Assembly to the government to be tough with those opposing India's support to the British War effort.[119] Premier Sir Sikander Hayat, however, considered sabotaging of the War effort as 'treachery, a stab in the back and even un-Islamic'.[120]

There is need also to remember that during the War years (1939-45) all political decisions were essentially influenced by British perceptions of problems. The Unionist government was bound by the decisions taken by the British administrators and as such in no case were the Unionists in a position to alter important decisions particularly those that related to the economy as well as the ones that influenced the party's relations with the Congress. This is not to absolve the Unionists of their responsibility of acting as extended hands of British administrators. But perhaps there is need to diffuse the level of criticism of the Unionist Party by suggesting that it is imperative to study the Unionist relations with the Congress in the inhibitive background and circumstances in which the Unionist Party was operating during the War years.

When it concerned law and order and important economic decisions, governments under provincial autonomy had no option other than to toe the British bureaucratic line. An example that substantiates this is available in the fixing of prices of food grains in Punjab. The government wanted to purchase grain from the Punjab farmers at prices which were well below the prevailing market prices so as to dispatch grain to Bengal which was then under famine conditions. However, encouraged by some Unionist leaders particularly Chhotu Ram, the peasantry in Punjab began hoarding grain. The government resorted to forced requisitioning and called the attitude of leaders like Chhotu Ram, 'ruthless opportunism'.[121] Chhotu Ram was warned and threatened with dismissal.[122] An angry Chhotu Ram even offered to resign on the issue.[123] This crisis was averted only with the passage of time and some easing of the situation but more perhaps because the British still valued Unionist support in Punjab. The situation would have been dealt with in a totally different manner with far more ruthlessness by the British had they been called to handle a similar situation in more peaceful times. Chhotu Ram would surely have lost his seat as minister. Such were the realities of power enjoyed by ministers for which they were held responsible under provincial autonomy.

The Unionist Party's relations with the Akalis and the Khalsa National Party were less complex and consequential when compared to the relations with the Muslim League and the Congress. A section of the Sikhs represented by the Khalsa National Party and its important leader Sir Sunder Singh Majithia were like the Unionists closely associated with the British government in Punjab. As such the two were natural allies. Sunder Singh Majithia was chosen by Sikander Hayat as a representative of the Sikh community in his Ministry in 1937. The support extended by the Khalsa National Party to the Unionists was also influenced by the economic background of its constituents. Most of its influential members were big landlords having similar socioeconomic interests as the Unionists. This bond was further strengthened because of the various pro-agriculturist legislative measures initiated by the Unionist Party during the period 1937-42.

The Unionist Party's political relations with the Akalis on the other hand were consistently influenced by their relations with the Muslim League. The Akali policy of maintaining a distance from the Unionists was based on the belief that a predominantly Muslim ministry in Punjab was not in the interest of the Sikhs. The Akalis even organized an anti-Unionist government day on 3 August 1941. The closer the top leadership of the Unionist Party got to the Muslim League the more distance was created between them and the Akalis. The other major issue of difference between the Unionists and the Akalis was the importance given by the Unionist leadership to Sunder Singh Majithia and his Khalsa National Party. For the Akalis this was totally unwarranted. For as long as Majithia was alive the Akali leaders maintained a distance from the Unionist Party. However, with his death on 2 April 1941, the differences between the Khalsa National Party and the Akalis were somewhat narrowed, leading in the first instance to the creation of the Khalsa Defence of India League in the same year. This also quite naturally brought the Akalis closer to the Unionist Party.

By March 1942 Sardar Baldev Singh was able to form the Punjab Sikh United Party in the Punjab Legislative Assembly comprising some members from the Khalsa National Party, some independent Sikh legislators and some Akalis in order to find a solution to common grievances of the Sikhs.[124] An agreement was reached between the Unionist government and a fairly representative section of Punjab Sikhs in the form of the Sikander-Baldev Pact on 14 June 1942.[125]

Issue of Jhatka

It was agreed that instructions would be given to the government and semi-government institutions to allow every community to cook and use meat slaughtered according to its own rituals and rites.

Teaching of Gurumukhi

It was decided that wherever an adequate number of Sikh students sought to study it, the government would try to make arrangements for teaching of Punjabi through Gurumukhi. Provision was also to be made to restore the status of Punjabi as a second language in the province.

Legislation regarding religious matters

Members of the Legislative Assembly would be free to take decisions on religious matters concerning their community.

Recruitment criterion

A recruitment policy with a fixed proportion for recruitment of members of various communities to government jobs was in existence in Punjab under which Sikhs had been allotted a 20 per cent share, but this share had seldom been given. Sikander Hayat agreed that he would ensure that the 20 per cent reservation for Sikhs would not henceforth be ignored.

Sikh representation at the Centre

Sikander Hayat further assured that whenever there was any reshuffle or change in the Executive Council of the Viceroy, the Sikh claim to the vacant seat would have his full sympathy and support. He would also give his support to the Sikh claim for a due share in the central services.

From the British point of view the agreement was a suitable and advantageous development. In the first place the agreement made the sailing more smooth for Sikander Hayat and also diffused communal tension. But even more important was the fact that in this union one martial race had joined hands with another with both extending full committed support to the British War effort.[126] On the overall political scene of Punjab too the agreement had significant implications. For the Congress it was a major setback because it eroded the already meagre support the party possessed among the Sikhs. It is important to note that Master Tara Singh the chief spokesman of the Akalis viewed this agreement as an achievement for the Sikhs in general and did not consider this as a political agreement. He was of the view that political differences with the Unionists persisted and would continue to be fought.[127]

Master Tara Singh's assessment of the pact seems fairly correct because in reality the terms of the agreement between the Unionists and Baldev Singh were more in the form of assurances, acceptance and appreciation of sociocultural-cum religious sentiments rather than a calculated political initiative or understanding like the Sikander-Jinnah Pact. For Baldev Singh personally the agreement proved advantageous, as, soon after it, he joined the Unionist ministry (26 June 1942).[128] In due course Sardar Joginder Singh was nominated to the Viceroy's Executive Council and given the charge of education, health and lands.[129]

An indirect fallout of the Sikander-Baldev Pact on the politics of Punjab was that Jinnah felt slighted because he had considered the Sikhs a hurdle in his two nation theory. Jinnah's annoyance was further underlined because he felt that Sikander should not have reached an understanding without Jinnah's consent. He viewed the Unionist agreement with the Sikhs as a betrayal of the Muslim League's cause and also a violation of the 1937 Lucknow pact between the two parties. The removal of Sikander Hayat from the Muslim League Working Committee in July 1942 in fact was a fallout of the Unionist Party's agreement with Baldev Singh.[130]

The Hindu Election Board or the National Progressive Party also merits mention in a review of the Unionist Party's political relations because it won 15 seats in the election to the Punjab Legislative Assembly in 1937. Three of these seats were, however, lost in the ensuing bye-elections.[131] The political relations of the National Progressive Party with the Unionists reflect a remarkable contradiction. With fundamental differences particularly in economic policy it is difficult to understand how the two could get along. Once again the only common factor between the Unionist and the National Progressive Party was their common collaborative attitude towards British rule. This factor appears to have been instrumental in enabling both the parties to ignore their other important differences.

The Unionist Party had grown into a formidable political power by a sustained pro-rural economic bias. Its popularity in rural Punjab grew quite in proportion to the level of its attack on the 'moneylenders', and other commercial classes. On the other hand, the National Progressive Party's very existence depended on its ability to oppose the rural-biased economic programmes of the Unionist Party. Proceedings of the Punjab Legislative Assembly are replete with clashes between Unionist legislators demanding more share in development grant for rural areas and stricter statutory provisions against moneylenders, etc., on the one hand and members of the National Progressive Party opposing such proposals tooth and nail. In fact the so-called urban versus rural divide that came to symbolize the political scene of Punjab in the 1930s and 1940s was based on the fight between these two parties.

Chhotu Ram was among the important Unionist leaders who persistently opposed the Nationalist Progressive Party and virtually everything it represented. However others like Fazl-i-Husain and later Sikander[132] maintained cordial relations on a personal level with leaders of the party. Chhotu Ram's animosity was based on the belief that the Nationalist Progressive Party represented those sections of people who he believed were responsible for the economic plight of the peasantry. He was supported in this conviction by many middle-rung leaders of the Unionist Party. Even prior to 1937 there were frequent clashes between members of the two parties in the Legislative Council as also outside. Raja Narender Nath in particular and Gokul Chand Narang were the two main critics of the Unionist economic policies during the 1920s and 1930s. The Punjab Moneylenders Bill (1925), for example, was vetoed by the governor even though it had been voted by 46 votes in favour with only 20 against.[133] This happened mainly because influential Nationalist Progressive Party leaders were able to influence the government. Signatures of 21,000 people were collected by the Punjab Money-lenders Association against the Bill.[134] The large-scale mobilization that took place against such Unionist Party sponsored legislative measures was due to the efforts of the National Progressive Party.

The most well-presented criticism and opposition to the Unionist Party's economic policies particularly with regard to its emphasis on rural areas are found in the writings and statements of Raja Narender Nath.[135] *The Punjab Administration Report, 1931,* for example, states that of the 20 Nationalist Progressive Party members in the Punjab Legislative Council, 9 were persistent and bitter critics of the Unionist economic policies and legislative proposals.[136]

The fact that such unfailing opponents could join hands for political advantage can also be understood in terms of the fact that both parties were 'top heavy' ones with little grassroot support. The Unionist Party as we have already seen was never homogeneous or well knit, rules, regulations and creeds were only on paper. The party was held together by individual personalities on personal and usually subjective issues, individual vested interests alone were usually the most predominant factors influencing decisions. The only element more important was British authority, which usually acted tactfully and in a remote-controlling manner. From 1938 onwards, the Nationalist Progressive Party members generally opposed most of the economic legislative reforms sponsored by the Unionists and frequently voted against the party. Yet Raja Narender Nath's nominee Sir Manohar Lal operated the important portfolio of finance in the Unionist ministry.

The Unionist Party's political relations with other important parties in Punjab at the time were ambiguous and remarkably contradictory. The most important feature was opportunism. Ideals, principles and ideologies had no place in the party's political functioning. One factor, however, was overriding in its impact and influence, the remote controlling character of British bureaucracy. The party's relations with the Congress, Muslim League, the Sikhs and National

Progressive Party were only as good or as bad as the British had wanted them to be. The Unionist Party's political character symbolized by vested interest in decision-making, internal intrigue and dissension, was typical of a party which had more top leaders than ordinary workers. The fact that almost all important leaders of the party were in some way or the other beneficiaries of British patronage perpetually overshadowed the party's response to problems, situations and relations with other political organizations. This subconscious bond of loyalty towards British rule in India within the top leadership of the Unionist Party as well as its main supporters gave a predictable character to its politics. While the British took it for granted, its political rivals seldom took it seriously knowing that in any case the kind of politics practised by the Unionists did not have a bright future. In a decade when confrontation and challenge were the key words to political progress, the Unionist Party represented the politics of compromise.

NOTES

1. L.H. Griffin and C.F. Massey, *Chiefs and Families of Note in the Punjab*, ed. by G.L. Chopra, vol. II (Lahore, 1940), p. 332.
2. Ibid., p. 333.
3. Ibid.
4. Ibid., p. 334.
5. Ibid.
6. Ibid.
7. Ibid., p. 335.
8. Ibid.
9. Ibid., p. 336.
10. Ibid., p. 204.
11. Ibid., p. 207.
12. Ibid.
13. Craig Baxter, 'The Peoples Party Versus The Punjab Feudalists', *Journal of Asian and African Studies*, vol. VIII: 3 and 4 (July-October 1973), pp. 167-89.
14. Waheed Ahmad (ed.), *Letters of Mian Fazl-i-Husain*, p. 592; D. Gilmartin, 'Religious Leadership', p. 493.
15. See Louis Dumont, *Homo Hierrchius: The Caste System and Its Implications* (Delhi, 1970), p. 20.
16. Isphani, *Quad-i-Azam*, p. 20.

17. Syed Nur Ahmad, *Martial Law*, p. 100.
18. Ibid.
19. Yadav, *Elections*, p. 84.
20. *The Tribune*, 16 October 1937.
21. Ibid.
22. Isphani, *Quad-i-Azam*, pp. 49-54.
23. See Talbot, *Punjab and the Raj*, p. 124.
24. Imran Ali, *Punjab Politics*, p. 19.
25. See Jahan Ara Shah Nawaz, *Father and Daughter*, p. 164; also Syed Nur Ahmad, *Martial Law*, p. 146.
26. *The Tribune*, 7 October 1937.
27. Amlendu De, 'Sahid Ganj Agitation and Khaksars', *Punjab Past and Present*, vol. XI, 1975, p. 384.
28. Khizr Hayat, 'The 1937 Elections and the Sikander-Jinnah Pact', *Punjab Past and Present*, vol. X-II, October 1976.
29. *Indian Year Book*, 1938, p. 823.
30. *The Tribune*, 19 October 1937 and 23 October 1937; Yadav 'Partition of India'; also Khaliquzzaman Choudhry, *Pathway to Pakistan* (Karachi, 1961), p. 171; and Isphani, *Quad-i-Azam*, pp. 50-1.
31. See Khaliquzzaman, *Pathway to Pakistan*, p. 290; also Talbot, *Punjab and the Raj*, p. 725.
32. *Linlithgow Collection*, vol. 92, Glancy to Linlithgow, 21 July 1943, p. 62.
33. S.Q.H. Jafri and S.A. Bukhari (eds.), *Quad-i-Azam's Correspondence with Punjab Muslim League Leaders* (Lahore, 1977), p. 48.
34. *The Tribune*, 22 October 1937.
35. Stanley Wolpert, *Jinnah of Pakistan* (New York, 1984), p. 156.
36. I. Talbot, 'Deserted Collaborators: The Political Background to The Rise and Fall of the Unionist Party, 1923-47', *Journal of Imperial and Commonwealth History*, vol. XI, No. 1, October 1982, p. 82.
37. Letter of Ahmad Yar Khan Daultana to Jinnah, 15 November 1937, cited in Talbot, *Punjab and the Raj*, p. 139.
38. Ibid.
39. Sayed Nur Ahmad, *Martial Law*, p. 187.
40. *The Tribune*, 7 June 1938.
41. See Talbot, *Punjab and the Raj*, p. 129.
42. Ibid.
43. See ibid., pp. 126-9.
44. *Linlithgow Collection*, vol. 86, Emerson to Linlithgow, 4 March 1938, p. 58.
45. S.S. Pirzada, *Muslim League Leaders Correspondence with Jinnah* (Bombay, 1944), pp. 277-86.
46. *The Hindu Outlook*, 29 August 1939.
47. *The Tribune*, 29 August 1939.

48. *PLAD*, vol. XIV, 26 November 1940, p. 436.
49. *Linlithgow Collection*, vol. 89, 21 March 1940, p. 40; also *The Tribune*, 23 March 1940.
50. *The Tribune*, 11 September 1940.
51. P. Moon, *Divide and Quit*, p. 20.
52. Syed Nur Ahmad, *Martial Law*, pp. 151-4.
53. Ibid.
54. *The Tribune*, 18 April 1941.
55. C. Baxter, 'Union or Partition: Some Aspects of Politics in the Punjab 1936-46', in L. Zirring (ed.), *Pakistan the Long View* (Durham, 1977); also Syed Nur Ahmad, *Martial Law*, p. 153. For deliberation and text of the Conference see, Pirzada, *Muslim League Leaders Correspondence*, vol. II, pp. 325-40.
56. Jafari and Bukhari (eds.), *Quad-i-Azam's Correspondence*, op. cit., p. 371.
57. *The Tribune*, 14 March 1941.
58. *Indian Annual Register*, vol. I, 1941, pp. 242-3.
59. Ibid.
60. *The Tribune*, 22 August 1941.
61. *Linlithgow Collection*, vol. 90, Craik to Linlithgow, 4 March 1941, p. 20.
62. Ibid., vol. 10, Linlithgow to Amrey, 1 March 1941, p. 63.
63. Ibid., vol. 90, Amrey to Linlithgow, 19 March 1941, p. 50.
64. *Indian Annual Register*, vol. II, 1942, p. 293.
65. Jafari and Bukhari (eds.), *Quad-i-Azam Correspondence*, op. cit., p. 372.
66. Pirzada, *Muslim League Leaders Correspondence*, p. 184.
67. Ibid.
68. *The Tribune*, 4 September 1941.
69. Ibid.
70. Ibid., 22 August 1941.
71. Ibid., 12 June 1942.
72. Isphani, *Quad-i-Azam*, p. 58.
73. A day before his death, Sikander solemnized the wedding of two sons and a daughter. His body was placed in the same *pandal* in which the marriage ceremonies had been performed.
74. Also see Talbot, *Punjab and the Raj*, p. 167. Talbot suggests that Khizr Hayat was the choice of the government essentially because of his elite and feudal social background apart from the fact that loyality of the Tiwanas to the British was unquestioned over the past hundred years. See *Punjab and the Raj*, p. 168.
75. *The Times of India*, 30 December 1942.
76. *The Transfer of Power*, vol. III, p. 487.
77. P. Moon, *Divide and Quit*, p. 59.
78. *The Civil & Military Gazette*, 21 December 1943, cited in Talbot, *Punjab and the Raj*, p. 169.

79. P. Moon, *Divide and Quit*, p. 58.
80. *Linlithgow Collection*, vol. 92, Glancy to Linlithgow, 21 July 1943, p. 52.
81. *The Indian Year Book*, 1942-43, p. 859.
82. Jafari and Bukhari (eds.), *Quad-i-Azam's Correspondence*, op. cit., pp. 189, 204.
83. *The Tribune*, 12 June 1943.
84. Ibid., 22 November 1943.
85. G. Alana, *Pakistan Movement*, p. 237; also see Talbot, *Khizr Tiwana*, p. 115.
86. *The Transfer of Power*, vol. IV, p. 879.
87. *The Tribune*, 29 April 1944.
88. Talbot, *Khizr Tiwana*, p. 79.
89. *The Transfer of Power*, vol. IV, Wavell to Amrey, 18 April 1944, p. 898.
90. Ibid., Wavell to Glancy, 15 April 1944, p. 882.
91. *The Hindustan Times*, 15 April 1944.
92. Talbot has given a detail account of these meetings between Khizr and Jinnah, see his *Khizr Tiwana*, pp. 116-22.
93. Ibid.
94. Imran Ali, *Punjab Politics*, p. 569.
95. *The Tribune*, 4 June 1944; also *Indian Annual Register*, vol. I, 1944, p. 224.
96. Talbot, *Khizr Tiwana*, p. 122; also Jamil-ud-Din Ahmad, *Some Recent Speeches and Writings of Mr. Jinnah*, vol. 2 (Lahore, 1976), p. 42.
97. See Talbot, *Khizr Tiwana*, p. 123.
98. *The Transfer of Power*, vol. IV, pp. 503, 954.
99. Talbot, *Punjab and the Raj*, p. 184.
100. Imran Ali, *Punjab Politics*, p. 42.
101. Ibid., p. 43.
102. Tikka Ram, *Sir Chhotu Ram: An Apostle of Hindu Muslim Unity* (Lahore, 1946), p. 104; also Yadav, 'Partition of India', p. 137.
103. *Indian Annual Register*, vol. I, 1944, p. 233.
104. In the Assembly 28 of the 75 Muslim seats were in Multan Division. Rawalpindi Division had 20 Muslim seats, while Lahore Division had 18. See Yadav, *Elections*, p. 136; also Talbot, *Punjab and the Raj*, p. 173.
105. Talbot, *Punjab and the Raj*, p. 173.
106. Ibid., p. 161.
107. Azim Husain, *Mian Sir Fazl-i-Husain: A Political Biography*, p. 96.
108. See ibid. Also N.B. Sen (ed.), *Punjab's Eminent Hindus* (Lahore, 1943).
109. Azim Husain, *Mian Sir Fazl-i-Husain: A Political Biography*, p. 96
110. Y.P. Bajaj, 'Chhotu Ram and The Indian National Congress', *Punjab Past and Present*, vol. XII-I, April 1978, p. 182.
111. Ibid.
112. Azim Husain, *Mian Sir Fazl-i-Husain: A Political Biography*, p. 123; also Syed Nur Ahmad, *Martial Law*, p. 182.

113. H. Harcourt, *Sidelights of The Crisis in India* (Bombay, 1924).
114. Ibid.
115. *The Tribune*, 12 October 1937.
116. *Gopi Chand Bhargava Papers*, Nehru to Bhargava, 3 March 1937.
117. Ibid.
118. *The Tribune*, 12 October 1937.
119. *PLAD*, vol. X, 27 November 1939, p. 1049.
120. Ibid., vol. X, 30 October 1939, p. 316.
121. *The Tribune*, 2 November 1940.
122. Talbot, 'Deserted Collaborators', pp. 79-93; also his *Punjab and the Raj*, pp. 152-4.
123. *The Transfer of Power*, vol. IV, p. 179.
123. Ibid., p. 520.
124. *The Tribune*, 12 June 1942.
125. Ibid., 16 June 1942.
126. P. Moon, *Divide and Quit*, p. 37.
127. *The Tribune*, 25 June 1942.
128. L.R. Nair, *Sikander Hayat Khan*, p. 58.
129. K.C. Gulati, *The Akalis Past & Present* (New Delhi, 1974), p. 82.
130. Isphani, *Quad-i-Azam*, p. 58.
131. Yadav, *Elections*, p. 134.
132. Syed Nur Ahmad, *Martial Law*, p. 124.
133. *The Tribune*, 7 February 1925.
134. Ibid.
135. See Raja Narender Nath, 'The Punjab Agrarian Laws and Their Economic and Constitutional Bearings', *Modern Review*, 65, p. 30.
136. *Report of the Administration of Punjab*, 1931, p. 32.

CHAPTER 6

Eclipse of the Unionist Party

THE LAHORE Muslim League Session of 1940 was not only a major milestone in the Muslim League's progress towards emergence as a formidable political machine but it was also an important turning point in the political history of Punjab. In a way Punjab was never really to be the same again as the Pakistan Resolution approved in the Lahore Session not only threatened the political structure of the region but even disputed and challenged the fact that Muslims had been for centuries an intrinsic part of Punjab's multi-ethnic social fabric. The Muslim League's resolve to demand Pakistan by dividing Punjab was not only a master political stroke but a devastating political agenda that would in due course sweep aside centuries of sociocultural and economic coexistence between Hindus, Muslims and Sikhs. The demand for a separate nation state was based essentially on differences of religion and belief, and as expected by the people who conceived the idea it soon gathered a political momentum that pushed aside all opposition into irrelevance. The Unionist Party too was swept away into the oblivion of history. In fact the same would have happened with even the most well entrenched political organization, such was the tumult that followed the Muslim League's demand for a separate Islamic state. Even though the formal demise of the Unionist Party took place only on 23 June 1947, the day when the East and West Punjab sections of the Legislative Assembly met separately to approve the Bill to partition the Punjab, its death knell had been sounded loud and clear by the Pakistan Resolution. Every passing day after 1940 was a day of new crisis for the Party. As K.K. Arif has pointed out 'The Pakistan Resolution . . . caught the public imagination . . . almost overnight the Muslim League turned into a political movement taking India by storm.'[1] Sikander Hayat's death in 1942 and Chhotu Ram's death in the beginning of 1945 were factors that greatly added to the party's problems and further served to expedite its elimination.

Chhotu Ram's death in particular came at a critical juncture in the Unionist Party's beleaguered journey. He was the last of the old Unionist stalwarts but more importantly, he was the most assertive opponent of the Muslim League's two-nation theory. This is not to suggest that he could alone have withstood the political pressure that followed the League's divisive agenda, but perhaps he could have emerged as a catalyst of opposition to the scheme of Partition. His death in fact appears to have left the field clear for the Muslim League. In the dramatically altered political situation that came to confront Punjab in the early 1940s, even while the Unionist Party had been reduced to irrelevance, there were other important factors too that influenced its decline. Some of these had their genesis in the party's inherently contradictory composition and were thus unavoidable while others were the result of circumstances and events over which the leaders of the Unionist Party had no control or influence.

The world that emerged from World War II was profoundly altered. The end of the War was marked by far-reaching social, economic and political changes. As in numerous colonized countries across the world, in India too the War's end saw resurgence in nationalism and anti-colonialism. Then peculiar conditions and demands of the War had influenced the economies not only of countries that were directly involved in it but also of their colonial empires. In the case of India the War completely changed the political scene all over the country. In Punjab the dramatically changed political scene mainfested itself in seriously eroding the political influence of the Unionist Party.

In the initial years of the War, the Unionist leaders had worked earnestly to boost the British government's War effort particularly in its drive for the enlistment of soldiers. Due mainly to economic benefits that followed from enrolment into the army a large number of Punjab's youth showed considerable enthusiasm towards enlistment. For most young men, joining the armed forces opened better avenues of employment and a life of assured dignity and respect. Financially too it was rewarding as soldiers were able to send good sums of money to their kin most of whom were in the villages. This helped in improving the economic conditions of their families at home. Money sent by enlisted men during the War years played an important role in the economy of rural Punjab.[2]

However, the economic benefits that derived from the War were naturally short-lived and as the War progressed, enthusiasm among the youth for recruitment disappeared. Fighting wars in distant lands, in harsh conditions under foreign commanders was not something for which the youth of Punjab were mentally prepared. Large-scale desertions reportedly followed. Knowledge of the harsh realities of War had a rapidly dispersing influence which discouraged even those who were earlier inclined to be enlisted. In a matter of months the impression had spread around that enlistment must be avoided at all cost. As a result, keeping the supply chain of recruits unbroken became a major issue of concern for the government of Punjab. As pressure mounted for more men, government machinery was applied to enforce recruitment.[3] The situation reached a point where able-bodied youth disappeared from their villages for fear of being forcefully enlisted. The Unionist Party was left to face the back-lash because howsoever nominal and superficial its control over government policy may have been, the Unionists were considered responsible for the policy of enforced recruitment and the con-sequential plight of a large number of rural families.

The economic consequences of the War also proved seriously detrimental to the future of the Unionist Party. During the War years there was widespread scarcity of essential commodities of daily use. In particular food, cloth and kerosene became extremely scarce and were not available to people with limited means[4] resulting in blackmarketing and price rise. Reports of corruption in the supply distribution system and misuse of supplies had become common, something for which the Unionist Party was again held responsible. The government's decision to send wheat from Punjab to the famine stricken areas of Bengal and Bihar also served to seriously com-promise the position of the Unionists in the eyes of the Punjab peasantry. About 2,65,100 metric tonnes of food grain was sent to Bengal in the middle of 1943.[5] The exporting of wheat had been opposed all along by the Unionist leaders. For example even in 1942,

Mustaq Ahmad Gurmani, had criticised his own party leadership on the floor of the Assembly on the issue.[6]

The initial opposition to the export of grain from Punjab to Bengal was mainly due to the fact that requisition of grain for export was being forcefully made at prices which were well below the prevailing market prices. The crisis was further fuelled by the fact that the availability of grain in Punjab had already been effected by the demands of war. Because of the severity of the famine in Bengal and the pressures of War on the economy, Punjab was faced with a severe shortage of food grain in 1944-5. To meet the grave situation the government further intensified the forcible requisition of grain from the villages.[7] This caused even greater resentment among the people, leading to disturbances in various parts of the state in the winter of 1945.[8]

To effect improvement in the condition of the supply of essential goods a rationing system was introduced. However, in this exercise too, some serious problem arose. As it happened, the civil supplies distribution network was mostly in the hands of the Hindus or more specifically in the hands of the Hindu trading classes more commonly referred to as the Banias. It appears that the traders tightened control over the distribution system hoping naturally to profitably utilize the conditions created by the scarcity. The shortage of essential commodities, the shortcomings in the distribution system added a third unfortunate dimension, that of communal biases.[9] However, it needs to be remembered that trading classes in Punjab or for that matter any where else are rarely known to subordinate profit to class or communal biases. Successful traders rarely differentiate among customers on the basis of community. The Muslim League was in any case consciously building communal tension and used the failures in the distribution only as a handy excuse to put pressure on the government.

The result of the alleged irregularities in the supply distribution system was that a simple economic problem soon assumed a communal dimension. Six resolutions complaining against the rationing and distribution of cloth were passed in the leading mosques of Lahore in mid-1945.[10] In May 1945 Muslim League activists convened a protest meeting in Lahore against the food ration and distribution system.[11] A similar situation prevailed in various other towns of Punjab, even while the problem was serious in itself, the communal colour only served to aggravate it.

Large scale corruption in the distribution system also decreased supplies that were meant for rural areas because they were frequently siphoned off en route and distributed in towns where people had a better paying capacity and were in a position to pay more for the same commodity. Ambala division in particular suffered considerably due to this.[12] All put together, the Unionist Party was placed in an unenviable position, unable to function effectively as the vehicle of peasant interests and unable to attack the commercial classes for having created the crisis because of the fear of losing their support in the elections (1946). In any case most of the Unionist party leaders being big landowners were themselves major beneficiaries in the crisis that resulted from the shortage of food grain. It was the common man who bore the burden of shortages and price escalations. A direct fallout of the crisis of food grain shortage was that internal contradictions in the Unionist Party's composition emerged on the forefront. The ironic socioeconomic paradox of large landholders of Punjab claiming to represent the small and middle peasantry had finally manifested itself and began to mock the Unionist leadership with consequences that would in due course prove to be disastrous.

The end of the World War confronted the Unionist government in Punjab with new and unforeseen problems. Among the more consequential of such problems was that with the War's end a large number of soldiers were demobilized and sent home.[13] The soldiers had at the outset been recruited under promises of brighter and better prospects on their return from the War. But when they returned to Punjab without adequate pension and alternate jobs they were disillusioned. The government on its part was in no position to offer alternate employment. Talbot absolves the government from its responsibility of taking care of the returning soldiers because, the War came to a sudden end and the government was not adequately prepared for resettlement.[14] But it could well be added that the promises made by the Unionists while encouraging people to enlist in the first place were more to meet the immediate demand of recruits without really having thought sincerely of the details. Not only did the War's end remove the pressure from the Punjab government but the changed political situation also added to the growing indifference of the government to such problems. As a result thousands of able hands were left idle. Some of these men had travelled during the course of the War to different countries and had interacted with other nationalities with higher standards of living and more progressive ideas. In sum they returned home enlightened and perhaps more conscious and hopeful of their rights. It was the large number of such soldiers who believed that the Unionists being the government were responsible for their problems or at least as much so as the British. This anger was converted into effective support for the Congress and the Muslim League at the obvious cost of the Unionist Party.

Quite in proportion to its mounting problems and declining fortunes the Unionists also had to face other problems that were linked to the declining interest the British had begun to take in welfare. British support to the Unionists which was so apparent during and before the War years had decreased considerably with its end. The changed political situation manifested particularly in the growth of the Muslim League's influence in Punjab had made the British realize that they could no longer ignore the Muslim League, more so when the advantages of supporting the Unionist party politically were no longer as valuable and attractive. The loss of unstinted British support to its cause was a major set-back to the party.

The change in British policy towards the Unionist Party was essentially influenced by the fact that Jinnah had successfully donned the mantle of the chief spokesman of the Muslims in India. British policy was merely a result of the changed political scenario which from the British point of view reflected not only the increasing role of the Muslim League but quite in proportion the falling importance of the Unionist Party. The rapid decline in Unionist fortunes following the change in British attitude was expected because the party had come to depend extensively on British support. This flawed Unionist policy was among the main reasons for its rapid decline.

The Unionist government's policies and style of functioning during the World War II years as also the rapidly changing political situation together led to a considerable erosion of its support in rural Punjab. The small peasant and the tenant farmer had benefited by the pro-agriculturist legislation initiated by the Unionist government between 1937-41, but the benefits that they derived were wiped out during the War years. The big landlords of course had realized well in time the new direction of the political wind and had begun changing sides well in time, a fact that stands substantiated by the rapid increase in desertion from the Unionist Party in favour of the Muslim League and the Congress in the last year of the War and the couple of years that followed.

The release of the Indian National Army soldiers from detention after the surrender of Japan also influenced the political fortunes of the Unionist Party. A large number of INA men were from rural Punjab. The Congress had played an important role in their release and was thus considered by the released men as a natural ally.[15] The enthusiastic response the released INA men received all over the country as also the political encouragement from the Congress and the Muslim League naturally interested them towards active political participation.[16] The Congress and the Muslim League derived considerable political advantage and benefit from the fact that the ex-INA men were able to effectively start an erosion in the base of the Unionist Party in the villages. This was possible because in the eyes of the villagers the INA men were heroes and worthy of trust and respect. War veterans, be they from the INA or demobilized British units played an important role in helping the peasantry to make decisions. Even today such ex-servicemen settled in the villages remain important consultants for fellow villagers with people generally looking up to them for guidance in most matters. Leading regulated and disciplined lives they act as 'role models' for the entire village.

The Labour party's victory in the General Election in Britain in 1945 raised, among Indian leaders, a ray of hope for political relief, even freedom and added a surcharged element to the politcal scene in India. In Punjab the Muslim League further intensified its demand for a separate state. As the possibility of Pakistan and free India drew near, it was felt that the Muslim League and the Congress alone were viable political options. This widely-held belief among the masses was to prove an important cause for the embarrassment and humiliation that the Unionists were later to face. The shift in loyalty was in a way a natural process, in line with the common desire of being on the winning side.

The breakdown of the Simla Conference (July 1945) further underlined the opinion commonly held among the Muslim masses that henceforth the Muslim League would alone be considered the representative of Muslim opinion in Punjab and in any case the chances of securing patronage were far better while supporting the Muslim League. The Unionists were a party of the past, the League a party of the future. For a long time Jinnah, the League supremo, had worked to create a situation where he and his party would become solemnly responsible for the expression of Muslim political sentiment. Jinnah by asserting at the conference that the nomination of a Muslim to the Viceroy's Executive Council could be done only by the Muslim League with his (Jinnah's) consent and that any decision of the Executive Council to which the Muslims objected would require a two-third majority for approval were obviously not accepted by the viceroy.[17] Even since the Sikander-Jinnah Pact (1937) Jinnah had insisted that the Unionist Party could not claim to represent Muslim opinion. His tough attitude at the Simla Conference was a display of political genius. By ensuring the breakdown of the talks he was able to establish finally that he and his party alone were the spokesman of the Muslims of India and that the British and the Congress however unwilling had no other option than to attach significance to the Muslim League alone.[18] Talbot says that, 'Khizr to his, dying day regarded Wavell's 'capitulation to Jinnah at Simla a major British betrayal.'[19]

The announcement of elections to the Punjab Legislative Assembly was made on 21 August 1945. The political agenda of the principal participants, both the Muslim League and the Congress was clear and well known. The Muslim League stood for Pakistan and the Congress for India's freedom. On the other hand the Unionist Party had only its past 'glory' to project. The party's election manifesto released in November 1945 was a painfully contrived attempt to seek credibility. When the whole country was in political ferment, the Unionists were talking in terms of 'attainment of independence by constitutional means'.[20] While the situation demanded an all India perspective, the Unionist leadership was talking of benefits to 'Punjab and Punjabis'. The Unionist Party's emphasis on provincial prosperity had no significance or even relevance when compared with the Congress party's 'Quit India' slogan and its pronounced objective of complete freedom, as also the Muslim League's demand for the new state of Pakistan.

Faced with loss of its goodwill in rural areas the Unionist party began to depend increasingly for survival on the government. In the surcharged anti-imperial and anti-colonial sentiment that swept the world after World War II the policy of seeking support from the very people who were thought to be symbols of colonial exploitation proved unforseenly counter-productive. At about the same time that the Unionists were seeking the assistance of the British bureaucracy in Punjab, many of the world's colonial ruled countries had started their fight of freedom, making colonial rulers extremely unpopular among the native people. When the Unionists attempted to use colonial assistance and force to coerce people to support them it obviously harmed their image. The Unionist Party had for long been an 'aloof body, seasonally resident in Lahore or Simla, remote and for all purposes out of touch with the people'.[21]

On the other hand the Muslim League while enjoying the concealed support of the British bureaucracy strengthened and consolidated its position. The party opened branches in a large number of towns and put great emphasis on propaganda particularly a kind that focussed on the rural Muslim masses who had traditionally been the supporters of the Unionist Party. The League's effort at wooing rural Muslims by a purely religious appeal did not quite succeed initially. Muslim League leaders soon realized that the rural Muslim population of Punjab would accept the League's Islamic appeal only if it was propagated by men known and respected by the rural population. The League leadership was conscious of the fact that the Unionist Party had derived great advantage in the 1937 elections from the support of leading *pirs*. The Muslim League thus endeavoured to pursue the same strategy to enhance its acceptability among the Muslim masses. It launched a systematic plan to secure the support of influential *pirs*. The considerable success achieved in this effort by the League was among the most important causes for the elimination of the Unionist Party's influence from among the Muslim population of rural Punjab.

The level of success secured by the Muslim League in effecting desertion of *pirs* and *sajjada nishins* from the Unionist Party in its favour was conveniently facilitated due to the fact that relations of the Unionist Party with the *pirs* had never really been congenial, they were in fact purely of self-interest and preservation, apart from being a totally motivated and self-seeking understanding, there was little else between the two. Besides the socioreligious and ideological distance between the Unionists and their religious supporters enabled the Muslim League to offer a political alternative to the *pirs* dressed in a fundamentalist ideology. For the *pirs* the Muslim League's offer was a welcome opportunity as it would enable them to create a new religious-cum-political platform. The most significant political advantage that was derivable from the Muslim League's Islamic appeal[22] was that it cut across rural and urban lines, a phenomenon unique to Punjab's political life. The *pirs* were thus joined even by the *ulemas*, to unitedly propagate the League's cause. The transfer of loyalty of this socially, religiously and politically vital segment of Muslim society made the majority of Muslims believe that the Unionist Party's non-communal approach to politics, or rather somewhat liberal and less communal approach had outlived its *raison d'être*.

It was the socioreligious leaders like the *pirs*, etc., whom the Muslim masses were inclined to trust and follow. Their extensive following enabled them to start a massive propaganda on behalf of the Muslim League that the idea of Pakistan was a sort of 'heaven' (*Bahista*) on earth. Pakistan, it was said, would provide a panacea for all the ills that engulfed Punjab's Muslim population. There would be no poverty, no harassment, no exploitation by the Hindu 'moneylender' in the 'pure land'. For the poverty-stricken Muslim peasantry such assurances were like words from heaven. Such propaganda also attempted to make the Muslim masses believe that the Muslim League had answers for the common man's financial and daily needs, in sum the masses were promised that the League would give them much more through an Islamic idiom,[23] than what the Unionists were giving through a 'secular' idiom. For the deeply religious Muslim peasantry the options being offered by the Muslim League appeared more attractive.

The political policy of the Muslim League was based on an

assessment of what the common Muslim masses actually needed,[24] the approach was in fact a kind of psychological war. The League leaders were conscious of the fact that they were a 'Muslim party without the Muslim masses'.[25] The Muslim League sought political support in the villages by assurances of help to the peasant in overcoming economic problems. The main emphasis of the League workers was to implant in innocent minds particularly in rural Punjab the impression that the Unionists were not only responsible but were the main cause of all their problems and that the best alternative for them was Pakistan. The two nation theory implying the demand for Pakistan was also explained by the League activists to the peasantry by providing the interpretation that the Muslims of India had always constituted a separate nation and it was the responsibility of the Muslim League to assert this fact on behalf of the Muslims.[26] The Muslim League politics in Punjab thus came to be based on the policy of arrogating to itself the right to represent the Muslim masses. With this being the principal objective it even had *fatwas* issued by some religious leaders stating that the Muslim League was the only Islamic party and those that did not vote for it were *kafirs*.[27] Firoz Khan Noon a staunch Unionist earlier, even said that 'a vote for the League was a vote for the Prophet'.[28] But as Christina Lamb points out the Muslim League was a party run by the elite 'who cried Islam in danger when it was their own positions, never their religion that was at risk'.

The ferocity of the religious appeal by the Muslim League made even the Unionists issue their own religion-based appeals to the masses. Some Unionists following the example of the League began flying Islamic flags at their political meetings. In fact even Chhotu Ram had just before his death, drawn a plan to employ religious preachers to campaign for the Unionist party.[30] Even Khizr Hayat had begun to use in his speeches verses from the Holy Koran.[31] Khizr attempted to highlight the economic benefits derived from the Unionist rule by providing explanation in Koranic terminology. For example, in a speech in Gujarat he used the first verse of the *Sura Fatiha* to prove that the Unionists had greater moral and religious justification to guide the destiny of the Muslims than the Muslim League. Khizr's point was that *Allah* was described in the Koran as *'Rab-u-alameen'* (Lord of everything and every one not just the Muslim).[32]

Khizr Hayat's attempt to counter the growing influence of the Muslim League by projecting the Unionist Party as having more moral and religious credibility, a claim he based on interpretations of the Koran, lacked conviction. His approach was predestined to failure. The policy of defending the Unionist Party's politics in Islamic idioms while at the same time attempting to maintain the party's secular approach failed totally to counter the Muslim League's provocative propaganda mechanism. After having dwelt on secular credentials and having nurtured the image of being a secular party the sudden change in colour could not possibly have yielded enough advantage to check the growing influence of the Muslim League.

By the beginning of 1946 the Unionist Party had lost the support of almost all leading *pirs* and *sajjada nishins* and as such had been replaced from its stronghold of Muslim support in rural Punjab. The loss of this vital section meant that the party also lost control over the network through which it had mobilized its supporters in the villages. The large-scale desertions that began to take place during 1945-6 from the ranks of the Unionist Party in favour of the Muslim League among the Muslims and the Indian National Congress, among others, reflected the growing irrelevance of the Unionist Party and its programmes. The exodus from the Unionist Party was like the search for 'greener pastures'.

For the Unionists to survive politically and for their support to be kept intact it was imperative that the party's significance as a political entity be maintained and emphasized by the British. This was so because peasant societies like Punjab which are deeply embedded in feudal attitudes, political support has always been dependent proportionately on the utility of the leader or party concerned. When the Unionists began losing their clout with the government, the peasantry realized that supporting the Unionists was like betting on a sick horse which had outlived its utility. It did not take too long for the Punjab Muslim landlords and other influential power brokers to realize that access to positions of importance or service would be cut off if they remained outside the Muslim League ranks any longer. This fear played an important role in the exodus of the rural elite of Punjab from the Unionist Party.[33] The Unionist Party had all along been looked upon for patronage and protection of vested interests. It was in fact a vehicle of opportunism which operated on the principle of receiving patronage from the British administrators and distributing it to henchmen in lesser degrees. When the significance of its leaders declined they failed to receive patronage, they were therefore obviously unable to distribute it lower down the ladder. When the future of the party itself became uncertain, people deserted it rapidly.

The Muslim middle class had greater stakes in the partition of the country and played an instrumental role in the swelling of Muslim League's ranks. This whole exercise came to be influenced by the fact that the middle and educated sections of Muslim society believed and quite rightfully so that the new state would provide immense opportunities. They also saw in the formation of the new state a chance to control the vast commercial avenues that would emerge. In fact for the privileged Muslim middle class 'Pakistan' meant a chance to develop early monopolies in trade and business. As time was to prove they did succeed to a great extent in this endeavour. In fact the Muslim League's two nation theory propaganda had from the very outset promised something or the other for all sections of Punjab's Muslim society. If for the traders the new state was supposed to have the advantage of no competition from the Hindu business classes, for the peasantry Pakistan was to be emancipated from the clutches of the Hindu moneylenders. As pointed out by W.C. Smith:

> Being sure of the British going away from India they (the Muslim middle class) realized one after another that their chances of class success, pitifully meagre in the present order and, as individuals, none too bright even in a free capitalist India, could be immensely increased if they would stand together as a corporate Muslim middle class and fight for power. If Pakistan were achieved, they would have an opportunity of investing their money, or dominating commerce. They have said that Muslims and Hindus are so different that they cannot live together in one State. What they have meant is that the Muslim bourgeoisie and the Hindu bourgeoisie are competitive, that they cannot both own the banks and industries, run the commerce do the professional and other jobs, in one capitalist state.[34]

Such was the speed of exodus from the Unionist Party that by the autumn of 1945 even staunch Unionist families like the Hayats, Noons, Daultanas had shifted their loyalties to the Muslim League.

Their change of loyalty was well in line with the feudal tradition of being perpetually in search of power, the consequence was a major set-back to the Unionist power structure. This was mainly because such families wielded immense social and economic power in their home districts as also in their *biradaris*. The transfer of loyalty by such families delivered not only a crippling blow to the Unionist Party but was a cause of demoralization and came to have a snowballing effect. The Muslim League on its part spared no effort to consolidate into its fold the support of people who were deserting the Unionist Party.

The League's leadership in Punjab in fact consciously recognized the peculiar character of Punjab's rural society, the uniqueness of which is best reflected in the manner in which influential families and *biradari* leaders controlled the political destiny of the vast number of people in their respective regions. The success that could be achieved by the use of influential families as intermediaries stood testified by success of the Unionists, in the 1937 elections. The Muslim League had merely to follow suit. Talbot points out that it was in pursuance of this policy that the Muslim League organized a special conference of the Gujjar *biradari* at Lahore, which was presided over by Captain Chaudhri Shamshir Ali. The conference appealed to the Muslim Gujjars, not only of the Punjab, but of the whole of India to 'sacrifice body, heart and wealth for Pakistan, so that, like every other *biradari* our *biradari* should gain a Divine Reward'.[35] The constituents of different *biradaris* were similarly mobilized throughout the province.

The Muslim League also enrolled student volunteers in large numbers and imparted to them training for political propaganda purposes. This task was performed mainly by the Punjab Muslim Students' Federation, led by Abdul Sattar, Khan Niazi, Ibrahim Ali Chisti and Hameed Nazami.[36] The majority of its members came from Islamia College, Lahore.[37] The League also developed close links with Muslim social and educational organizations including the Anjuman-i-himayat-i-Islam.[38] The contribution of the student volunteers towards consolidating the Muslim League's hold over the masses can never stand over-emphasized. The Punjab Muslim Students' Federation in particular strongly supported the demand for Pakistan and established a Pakistan Rural Propaganda Committee with Niazi as its Secretary. This committee worked among the Muslim peasantry in specific to make them consciously participate and contribute towards the demand of Pakistan.[39] The enthusiasm with which the students worked for the cause of the League went a long way in demoralizing the little that was left of the rank and file in the Unionist Party. There is also little doubt that the enthusiastic support given by the students to the Muslim League particularly within the context of the two nation theory[40] derailed the little chance the Unionist Party ever had of successfully confronting the League's scheme of dividing Punjab. The dedication and zeal of these youth to the cause of the Muslim League and Pakistan was among the most important causes for the total isolation of the Unionist Party and the few leaders who still owed some loyalty to it from among the Muslim masses.

The main method adopted by the activists was to raise religious feelings and passions to frenzied heights. These youth showed a remarkable ability to saturate the Punjab villages with the Muslim League's political views in the garb of Islamic fundamentalism. Politics in the disguise of religion was bound to prove an unbeatable combination. The impact of such propaganda proved extremely effective because these volunteers often began their political speeches with verses from the Koran. Political meetings were frequently organized by them after the Friday prayers in the local village mosques. The Unionist Party was greatly handicapped with regard to youth support, in fact the party did not even have a student wing. Herein lay an important cause for the victory of one and the defeat of the other.

By the time elections were actually held (February 1946), the Muslim League had for all practical purposes replaced the Unionist Party in the minds of the Muslim masses of Punjab. Having started from scratch in less than a decade it built a cadre of about two lakh members.[41] The Unionist had lost relevance, their influence being confined to the walls of the Assembly[42] and the grandeur of Simla and Lahore. They had become out of touch with the ground realities of Punjab and had failed to appropriately react to the rapidly changing socioeconomic and political situation. The Unionist Party had in fact been simply outplayed.

The 1946 election to the Punjab Legislative Assembly proved to be an important turning point in the history of Punjab as also in that of the Unionist Party. The elections differed from the 1937 elections importantly in the sense that they were fought more on party basis and on specific issues. While for the Muslim League the main political agenda was the formation of Pakistan, for the Congress it was freedom of India. The Unionists with no political agenda worth the name simply drifted along into growing irrelevance. While party symbols and affiliations played an important role in wooing the voters, just as caste and *biradari* associations and linkages too played an important part. The elections were held in February 1946.

Of the 86 seats designated for Muslims (including rural and women) the Muslim League won 73. The 19 seats won by the Unionists were all rural.[43] The Muslim League got 66.4 per cent of the votes and the Unionists who contested only in the rural areas, got 26.7 per cent.[44] Jinnah was overjoyed at this success. He said, 'I am more than happy that the Congress won 40 seats of which only one was a Muslim.' The Muslim seat won by the Congress was that of Maulana Ghaznavi, President of the Punjab Congress Committee. The voting also showed that Punjab had finally and totally been divided on communal lines and also that the Unionist Party had in essence been reduced to the status of an insignificant political organization existing only in the shadow of the Muslim League. But even more importantly the voting pattern and the results further

TABLE 6.1: PUNJAB LEGISLATIVE ASSEMBLY, 1946: ELECTION RESULTS

Party	Seats
Muslim League	73
Congress	51
Unionist Party	19
Akali Dal	21
Independents	11
Total	175

SOURCE: *Indian Annual Register*, vol. I, 1946, pp. 229-30; also Yadav, *Elections*, p. 106.

confirmed the fact that a deep wedge had emerged among different communities in Punjab.

Soon after the elections the communal divide influenced the claims that were put forth for the formation of the ministry. The frenzy and passion of the election days spilled over into the formation of the ministry. The Muslim League claimed its natural right, being the largest single party. The Akalis with 21 seats also held an important position. Initially both the League and the Akalis explored the possibility of forming a coalition government which however could not materialize. The difference in opinion was serious and was based mainly on the League's demand of Pakistan being confronted with the Akali objective of Khalistan.[45]

The third important political force in Punjab at the time, the Congress, once again reflected indecision even though its objective of preventing the Muslim League from forming a government was clear enough. Maulana Azad on the other hand worked to materialize a Congress-Akali-Unionist coalition. Sardar Patel supported Azad's view as also did Mahatma Gandhi.[46] Nehru, however, was against the coalition primarily on the ground that the Congress should not support the Unionists, who all along had collaborated with the British.[47] Nehru's hesitancy to join force with the Unionists notwithstanding the Congress, entered the coalition mainly because it really had no other option. The Unionists were obviously considered lesser of the evils among the options available. *The Tribune*[48] considered the proposal of this coalition as being in the nation's interest on the ground that the Unionists had all along been opposed to the proposal of Pakistan. Another factor that appears to have influenced the Congress is that the only agenda for the Muslim League had been the Partition of India. Opposition to the League at this stage therefore actually meant opposing the prospect of Pakistan. Therefore, other things apart, avoiding the Partition of India was now considered by nationalist parties like the Congress as being more important.

The formation of a Congress-Unionist-Akali coalition ministry became possible on 6 March. Khizr Hayat the outgoing Unionist Premier was invited to once again lead the government. For the

Muslim League, however, the British government's decision to allow such a coalition was a major political set-back. The League being the largest single party in the Assembly obviously felt deprived and cheated.[49] In protest the Muslim League observed a mass hartal on 7 March. Traitor's Day was organized on 9 March.[50] From this point of time onwards, immense pressure came to be mounted on Muslim Unionist legislators to desert the Unionist Party.

The swearing in of the new ministry on 11 March 1946 could not have come at a more inappropriate time. Apart from Khizr Hayat, as Premier, the ministry included Bhim Sen Sacchar, Congress (Finance), Ch. Lehri Singh, Congress (Public Works), Sardar Baldev Singh, Akali (Development), Nawab Muzzafar Ali Khan Qizilbash, Unionist (Revenue) and Mohammad Ibraham Barq, Unionist. The highly opportunistic character of the coalition defied ideological reasoning and was destined to chaos and confusion from the very beginning. There was total lack of understanding between the legislative groups of the parties both on the floor of the house as also off it. Political reports submitted by Evan Jenkins, Governor of Punjab to the Viceroy repeatedly show that the political system was heading towards chaos.[51]

Not only the formation but later even the functioning of the new government appears to have been confined to theory alone. The new Assembly attempted the formality of conducting an Assembly Session in March. The occasion provided to the Muslim League legislators an opportunity to chide and taunt the Muslims among the Unionist Party as traitors and 'banaspati Muslims'.[51] Mohammad Hassan even addressed Sir Khizr Hayat as, 'Malik Sir Ghaddar Hayat Khan'.[53] Ghazanfar Ali Khan attacked the coalition as a 'combination of heterogeneous elements united merely by their hatred for the League'.[54] Even senior leaders like Firoz Khan Noon threatened mass destruction by direct action if the British did not make amend 'will put to shame the deeds of Haluka Khan and Chengiz Khan. . . .'[55] The mass hysteria and violent fanaticism advocated by some of the Muslim League leaders provided early indication of the troubled times that lay ahead.

Even though the chances of success of the coalition government were bleak, the Congress leaders of Punjab expedited to a considerable extent its early demise. Oblivious of the fact that their parent body was the symbol of India's political will the Congress leaders of Punjab were busy in petty squabbles[56] leading to a situation where the coalition ministry became ineffective and meaningless. As the more important member of the coalition with the largest numerical strength, the Congress in Punjab should have effectively supported Khizr Hayat in facing the onslaught of the Muslim League. Its complete failure in doing so exposed the coalition government to avoidable embarrassment.

Starting with the formation of the coalition ministry, every passing day was a step closer to the holocaust that soon engulfed the province. 'Communal and political tension is increasing . . . communities are preparing for . . . rioting . . . private armies . . .' reported the governor to the viceroy on 2 May 1946.[57] The governor attributed the anger and hatred of the Muslim League to the commonly held belief that it had been betrayed by the British. As for the governor, however, he was inclined to believe that Jinnah had simply been outmanouevred the Congress.[58] The League's point of view was simple in the sense that being the largest single party in the Assembly the formation of ministry was its right. In any case the Muslim League was convinced that the sole objective of the coalition was to keep the Muslim League out of power. There was also considerable basis in the League's belief that a coalition of the Congress and the Unionists was possible only because of their common hatred for the League. The League leadership also believed that the Muslims in the Unionist Party had betrayed the Muslims of Punjab. All put together the leaders of the Muslim League were convinced that they had no option other than whipping up of passions. In a way the League's prevention from ministry formation proved a blessing in disguise as it certainly hastened the partition of Punjab. These developments provided to the Muslim League a kind of moral right to mobilize the Muslim masses and paralyse the coalition government.

The League's slogan of 'Islam in Danger' and its programme of 'Direct Action Day' for 16 August 1946 was keeping in line with its policy of bringing to a halt the government of Punjab. The violent nature of the League's plan was like a call to civil war, the other two major communities were not too far behind in cobbling to the problem.[59] The Lahore Action Committee of the Muslim League organised a meeting of the *ulemas* and *pirs* and had a *fatwa* issued in favour of *jehad*.[60] By June 1947 the RSS had 58,000 members, the Muslim League National Guard 39,000 members and the Sikh Akali Fauj 8000 members.[61]

The communal violence that engulfed Punjab in the months that followed was a natural sequal to the unbridled and provocative propaganda with which the people of Punjab had been continuously blasted beginning from the end of 1945 and throughout 1946. Initially the level of communal violence was contained to some extent as a result of quick responses from the administrative machinery. As such Punjab was spared the initial violence that had erupted elsewhere in the country. However, the communal situation in Punjab began deteriorating rapidly with events racing towards disaster particularly as news of communal violence in Bombay, Bihar, etc., began spreading in the region. Initially the government reacted sternly and effectively in enforcing law and order, freely using the Punjab Public Safety Ordinance from November 1946. All forms of provocative activity like demonstrations, carrying of weapons and processions were banned. The Muslim League and the RSS were both declared unlawful bodies. The communal passions in Punjab had unfortunately been so intensely aroused that even the strictest of administrative measures could provide only temporary relief. It is, therefore, not surprising that the activity of the Muslim League National Guard as well as that of the RSS instead of being restricted actually got further intensified. The government raided the Muslim League and RSS offices all over Punjab, but nothing significant came out. In Lahore, however, obstruction in the searches of the League headquarters led to the arrest of important leaders like Shaukat Hayat, Mumtaz Daultana, Firoz Khan Noon, etc.[62] There arrests, however, proved to be rallying points towards violence[63] and even greater intensification of communal passions. The search in the League's headquarters at Lahore also unearthed 2000 steel helmets.[64]

Jinnah, the master of political strategies that he was, saw in the banning of the Muslim League National Guard an ideal opportunity to launch an 'all out' struggle, a breaking point so to say.[65] Henceforth the pressure mounted by him and his party on the government was immense, causing the government to practically come to a standstill. A demoralised government ordered the release of the Muslim League leaders on 27 January 1947 and lifted the ban on the Muslim League National Guard the next day.[66] The lifting of the ban and release of the arrested leaders appears, as Talbot has suggested, to have been influenced by the Governor Jenkin's conciliatory attitude at this stage. He reminded Khizr that 'it was easier to send people to jail than to get them out of jail in a cooperative frame of mind'.[67] The soft approach, however, failed to pacify sentiment and did not in any way alter or diffuse the tense situation with the chances of conciliation had by then been totally diminished. For the Muslim League, the release of its activists as also its demand for lifting the ban on its National Guard as also the demand for restoration of civil liberties were only part of a broader strategy. The real objective was the overthrow by force of the coalition ministry in Punjab.[68] The climbdown by the Punjab government even though belated was on expected lines and reflected the actual political condition and compulsions of Punjab. Far from being in a position of enforcing tough administrative decisions the government was scarcely in a position to even defend itself. Even Khizr Hayat's own life was in constant danger, compelling him even to change his place of residence frequently.

On 20 February 1947 the British government announced its decision to transfer power by June 1948. The Unionist Party had already ceased to be of any political significance since its defeat in the elections but even as a part of the coalition ministry the Unionist ministers and legislators had come to be treated indifferently mainly as the party no longer appeared to be of any relevance. With the announcement of the handing over of power not only was Punjab engulfed in a state of complete anarchy but even the coalition ministry and its Premier Khizr Hayat suddenly became totally irrelevant. The little authority that they had lost credibility. But more importantly the sudden decision of the British to quit India made the coalition government lose the will and determination to face the turmoil which the Muslim League's call for civil disobedience had created. In sum a demoralized Khizr Hayat was expected to lead an even more demoralized and disinterested government to restore the credibility of law[69] in the face of a population which had been continuously poisoned by communal rhetoric. The Muslim League's policy of mobilizing the masses to support the partition of India had finally begun to pay dividends.

The situation deteriorated so rapidly that a double-minded Khizr Hayat being unable to bear the pressure of office finally decided to succumb and resigned as premier on 1 March 1947. Khizr explained his resignation by saying 'parties in the province must now be brought face to face, it is now incumbent on me to leave the field clear for the Muslim League to come . . . make arrangement with other parties'.[70] The coalition ministry formally resigned on 5 March 1947. It had been in office for almost a year to the day. Not on one occasion during the whole year did the ministry appear to be in command. Yet in the context of Khizr Hayat, personally a well-meaning and earnest man it was a sad end to an eventful political career. Like Chhotu Ram he was a remarkable man believing that partition of Punjab implied not only the partitioning of a province but destruction of a way of life based on centuries of sociocultural interaction.

The east and west sections of the Punjab Legislative Assembly met separately for the last time on 23 June 1947. The session was a mere formality. With Punjab engulfed in the flames of communal passion, the only agenda was division of Punjab. The Assembly voted for partition. All Muslim legislators of the Unionist Party voted in favour of Pakistan.[71] The fact that some Muslim Unionist legislators waited for as long as the last session of the Punjab Legislative Assembly to support the partition resolution is a significant pointer to the tragedy that the whole scheme of Partition actually was. The few non-Muslim Legislators that remained within the Unionist Party after 23 June 1947 drifted in the course of time into the Congress. The Unionist Party disintegrated and disappeared into the oblivion of history. It had been born suddenly without the pains of labour. Over the years it appeared to do well, but it passed away painfully, agonizingly and sadly without leaving a trace almost in line with the suddenness of its creation. The Unionist system of concensus as Talbot too has suggested[72] was the surest way of maintaining peace in a society that was unable to isolate itself from the frenzy of religious passion so vehmenently propogated by leaders in search of political power.

The dimensions and implications of partition need to be understood in view of the fact that seventeen million people were compelled by circumstances to leave their homes and search for new ones, between six lakhs to one crore lost their lives.[73] Another estimate puts the number of women abducted and kidnapped at over one lakh. For students of history the traumatic happenings of 1947 contain the drama, the tragedy, the unresolved and unending queries leading to a situation where Partition has come to mean different things to different people. The reasons for the chilling scenes, the sudden relish for violence still remain rationally unexplained. To whom should the finger of responsibility point? There is obviously no simple answer.

In a more generalized manner the roots of the violence can be traced to the sustained nurturing of distrust and hatred between major communities even though for Ayesha Jalal a great part of the blame rests on the shoulders of Mountbatten:

> While Punjab writhed and turned under the impact of decisions taken in distant places, Mountbatten boldly claimed credit for having accomplished . . . one of the greatest administrative operations in history. On behalf of the Hindus, Sikhs and Muslims who were slaughtered in their hundreds of thousands, and the refugees who in their millions stumbled fearfully across the frontiers of the two states, the historian has a duty to challenge Mountbatten's contention and ask whether this 'great operation' was not in fact an ignominous scuttle enabling the British to extricate themselves from the awkward responsibility of presiding over India's communal madness.[74]

It is commonly believed that the flaring up of communal passion was mainly the result of a conscious British imperial policy. While there may be some element of truth in this belief, this attitude, at the same time, appears to betray signs of nationalistic emotionalism and in the process also conceals the failures of political parties and their leaders. A worried Sir Evan Jenkins, Governor of Punjab wrote to Mountbatten: 'no leader appeared concerned towards the implications and difficulties of partition'.[75] When Khizr Hayat, for example, was compelled by the agitations of the Muslim League to resign as Premier of Punjab on 2 March 1947, Master Tara Singh standing on the steps of the Punjab Legislative Assembly dramatically unsheathed his sword and said, 'the time has come when the might of the sword alone shall rule. The Sikhs are ready. . . .'[76] Two days later (5 March) *The Hindustan Times* commented:

Sikhs are much better organized and better armed than the Muslims . . . a British official told me that if they had to face a similar movement as like that of the Muslim League against Khizr Hayat the problem would have been far more serious . . . when the rival claims of communities are submitted to the arbitration of force the Sikhs are also likely to have the powerful support of the RSS.

While examples of provocation from both sides are unending there is need also to mention that the growing rift between communities was not simply the result of communal madness. This is so because there were some vital elements of economic interest involved. It is hardly surprising that some important leaders in Punjab were actually conscious of the problems that were likely to follow the partitioning of Punjab. The Unionist Premier Khizr Hayat, for example, was against the very concept of dividing Punjab to form Pakistan:

It will be ruinous for all communities to split up the Province into bits. I had, in a Press interview some weeks back, expressed my opposition to any scheme involving partition of the Punjab. I notice now that section of the Press has doubted the authenticity of that statement. I have in fact on many occasions in the past expressed the view that it would be ruinous for all communities to split up the Province into bits. The present Punjab boundaries make the Province a self-sufficient economic unit. The irrigation system, the electricity scheme, and the extensive development programme of the future, if torn apart, would lead to an impoverishing of both the western and the eastern Punjab. It will be a catastrophic calamity if this comes about and all sections of the Punjabis should consider its dangerous implications, particularly the Hindus and Sikhs in the west and Muslims in the east of Punjab.[77]

Even Feroz Khan Noon among the most vocal supporters of the concept of Pakistan had in fact foreseen the problems that would arise from the partition of Punjab:

We, the Muslims, are not willing to surrender one inch of the Punjab's territory. If we divide the land of the five rivers with its common irrigation system we are laying the foundation for future wars. An unjust peace is likely to force the two India's to begin to arm themselves in self-defence. Resources sorely needed for our economic development will be frittered away on unproductive defence channels. The Congress realizing that a division of India is inevitable are now using every device to make Pakistan not worth living. But the Muslim prefers his freedom to everything else.[78]

For the Sikh population the division of Punjab was a move pregnant with serious implications but at the same time unavoidable. Even though the Sikh population at the time was just 45 lakhs of Punjab's 2.8 crores, the community's tendency for hardwork and dynamism had led to a situation where large tracts of fertile land across the Punjab were cultivated by them. Partition implied that the community would be uprooted not only from their ancestral homes but divested of lands which they had brought by sheer dint of hard work into high levels of productivity. Besides, the partition of Punjab also meant that the Sikh peasantry would lose control of the vast irrigation networks of west Punjab. The unfortunate fact is that serious economic grievances got clouded and covered in communal colours as a sequel to the kind of propagandist politics that had been going on in Punjab for some years. The violent reaction of the people was also in a way the natural consequence of a disturbed society in which strange elements had come to the fore. When the holocaust finally struck, Mountbatten showed inexplicable hurry to leave India and hand over Pakistan to Mohammed Ali Jinnah, and India to Jawaharlal Nehru. The advancing of the transfer of power by almost a year proved a disastrous decision since it was the most important cause for the massive loss of life and property witnessed in different parts of India, specially Punjab.

The fault of Mountbatten is not merely an error of judgement but a conscious evasion of tackling an emerging crisis by handing over the administration at the fateful moment to leaders who had no experience in managing such a situation. Besides, there are other issues, some emotional and others practical for which scholars will perhaps criticize Mountbatten and his 'masters' in London. For example, a nation that had been united for thousands of years was to be divided into two within 40 days. Millions of families were forced to find new homes overnight, with no security or assistance. The surprising fact is that the British appear to have actually visualized the problems that could result from such speedy 'partition'. The anarchy and chaos witnessed in the western districts was rooted in the simple fact that the administration was not even prepared for action. The viceroy very bluntly put it: 'Administratively it is the difference between putting up a permanent building, a nissen hut or a tent. As for Pakistan is concerned we are putting up a tent. We can do no more.'[79]

'The range of effective decisions open to human beings' as V.N. Datta points out, 'is more limited than often imagined.'[80] With this in mind the blame for the communal holocaust it appears must also be placed on leading Indian politicians of the time, particularly of the Congress, as the viceroy is known to have rarely differed with some of these leaders. The British on their part claim to have done everything 'humanly possible' to control the situation, and stress the fact that 'the situation was long past mere military action and required political leadership of a very high order'.[81] If anything it was a complete failure of responsible political leadership which had brought anarchy to Punjab. Datta has very aptly termed the men who mattered during those traumatic month as the 'heroes of retreat'.[82]

The butchery that occurred in Punjab can therefore also be attributed to the ambiguous manner in which both political leaders and administrators handled the crisis. Countless are the stories of families who left their homes at a few minutes notice, some did not even have the time to wait for members who were away from home. Thousands of families who were living prosperously thus joined the 'convoy' of partition with only the clothes they were wearing. The tales of horror and barbarity of human behaviour have naturally over-shadowed the economic social and cultural disaster that partition created for millions of families. One can only imagine—what if more time had been given, adequate security, and means of transport, provided? Would the story of Punjab's partition still have been the same sad one that it is today?

The most profound irony of the whole situation is that power was handed over to two government mechanisms which did not even know the exact boundaries of their new dominion. As Jalal points out, Mountbatten consciously delayed announcing the details of the Boundary Commission awards up to 18 August because he was apprehensive that the strong disagreement that was likely to emerge among the leaders might shatter the whole exercise. Thus, we have a situation where leaders agreed to accept the reigns of power without having assessed what the new boundaries would imply for millions of innocent people.

The sudden demise of the Unionist Party was rooted in the changed political situation both in Punjab as well as all over India. In the new political environment there was really no place for the Unionist Party or its politics of 'concensus'. The issues in 1947 were not regional or parochial, dimensions had become much broader, it was independence of India and the creation of Pakistan. No other issue seemed to matter. Within a span of six years (1940-6) as a result of the Muslim League's Pakistan Resolution, politics in Punjab had assumed a frenzied and vitiated complexion. For the Unionists the implication was that all their good work of economic development, communal harmony and sociocultural co-existence was wiped out without a trace.

The party's sudden eclipse can also be explained by the fact that both in quantity and quality its traditional support had come from sections of society that have always been known for shifting loyalties, the big landlords and the like. The unique feudal and political structure that operated in Punjab in the first five decades of the twentieth century and of which the Unionist Party was the most remarkable symbol was also, it must be remembered, a creation of British rule in Punjab. From the Unionist Party's point of view, however, there was an important drawback in the fact that its existence depended on the support of colonial mechanisms, that is for survival itself the strong and effective support of the British imperial administrative system became imperative. The moment this support decreased or lost its enthusiasm, or even when the fear and respect of the British administrative machinery began to decline the fortunes of those it had created or supported followed suit. The Unionist Party could obviously not have been an exception. Both the character and the future of the Party was too closely interwoven with the British administrative and political system to have been of any significance after the British had reconciled to leaving the subcontinent.

The Unionist Party dominated politics in Punjab for close to two decades. It enjoyed from 1937 to 1942 in particular the support of almost 68 per cent of the Punjab Legislative Assembly members. Even when it was practically routed in 1946 it did manage to rescue around 20 per cent of the votes polled.[83] The Unionist Party's success is, however, sometimes perceived as conditional, particularly when we realize that only a small part of Punjab's population was actually enfranchised. The party's success therefore can also be understood as the result of special circumstances.

These special circumstances essentially were restricted franchise and the hierarchical nature of rural Punjab. These circumstances ensured, as Talbot points out,[84] that right up to the eve of the departure of the British from India there was no real challenge to the politics of elite accommodation practised by the Unionists. It is not a coincidence that the fortunes of the Unionist Party began to decline the moment there was increased political participation.

The Unionist politics of elite accommodation based on proportion and the creation of a kind of 'grand coalition',[85] proceeded smoothly until the emergence of more important and superceeding political agenda—that of Pakistan and the freedom of India. The well meaning Khizr Hayat determinedly strove to keep Punjab united but obviously the special conditions that had enabled such sane voices to be heard and followed earlier had ceased to exist. Khizr's actions up to the very end represented the ability of the select elite to act independently and constructively even in conditions of extreme conflict. But his failure to change the destined course of Punjab's history also serves to underline the fact that the patron-client relationship which served as the bedrock of Unionist politics was challenged and destabilized even if only temporarily. This patron-client politics as we know re-emerged in Pakistan almost unscathed after 1947.

Even when the Unionist Party disappeared into oblivion it did leave a message for the communally cleavaged and strife-torn India and Pakistan—that the pursuance of 'intercommunal political accommodation can achieve a large degree of success, even in plural societies'.[86] The Unionist political philosophy serves to prove that communal differences can be meaningfully reduced if the similarities in sociocultural norms are emphasized. The Unionist policy particularly of its leaders Chhotu Ram, Sikander and Khizr of attempting economic development on a platform free from communal perceptions was an important factor that kept rural Punjab in particular free from the growing communal strife. The significance of the Unionist Party and its style of politics needs also to be understood in view of the fact that no sooner had the Unionist influence begun to weaken than almost simultaneously Punjab began to get engulfed in communal violence.

The most significant and lasting legacy of the Unionist Party remains however its policy of seeking and projecting cross-communal similarities, particularly in rural society. Its rural development and political agenda was based on the assumption that the peasantry of Punjab irrespective of community was bound in a profound manner by common economic compulsions and requirements.

NOTES

1. K.M. Arif, *Working with Zia: Pakistan's Power Politics, 1977-88* (Karachi, 1995), p. 5.
2. R.S. Nakra, 'Punjab Villages in Ludhiana district during the War' (Punjab Board of Economic Enquiry, No. 91) (Lahore, 1946), p. 8, vide Talbot, *Punjab and the Raj*, p. 144.
3. Talbot, *Punjab and the Raj*, pp. 145-6.
4. See Talbot, 'Deserted Collaborators'; see also his *Punjab and the Raj*, p. 146.
5. Talbot, *Punjab and the Raj*, p. 146.
6. Talbot, 'Deserted Collaborators'.
7. The problem has also been discussed by Talbot in his *Khizr Tiwana*, p. 100.
8. Talbot, 'Deserted Collaborators'.
9. Ibid.
10. Ibid.
11. Ibid.
12. *The Tribune*, 19 June 1945.
13. Talbot, *Punjab and the Raj*, p. 165.
14. Ibid.
15. Ibid., p. 165.
16. Ibid.
17. See *The Transfer of Power*, vol. V, pp. 1104-227.
18. Also see Talbot, *Khizr Tiwana*, pp. 137-40; and H.V. Hodson, *The Great Divide: Britain India and Pakistan* (London, 1969).
19. Talbot, *Khizr Tiwana*, p. 137.
20. *Civil and Military Gazette*, 29 November 1945.
21. Ibid.
22. Talbot cites numerous examples of these appeals, for example, the one by Fazal Ahmad Shah: 'I command all those who are in my Silsilah to do everything possible to help the Muslim League . . . those who do not . . . should consider themselves no longer members of the Silsilah', *Punjab and the Raj*, p. 211

23. *The Hindustan Times*, 26 February 1946.
24. W.C. Smith, *Modern Islam*, p. 333.
25. See Christina Lamb, *Waiting for Allah* (New Delhi, 1991), p. 23.
26. Khalid Bin Sayeed, *The Political System of Pakistan* (Boston, 1967), p. 8.
27. *Civil and Miliatary Gazette*, 29 January 1946.
28. Anita Inder Singh, *The Origin of the Partition of India, 1936-47* (Delhi, 1987), p. 38.
29. Lamb, *Waiting for Allah*, p. 23.
30. Madan Gopal, *Sir Chhotu Ram: A Political Biography* (New Delhi, 1977), p. 146; also Talbot, *Punjab and the Raj*, p. 162.
31. Talbot, *Punjab and the Raj*, p. 162.
32. Ibid.
33. W.C. Smith, *Modern Islam*, p. 331.
34. Ibid.
35. Talbot, *Punjab and the Raj*, p. 210.
36. Ibid., p. 157.
37. Ibid.
38. Ibid.
39. Ibid.
40. This extract from a letter of Niazi to Jinnah shows the level to which enthusiasm had reached: 'We have fully determined that to win the land of Pakistan we will launch one attack after another like Ghaznavi. . . . For a long time the Saints of Somnath have been waiting for another like him'. See ibid.
41. Khalid Bin Sayeed, *Pakistan: The Formative Phase*, p. 178.
42. *Civil and Military Gazette*, 4 September 1945.
43. *Indian Annual Register*, vol. I, 1946, pp. 229-30; also see Yadav, *Elections*, p. 106
44. Ibid.
45. *The Transfer of Power*, vol. VI, p. 1136, Punjab Governor to Viceroy, 11 March 1946.
46. Satya M. Rai, *Partition of Punjab* (New Delhi, 1985), p. 41.
47. Ibid.
48. *The Tribune*, 1 March 1946.
49. See, Talbot, *Khizr Tiwana*, p. 149; Syed Nur Ahmad, *From Martial Law*, p. 179; also Penderel Moon (ed.), *Wavell: The Viceroys Journal* (London, 1973), p. 220.
50. Penderel Moon, *Divide and Quit* (Delhi, 1987), pp. 72, 129.
51. *The Transfer of Power*, vol. XIII, p. 207.
52. *PLAD*, vol. XXV, 28 March, 1946, p. 192.
53. Ibid.
54. Ibid.
55. Allah Baksh Rajput, *Punjab Crisis and Cure* (Lahore, 1947), p. 39.
56. *The Transfer of Power*, vol. XIII, p. 373, Jenkins to Wavell, 31 August 1946.

57. Ibid., vol. VII, p. 400.
58. Ibid.
59. Home Political, Fortnightly Report, 2nd half of May 1946.
60. Ibid., 2nd half of August 1946.
61. Talbot, *Punjab and the Raj*, p. 233.
62. *The Tribune*, 25 January 1947.
63. P. Moon, *Divide and Quit*, p. 35.
64. Talbot, *Khizr Tiwana*, p. 155.
65. S.Q.H. Jafri and S.A. Bukhari (eds.), *Quad-i-Azam's Correspondence with Punjab Muslim League Leaders* (Lahore, 1977), p. 235.
66. *The Tribune*, 29 January 1947.
67. Talbot, *Khizr Tiwana*, p. 155.
68. P. Moon, *Divide and Quit*, p. 77.
69. *The Tribune*, 3 March 1947.
70. Ibid.
71. Ibid., 24 June 1947.
72. Talbot, *Khizr Tiwana*, p. 180.
73. H.K. Spate, *India and Pakistan: General and Regional Geography* (London, 1954), p. 119.
74. A. Jalal, *The Sole Spokesman Jinnah: The Muslim League and the Demand for Pakistan* (New Delhi, 1985), p. 293.
75. *Transfer of Power*, vol. X, p. 506.
76. Khaliquzzaman, *Pathway to Pakistan*, p. 376.
77. Ibid., pp. 378-9.
78. Ibid., p. 379.
79. C. Johnson, *Mission with Mountbatten* (London, 1951), p. 87.
80. Presidential Address, Indian History Congress (Chennai, December 1996).
81. Jalal, *The Sole Spokesman Jinnah*, p. 293.
82. Datta, Presidential Address.
83. I. Talbot, 'Back to the Future?', p. 67.
84. Ibid., p. 69.
85. Ibid., p. 68.
86. Ibid., p. 67.

Glossary

abiana	a tax levied by the government on landowners for use of canal waters.
banaspati	essentially meaning adulterated; the reference here relates to those Muslims who did not support the Muslim League in its struggle for the partition of India and the two nation theory.
Bania	an important Hindu caste, usually involved in commerce and business; significance here being related to money-lending activity in Punjab.
barani	land not having any source of irrigation other than rain.
begar	labour for which adequate compensation is not provided; the reference relates to exploitation of the deprived and helpless by big landowners.
benami	fictitious; used here in relation to transactions of money lending and sale/purchase of land so as to subvert and circumvent provisions of law.
biradari	'brotherhood', clan, kinship; a crucial factor in consolidation of political support in Punjab particularly south-east (Haryana), even to-day.
Chaudhari	a common title pre-fixed to names of people usually associated with land ownership; also frequently used to address headman and leaders in north India.
crore	ten million.
dargah	grave, tomb, shrine of 'sufi' saints, revered all over India by Hindus and Muslims alike; Khawaja Mouin-ud-din Chisti's 'dargah' being the most popular known example in contemporary India.
dehat/dehati	rural, belonging to rural area.
fatwa	ruling; also direction given by a Muslim judge or theologian, or even important leader on points of Islamic law, dimensions usually vary from technical interpretations of the Holy texts to political objectives.

ghaddar — actually meaning traitor, but more commonly applied to those who betray a wider cause, be it community, religion, union, etc.; applied here by Muslim League leaders on Muslim Unionists who did not support the two nation theory.

Idgah — a Mosque where Id prayers are held.

jati — meaning both caste and sub-caste, a critical factor in political support; a habit among aspiring Indian politicians is to appeal to 'jati' loyalties.

jatha — a group of volunteers a term usually applied when such a group participates in activity with concerted aims and objectives, usually political or religious.

jagir — grants of land made by rulers to people helpful to the government, or showing exceptional loyalty where it involved foreign rule as in case of the British.

jhatka — a term applied to slaughtering of animals for consumption by a single stroke, differentiating it from the Muslim method where the animal is usually beheaded slowly. The reference here is related to the Sikh community's demands upon the Unionist Premier Sikander Hayat.

jehad — essentially an Islamic term, meaning a holy war for the cause of the 'faith'.

kafir — essentially an Islamic term used to categorize those who are not followers of Islam; infidels or non-believers.

lakh — one hundred thousand.

lambardar — a title bestowed by the government usually on the largest landowner of the village responsible for the collection and deposit of land revenue; became a vital chain in the British policy along with the 'zaildars', etc., a backbone of the Unionist Party.

mandi — market usually dealing in wholesale of grain, vegetable, cloth, animals, etc.

maulvi — theologian, well versed in the Koran, essentially Muslim.

murid — a term used to describe people who were the followers of various sufi saints/'pirs'; very common in the region of Punjab particularly in what to-day forms Pakistan; many leading *pir's* had lakhs of 'murids' from different religions, but mainly Muslims.

murabba — a unit of land measuring 25 acre.

namaz — canonical prayer; strict Islam adherents perform it five times a day; Friday 'namaz' is of greater significance.

panchayat — a village council of arbitrators, earlier composed of village elders, but at present a symbol of the highly effective form

	of grass-root democracy in India; the word is derived from 'pan' (five) because in earlier times the council usually had five members; no legal powers to adjucate matters but usually decides on the basis of tradition, amicability, harmony, normally petty matters.
patwari	a official of the government hierarchically at the lowest of the revenue administration but by being constantly in direct contact with the people, a vital role; symbol of government authority for the common man.
pir	'Sufi' saint, a revered religious leader or spiritual guide; in Persian meaning elder; played an extremely important role in British policy of collaborative rule in Punjab; associated with mystical powers, both healing and spiritual.
rais	was a kind of title prefixed to the name similar to 'chaudhary' or 'malik', symbolising wealth and in colonial Punjab also influence and status; usually supporters of both the British and the Unionist Party.
safedposh	a lowly title given by the British to people selected by the administration on the basis of loyalty; associated in non-official capacity with revenue collection; usually men with lesser influence than the 'zaildars' and 'lambardars'; major supporters of the Unionist Party.
sajjada nishin	person incharge/custodian of 'Sufi' shrine, or the seat of prayer; supposed to have the mystical powers of the person whose shrine they look after; most of them had extensive influence both religious and socio-political; most were major collaborators of British colonial rule.
sardar	leader, usually associated with feudal societies.
sahukar	wealthy; mainly moneylenders; reference here relates to their responsibility for the debt-ridden plight of Punjab's peasantry.
shudhi	purification movement launched mainly by Arya Samaj to reclaim those Hindus who had converted to other religions mainly in the closing years of the nineteenth century and the beginning of the twentieth; main centres of activity were in Punjab and focus of the movement was against Islam.
silsilah	a 'Sufi' term essentially meaning a link; relevant mainly in the context of the '*sajjada nishins*', who provided a mystical connection between the 'murid' and the Sufi saint.
tabligh	an Islamic religious movement seaking conversion; also religious preaching.
taccavi	nominal grants of money given by the state to farmers usually in times of distress; at times such relief was provided

	by foregoing the demand of revenue; it remained a important focus of Unionist policies.
tehsil	revenue sub-division of a district under a subordinate but influential officer, tehsildar.
tanzim	an appeal to encourage education among Muslims; community consolidation.
thana	police station under the incharge known as thanedar; the most important part of the chain of civil administration; under the British; thanedar was extremely important, a good conduct report by him was imperative for any benefit from colonial rule.
tulai	to weigh; reference relates to corruption and cheating of farmers by fraudulent weighing.
ulema	Islam theologians, preachers, jurists; revered and very influential.
zamindar	landowner, individually or collectively receiving rent and paying land revenue; very influential; most bestowed loyalty on colonial rule and prospered from resultant patronage.

Bibliography

OFFICIAL PUBLICATIONS

A Collection of Acts Passed by the Local Legislature of Punjab in the Years 1926-41 (Lahore, 1942).
The Punjab Administration Reports, 1901-46.
Annual Reports on the Working of Cooperative Societies, 1938-46.
Annual Reports on the Working of Panchayats in Punjab, 1936-46.
Agricultural Statistics of Punjab, 1939-45 (Simla, 1950).
Board of Economic Inquiry: The Size and Distribution of Agricultural Holdings in Punjab (Lahore, 1925).
Board of Economic Inquiry: The Size and Distribution of Cultivators Holdings in Punjab (Lahore, 1928).
The Census of India, 1901 to 1941.
Punjab Legislative Council Debates, 1921-36.
Punjab Legislative Assembly Debates, 1937-47.
Punjab Government Gazettes, 1920 to 1947.
Eighteen Months of Provincial Autonomy (Lahore, 1939).
Report on the Committee on Indebtedness (Lahore, 1932).
Report on the Working of Debt Conciliation Boards from Inception upto December 1939 (Lahore, 1942).
Report of the Land Revenue Committee (Lahore, 1938).
Statistical Abstracts of British India, 1920-21 to 1930 (London, 1932).
Statistical Abstracts of British India 1929-30 to 1938-39 (Delhi, 1941).

NEWSPAPERS/WEEKLIES, ETC.

Dawn (Delhi).
Jat Gazette (Rohtak).
The Tribune (Lahore).
The Civil & Military Gazette (Lahore).
The Hindustan Times (Delhi).
Haryana Tilak (Rohtak).

OTHER NEWS PUBLICATIONS

Mitra, N.N. and H.N. Mitra (eds.) *The Indian Annual Register* (1921-3).
———, *Indian Quarterly Register* (1924-9)
———, *Indian Annual Register* (1930-47).
The Indian Year Book (1922-46).

PRIVATE PAPERS

Chhotu Ram Papers (Haryana State Archives)
Linlithgow Collection, 1936-43 (NMML)

PUBLISHED SOURCES

Ahmad, J. (ed.), *Some Recent Speeches and Writings of Mr. Jinnah* (Lahore, 1943).
Ahmad, W. (ed.), *Letters of Mian Fazl-i-Husain* (Lahore, 1976).
———, *Diary and Notes of Mian Fazl-i-Husain* (Lahore, 1976).
Ashraf, M., *Letters of Iqbal to Jinnah* (Lahore, 1956).
Dass, B.A. (ed.), *Letters & Writings of Iqbal* (Lahore, 1976).
Dass, D. (ed.), *Sardar Patel's Correspondence*, vol. II (Ahmedabad, 1972).
Hassan, M. (ed.), *Muslims & The Congress: Select Correspondence of M.A. Ansari* (Delhi, 1979).
Jafri, S.Q.H. and S.A. Bukhari (eds.), *Quad-i-Azam's Correspondence with Punjab Muslim League Leaders* (Lahore, 1977).
Jafri, S.Q.H., *Rare Documents* (Lahore, 1967).
Mansergh, N. and E.W.R. Lumby, (eds.), *Constitutional Relations Between Britain and India: The Transfer of Power*, vol. I-VI, 1942-4 (London, 1970, 71, 72, 73).
Mansergh, N. and P. Moon (eds.), *Constitutional Relations Between Britain and India: The Transfer of Power*, vol. V-XI, 1946-7 (London, 1974, 76, 77, 79, 80, 81, 82).
Pirzada, S.S., *Muslim League Leaders Correspondence with Jinnah* (Bombay, 1944).
Constitution Aims and Objectives of the Unionist Party (Urdu) (Lahore, 1936).

BOOKS, RESEARCH PAPERS, AND PH.D. THESIS

Abbott, F., *Islam & Pakistan* (Ithaca, 1968).
Agnihotri, H.L. and S.N. Mallick, *Ch. Chhotu Ram: A Profile in Courage* (Delhi, 1978).
Ahmad, A., *Islamic Modernization in India and Pakistan 1875-1964* (Karachi, 1967).
Ahmad, I. (ed.), *Caste and Social Stratification Among Muslims* (Delhi, 1973).
Ahmad, K.A., *The Founder of Pakistan: Through Trial to Triumph* (London, 1942).

Ahmad, Syed Nur, *Mian Sir Fazl-i-Husain, A Review: His Life and Work* (Lahore, 1936).

———, *From Martial Law To Martial Law*, ed. by Craig Baxter (Lahore, 1985).

Alana, G., *Pakistan Movement: Historic Documents* (Karachi, 1967).

Ali, I., *Punjab Politics in the Decade Before Partition* (Lahore, 1974).

———, 'Relations between the Muslim League and the Punjab National Unionist Party, 1935-47', *South Asia*, No. VI, December 1976.

Alibiruni, A.H., *Makers of Pakistan and Modern Muslim India* (Lahore, 1950).

Ali, Y., *Muslim Demand For Pakistan* (New York, 1942).

Ambedkar, B.R., *Pakistan or Partition of India* (Bombay, 1945).

Anwar, M., 'Forgotten Ahmad: Chaudhari Rehmat Ali and Concept of Pakistan', *Journal of the Research Society of Pakistan*, vol. VII, No. 1, 1970.

Arif, K.M., *Working with Zia: Pakistan's Power Politics, 1977-88* (Karachi, 1995).

Azad, A.K., *India Wins Freedom* (Bombay, 1959).

Azir, K.K., *The All India Muslim Conference 1928-35: A Documentary Record* (Karachi, 1972).

———, *The Making of Pakistan: A Study of Nationalism* (London, 1967).

Bajaj, Y.P., 'Sir Chhotu Ram and His Work' (unpublished Ph.D. thesis, Kurukshetra University, 1972).

———, 'Genesis of the Bhakra Dam Scheme (1914-48)', *Punjab Past and Present*, vol. XI-I, April 1977.

———, 'Unionist Politics and The General Elections of 1936-37: An Analysis', *Proceedings Punjab History Conference* (20th Session, March 1986).

———, 'Land Revenue Reforms of The Unionist Party', *Punjab Past and Present*, vol. X-II, October 1976.

———, 'Chhotu Ram and The Indian National Congress', *Punjab Past and Present*, vol. XII-I, April 1978.

Bajaj, Y.P. and Naresh Inder Singh, 'Congress Politics on the Eve of 1936-37 General Elections to the Punjab Assembly', *Proceedings Punjab History Conference* (19th Session, March 1985).

Barrier, N.G., 'The Formation and Enactment of the Punjab Aliention of Land Bill (1900)', *The Indian Economic and Social History Review*, vol. II (April 1965).

———, *The Punjab Alienation of Land Bill 1900* (Duke University, 1966).

Barrier, N.G. and P. Wallace, *The Punjab Press* (Michigan University, 1970).

Baxter, Craig, 'Union or Partition: Some Aspects of Politics in the Punjab 1936-46', in L. Zirring (ed.), *Pakistan the Long View* (Durham, 1977).

———, 'India and Pakistan' in J. Stossinger et al., *Divided Nations in and Divided World* (New York, 1974).

———, 'The Peoples Party Versus The Punjab Feudalists', *Journal of Asian and African Studies*, vol. VIII: 3 and 4 (July-October 1973).

Bhattacharya, N., 'Lenders and Debtors: Punjab Countryside 1888-1940', *Studies in History I and II*, 1985.

Bolitho, H., *Jinnah: Creator of Pakistan* (London, 1957).
Brass, P., *Language, Religion and Politics in North India* (Cambridge, 1974).
Calvert, H., *The Size & Distribution of Land Holdings in Punjab* (Lahore, 1925).
———, *Wealth and Welfare of The Punjab* (Lahore, 1922).
Chandra, B., *Communalism in Modern India* (Delhi, 1978).
Charlesworth, N., *British Rule and The Indian Economy* (London, 1982).
Chaudhari, K., *Pathway to Pakistan* (Karachi, 1961).
Chaudhary, P., *Punjab Politics and the Role of Sir Chhotu Ram* (Delhi, 1984).
———, 'Social Base of Chaudhary Sir Chhotu Ram's Politics', *Punjab Past and Present*, vol. X, 1976.
———, 'Agrarian Legislations of the late Thirties', *Punjab Past and Present*, vol. I, October 1976.
———, 'The Zamindar Ideology of The Unionist Party', *Punjab Past and Present*, vol. XVI-II, 1982.
Chhotu Ram, *The Nationalist Unionist Party* (Lahore, 1932).
———, 'Serving the Weak and Raising the Fallen', *Punjab Past and Present* (rpt), vol. VIII-I, April 1974.
Coupland, R., *Indian Politics 1936-42* (London, 1943).
Darling, M.L., *Punjab Peasant in Prosperity and Debt* (Bombay, 1925, rpt., New Delhi, 1977).
Datta, V.N., *Ideology of the Political Elite in Punjab 1900-1920* (Patiala, 1978).
———, Presidential Address, Indian History Congress, (Chennai, December 1996).
Daultana, A.Y.K., *Leaves from a Unionist's Diary* (Lahore, 1949).
De, A., 'Sahid Ganj Agitation and Khaksars', *Punjab Past and Present*, vol. XI, 1975.
———, 'Some Aspects of Communal Politics in the Punjab 1937-47', *The Oracle*, April 1979.
Dumont, L., *Homo Hierrchius: The Caste System and Its Implications* (Delhi, 1970).
Dungen, P.H.M., *The Punjab Tradition* (London, 1972).
Duni Chand, *Ulster of India: An Analysis of The Punjab Problem* (Lahore, 1936).
Durrani, F.K., *The Meaning of Pakistan* (Lahore, 1944).
Dwiki, S.J., 'The Impact of British Rule on Agriculture in Punjab: A Re-evaluation', *Economic Journal*, 3:1, January 1970.
Dwyer, Michael O', *India As I Knew It 1885-1925* (London, 1926).
Emerson, H., *A Note on The Land Revenue System in Punjab, 1937* (Lahore, 1938).
Gilmartin, D., 'Religious Leadership and the Pakistan Movement in Punjab', *Journal of Modern Asian Studies*, 13, 3 (1979).
———, '*Empire and Islam: Punjab and the Making of Pakistan* (New Delhi, 1989).
———, 'Tribe, Land and Religion in Punjab: Muslim Politics and The Making of Pakistan' (Ph.D. thesis, Berkeley, 1979).
Gopal, M., *Sir Chhotu Ram: A Political Biography* (New Delhi, 1977).

Griffin, L.H. and C.F. Massey, *Chiefs and Families of Note in the Punjab*, ed. by G.L. Chopra , 2 vols (Lahore, 1940).

Gulati, K.C., *The Akalis Past and Present* (New Delhi, 1974).

Hamid, A., *Muslim Separation in India* (Karachi, 1967).

Harcourt, H., *Sidelights of The Crisis in India* (Bombay, 1924).

Hardy, P., *The Muslims of British India* (Cambridge, 1972).

Hasan, M., 'Communalism in Provinces: A Case Study of Bengal and Punjab 1922-26', *Economic and Political Weekly*, 16 August 1980.

Hasan, M., (ed.), *India's Partition: Process, Strategy and Mobilization* (Delhi, 1994).

Hassan, S.S., *Plain Mr. Jinnah* (Karachi, 1976).

Hayat, K., 'The 1937 Elections and the Sikander-Jinnah Pact', *Punjab Past and Present*, vol. X-II, October 1976.

Heegar, G.A., 'Politics of Integration: Community, Party and Integration in Punjab' (Ph.D. thesis, Chicago, 1971).

Hodson, H.V., *The Great Divide: Britain India and Pakistan* (London, 1969).

Husain, Azim, *Mian Sir Fazl-i-Husain: A Political Biography* (London, 1946).

Husain, F., 'Punjab Politics', *Punjab Past and Present* (rpt.) vol. V-I, April 1971.

Ibbetson, D., *Castes of The Punjab* (Lahore, 1916).

Ikram, S.M., *Modern Muslim India and the Birth of Pakistan* (Lahore, 1977).

Islam, M.M., 'Darling and The Punjab Peasant in Prosperity and Debt: A Fresh Look', *Journal of Peasant Studies*, vol. XIII, 1985-6.

Isphani, M.A.H., *Quad-i-Azam: As I Knew Him* (Karachi, 1976).

Jalal, A., *The Sole Spokesman Jinnah: The Muslim League and Demand for Pakistan* (Cambridge, 1985).

Jinnah, M.A., *Muslim India Speaks* (Aligarh, 1942).

Johnson, C., *Mission with Mountbatten* (London, 1951).

Jones, K.W., *Arya Dharma: Hindu Consciousness in 19th Century India* (Berkeley, 1976).

Josh, B., *The Communist Movement in the Punjab 1926-47* (Delhi, 1979).

Joshi, V.C. (ed.), *Lala Lajpat Rai: Speeches and Writings*, vol. II (Delhi, 1965).

Khan, A.K., *Generals in Politics: Pakistan 1958-82* (Delhi, 1983).

Khan, U., *A History of Education in Punjab*, vol. I (Lahore, 1937).

Krishan, Y., *Mountbatten and The Partition of India* (Delhi, 1983).

Kulkarni, V.B., *Is Pakistan Necessary* (Bombay, 1944).

Kumar, R., *Essays in the Social History of India* (Delhi, 1983).

Lal, S., *Commentaries on the Punjab Alienation of Land Act* (Lahore, 1933).

Lamb, C., *Waiting for Allah: Pakistan's Struggle for Democracy* (New Delhi, 1991).

Lijphart, A., *The Politics of Accommodation: Pluralism and Democracy in the Netherlands* (Berkeley, 1968).

Ludden, D., *Peasant History in South Asia* (New Delhi, 1989).

Malhotra, S.L., *Gandhi and The Punjab* (Chandigarh, 1970).

Malik, Hafeez, *Iqbal: Poet Philosopher of Pakistan* (New York, 1971).

Malik, I. A., *A Book of Readings on The History of the Punjab 1799-1947* (Lahore, 1970).

Malik, I.H., *Sikander Hayat Khan: A Political Biography* (Islamabad, 1985).

Mehta, A. and A. Patwardhan, *Communal Triangle* (Allahabad, 1942).

Melano, J.H., 'Peasants, Money Lenders and Nationalists at the end of The Nineteenth Century', *The Indian Economic & Social History Review*, vol. I, September 1963.

Metcalfe, T.R., 'The British and Money Lenders in Nineteenth Century India', *Journal of Modern History*, vol. XXXIV, No. 4, December 1962.

Mittal, S.C., *Freedom Movement in Punjab 1905-1929* (Delhi, 1979).

Mishra, B.B., *The Indian Political Parties: An Historical Analysis of Political Behaviour upto 1947* (Delhi, 1976).

Moon, P., *Divide and Quit* (London, 1961).

Moon, P. (ed.), *Wavell: The Viceroys Journal* (London, 1973).

Mosley, L., *The Last Days of the British Raj* (London, 1961).

Mukhiya, H., 'Conversion to Islam in the Punjab during the 16th and 17th Centuries: A Preliminary Draft', *Punjab History Conference Proceedings*, 7th Session (September 1972).

Nagarkar, V.V., *Genesis of Pakistan* (New Delhi, 1975).

Nair, L.R., *Sikander Hayat Khan: The Soldier Statesman of the Punjab* (Lahore, 1943).

Nakra, R.S., 'Punjab Villages in Ludhiana district during the War' (Punjab Board of Economic Enquiry No. 91) (Lahore, 1946).

Narang, G.C., *Plight of the Punjab Minorities Under the so-called Unionist Government* (Lahore, 1941).

Nath, R.N., 'The Punjab Agrarian Laws and Their Economic and Constitutional Bearings', *Modern Review*, 65 (1939).

Nawaj, J.S., *Father and Daughter* (Lahore, 1971).

Nayar, B.R., *Minority Politics in the Punjab* (Princeton, 1966).

Najjar, B.S., *Punjab Under the British Rule, 1849-1947*, 3 vols. (Delhi, 1974).

Noon, F.K., *From Memory* (Lahore, 1966).

Nurullah, S. and J.B. Naik, *A History of Education in India* (Bombay, 1951).

Oren, S., 'The Sikhs, Congress and The Unionists in British Punjab 1937-47', *Modern Asian Studies*, vol. VIII, 1974.

Page, D., *Prelude To Partition: All India Muslim Politics 1920-32* (Delhi, 1982).

Pandey, G., *The Construction of Communalism in Colonial North India* (Delhi, 1990).

Philips, C.H. (ed.), *The Evolution of India and Pakistan, 1858-1947: Select Documents* (London, 1962).

Philips, C.H. and M.D. Wainright, *The Partition of India: Politics & Perspectives* (London, 1970).

Pirzada, S.S. (ed.), *Foundations of Pakistan: All India Muslim League Documents.* 1906-47, 2 vols. (Karachi, 1970).

Pradhan, S.D., 'Punjab's Manpower Contribution to the Indian Army during the First World War', *Punjab Past and Present*, vol. XII, April 1978.

Prasad, B., *The Hindu Muslim Question* (Lahore, 1943).

Puri, N., *Political Elite & Society in the Punjab* (Delhi, 1987).

Qanungo, K.R., *A History of The Jats*, vol. I (Calcutta, 1925).

Qureshi, S., *The Struggle For Pakistan* (Karachi, 1974).

Rai, S.M., *Partition of Punjab* (New Delhi, 1985).

———, *Legislative Politics & The Freedom Struggle in Punjab 1897-1947* (New Delhi, 1984).

Raj Pal, 'Agricultural Production in Haryana 1900-1966' (unpublished Ph.D. thesis, Kurukshetra University, 1996).

Rajput, A.B., *Punjab Crisis and Cure* (Lahore, 1947).

———, *Muslim League: Yesterday & To-day* (Lahore, 1948).

Robb, P. (ed.), *Rural India, Land Power and Society Under British Rule* (London, 1983).

Rose, H.A. (ed.), *Glossary of Tribes & Castes of Punjab & NWFP*, vol. I-III (first published 1883, rpt. Patiala 1970).

Rothermund, D. (ed.), *Islam in South Asia* (Wiesbaden, 1975).

Saini, B.S., *Social and Economic History of Punjab 1901-39* (Delhi, 1975).

Sayeed, K.B., *The Political System of Pakistan* (Boston, 1967).

———, *Pakistan: The Formative Phase, 1857-1948* (London, 1968).

Seal, A. and A. Jalal, 'Alternative to Partition: Muslim Politics Between the Wars', *Modern Asian Studies*, 15 March 1981.

Sen, N.B. (ed.), *Punjab's Eminent Hindus* (Lahore, 1942).

Sharma, D.C., 'The Truth About Mian Fazl-i-Husain', *The Modern Review*, January 1937.

Sharma, S.R., *Punjab in Ferment* (New Delhi, 1971).

Shastri, R.S., *Jeevancharita Chaudhari Chhotu Ram* (Hindi) (Rohtak, 1965).

Sherwani, L.A. (ed.), *Pakistan Resolution to Pakstan 1940-47* (Delhi, 1985).

Shukla, S.P., *India's Freedom Struggle and the Role of Haryana* (New Delhi, 1985).

Singh, A.I., *The Origins of the Partition of India 1936-47* (Delhi, 1989).

Singh, G., 'The Punjab Alienation of Land Act 1900: Its Background', *Proceedings Punjab History Conference, 1st Session* (November 1965).

Singh, Hari, *Agrarian Scene in British Punjab*, vol. I (New Delhi, 1983).

Singh, H., *Punjab the Homeland of the Sikhs* (Lahore, 1945).

Singh, K., *The Partition of Punjab* (Patiala, 1972).

Singh, P. (ed.), *Chhotu Ram in the Eyes of His Contemporaries* (New Delhi, 1992).

Smith, W.C., *Modern Islam in India* (London, 1946).

Spate, H.K., *India and Pakistan: General and Regional Geography* (London, 1954).

Talbot, I., *Punjab and the Raj 1849-1947* (Delhi, 1989).

———, 'Muslim Political Mobilization in Rural Punjab, 1937-46', in Peter Robb (ed.), *Rural India Land Power and Society Under British Rule* (London, 1983).

———, 'Deserted Collaborators: The Political Background to The Rise and

Fall of the Unionist Party, 1923-47', *Journal of Imperial and Commonwealth History*, vol. XI, No. 1, October 1982.

———, 'The Growth of The Muslim League in The Punjab, 1937-46', *Journal of Commonwealth and Comparative Politics*, vol. XX, 1982.

———, *Khizr Tiwana: The Punjab Unionist Party and the Partition of India* (Richmond, 1996).

———, 'Back to the Future? The Punjab Unionist Model of Consociational Democracy for Contemporary India and Pakistan', *International Journal of Punjab Studies*, vol. 3, No.1, 1996.

Talib, Gurcharan Singh, *The Muslim League Attack on Sikhs and the Hindu's in the Punjab* (Amritsar, 1950).

Tandon, P., *Punjab Century, 1857-1947* (London, 1961).

Tanwar, R., 'Tradition Versus Modernity: A Study of The Failure of Muslim Peasant Leadership in Punjab', *Journal of The Pakistan Historical Society*, vol. XL, Part III, July 1992.

———, 'Origin of the Punjab National Unionist Party: Feudal Elite and Legislative Politics', *Journal of the Pakistan Historical Society*, vol. XLIV, Part II, April 1996.

Tara, R.L., *Sikander Hayat and His Government as Reviewed by the Punjab Press* (Lahore, 1941).

Thorborn, S.S., *Musalmans and Money Lenders in Punjab* (Delhi, 1983).

———, *The Punjab in Peace and War* (New Delhi, 1979).

Tikka Ram, *Sir Chhotu Ram: An Apostle of Hindu Muslim Unity* (Lahore, 1946).

Tiwana, K.H., 'The 1937 Elections and The Sikander-Jinnah Pact', *Punjab Past and Present* (rpt.) vol. X-II, October 1976.

Trevaskis, H.K., *The Land of Five Rivers* (Oxford, 1928).

———, *The Punjab of Today*, vol. II (London, 1931).

Tuteja, K.L., *Sikh Politics 1920-40* (Kurukshetra, 1984).

Uprety, P.R., *Religion and Politics in Punjab in the 1920's* (New Delhi, 1980).

Vanden, P.H.N., *The Punjab Tradition* (Londan, 1972).

Verma, D.C., *Sir Chhotu Ram: Life and Times* (New Delhi, 1981).

———, 'Provincial Autonomy in the Punjab, April 1937-October 1939', *Indian Journal of Political Science*, vol. I, 1940.

Wallace, P., 'Political Party Systems of Punjab State, India: A Study of Factionalism' (Ph.D. thesis, California, 1966).

Wolpert, S., *Jinnah of Pakistan* (New York, 1984).

Yadav, K.C., *Elections in Punjab* (Delhi, 1987).

———, 'The Partition of India: A Study of Muslim Politics in Punjab 1849-1947', *Punjab Past and Present*, vol. XVIII-I, April 1983.

Zaheer, S., *Light on The League Unionist Conflict* (Bombay, 1944).

———, *A Case for Congress League Unity* (Bombay, 1944).

Ziring, L., H.W. Wriggins, and R. Braibanti (eds), *Pakistan The Long View* (Durham, 1977).

Index

Abdul Azia, Mian 141
Abdul Ghani, Sheikh 51
Abdul Haye, Mian Sir 109, 111, 141
Abdul Qadir 51, 52
Abdul Qayyam, Mir 99
Abdur Rahman Khan, Muhammad 99
Act of 1919 103
Afzal Ali Hasni, Syed 92, 141
Aga Khan III 90, 92
Ahmad Bakhash Khan 110
Ahmadiyah Movement 39
Ajmal Khan, Hakim 48
Akali Dal 41, 42, 79, 80, 98, 99, 100, 101, 110, 158-60, 184
Ali, Imran 136, 153
Ali, Shamshir 181
Alienation of Land Act 77, 93
Allaha Bakhash, Nawab, 92
Amjad Ali, Syed 141
Anant Ram, Rai Sahib 99
Anjuman-i-himyat-i-Islam 181
Arif, K.K. 168-9
Arya Samaj 39, 78
Ashiq Hussain 110, 141, 153
Azad, Maulana 184

Bajaj, Y.P. 120, 124
Balbir Singh, Rao 99
Barkat Ali, Malik, 99, 140, 141, 142
Barq, Muhammad Ibrahim 185
Bashir Ahmad, Mian 110
benami Bill, *see* Punjab Alienation of Land Amendment Bill
Bhai Parmanand 154
Bhakra Project 63
Bhargava, Gopi Chand 78, 86n91, 102, 124
Brahmo Samaj 78
British Indian Army 25, 52, 131
Butler, Harcourt 41

Central Sikh League 41
Chhotu Ram 40, 44, 48, 49, 50, 58n61, 63-79 *passim*, 82n3, 92-103 *passim*, 109, 118, 119, 120, 124, 125, 126, 133, 137, 139, 144, 147, 148, 151, 154, 155, 157, 161, 169, 178, 195
Chishti, Ibrahim Ali 181
Civil Disobedience Movement 78
Communal Awards 79
Communal Harmony Day 111
Congress Party 41, 48, 65, 66, 76-7, 78, 94-105 *passim*, 113, 135, 154, 173, 174, 176, 179, 183, 184, 185, 186, 193
Craik, Sir Henry 137
Cripps, Sir Stafford 150

Dandupat 73, 117
Das, C.R. 48
Datta, V.N. 193
Daulatana, Ahmad Yar Khan 37, 71, 89, 92, 105n7, 109, 140, 141, 147-8, 152
Daulatana, Mumtaz 149, 187
Debt Conciliation Boards 74, 117
Debtors Protection Act 73
Desai, Bhulabhai 96
Din Mohammad, Sheikh 51
Dumont, Louis 133

Duni Chand 78
'dyarchy' 60, 74, 81, 88, 102, 112

Factory Act 124
Faiz Mohammad, Sheikh 51, 109, 141
Fateh Khan, Raja 141
Fazl-i-Husain 40, 42, 43-52 *passim*, 57n55, 63, 65, 67, 68, 70, 71, 72, 75, 78, 79, 89, 90, 92, 96, 97, 98, 99, 104, 134, 147, 154, 161

Gandhi, Mahatma 40, 184
Ghaddar conspiracy 131
Ghani, Abdul 102
Ghazanfar Ali Khan 99, 109, 185
Ghaznavi, Maulana 183
Ghulam Ahmad 39
Ghulam Husain, Khwaja 99
Ghulam Mohyuddin, Maulvi 92, 141
Ghulam Rasul Khan 140, 141
Government of India Act 1935, 88, 101, 103
Gurmani, Mustaq Ahmad 171
Gurudwara Reforms Movement 80

Habibullah, Sardar 92, 102-3
Hailey, Sir Malcolm 51, 64, 67, 68
Hans Raj, Raizada 96
Hansraj, Bhagat 109
Harcourt, H. 155
Haveli Canal Project 120
Hindu Election Board 101, 103, 109, 110, 160-2
Hindu Law of Inheritance 37
Hindu Mahasabha 40, 42, 66, 77, 78, 79, 81, 99, 142
Hindu National Party 48, 68

Iftikhar-ud-din-Mian 102, 103, 110
Islamia College 181
Isphani 135, 136
Ittehad-I-Millat 95, 99, 100
Ittihad Party, *see* Punjab Unionist Party

Jahan Ara Shah Nawaz, Begum 92, 109, 110, 152
Jalal, Ayesha 190, 193
Jat Gazette 41, 82n3
Jenkins, Sir Evans 188, 190
Jinnah, M.A. 79, 96, 97, 98, 99, 134, 135, 138-53 *passim*, 160, 173, 175, 183, 187, 192
Josh, Sohan Singh 118, 124

Khalid Latif Gauba 99
Khalifa Shujaddin 141
Khalsa Diwan 38
Khalsa National Party 42, 80, 98, 101, 109, 110, 158-60
Khan Murtaza Ahmed Khan 141
Khan Niazi 181, 182
'Khattars' 153
Khilafat Committee 66
Khilafat movement 77
Kisan Conference 118, 119
Kisan Sabha 79, 80
Kitchlu, Saifuddin 48

Lal, Lala Harkishan 43, 78
Lal, Ch. Sham 109
Lal, Sir Manohar 67, 68, 84n40, 109, 111, 162
Lamb, Christina 178
Leghari, Sir Mohammad Jamal Khan 153
Lekh Ram 39
Liaqat Hayat Khan, Sir 153
Ludden, David 30

Maatab Ali, Syed 92
MacLagan, Sir Edward 43
Majithia, Sir Sunder Singh 48, 59n79, 63, 80, 89, 98, 109, 111, 158
Majlis-i-Ahrar-i-Islam 79, 80, 95, 100
Malaviya, Madan Mohan 65
Mamdot, Iftikhar Husain 149
Mamdot, Shah Nawaz Khan 92, 106n24, 110, 136, 140, 141, 149, 152
Mandi Act, *see* Punjab Agricultural Produce Market Act
Mann, Sardar Jagit Singh 109
Maqbool Mahmood, Mir 90, 92, 107n25, 109, 110, 141, 147, 152

Mazhar Ali Azhar, Maulana 99
Minimum Rates of Wages Bill 124
Mohammad Hassan 185
Mohammad Iqbal 66, 140, 141
Mohammad Yusuf, Khwaja 51
Muhammad Alam, Sheikh 99, 124
Muhammad Faiz Ali Khan 109
Muhammad Nawaz Khan 92
Muhammad Sadiq, Sheikh 51, 110
Muslim League 41, 42, 43, 79, 95, 96, 97, 99, 131, 134-53 *passim*, 168, 171, 173, 174, 176-90 *passim*; Lahore Action Committee of the 186-7
Muslim League National Guard 187, 188
Muzaffar Khan 89, 90, 105n6, 110
Naidu, Sarojini 99
Narang, Gokul Chand 52, 62-3, 71, 77, 113, 114, 117, 161
Nath, Raja Narender 48, 71, 89, 90, 99, 109, 114, 161, 162
National Defence Council 146
National Progressive Party 71, 160-2
Nau Jawan Bharat Sabha 78
Nazami, Hameed 181
Nehru, Jawaharlal 99, 119, 126, 142, 155, 156, 192
Nehru, Moti Lal 48, 65
Non-Cooperation Movement 40, 42, 153
Noon, Firoz Khan 60-1, 63, 67, 71, 82n2, 89, 90, 110, 178, 185, 187, 191; and his family 132
Noon, Sir Mohammad Hayat Khan 141
Nurullah, Mian 141

O'Dwyer, Sir Michael 19, 50, 51

Pakistan Resolution 143, 144, 145, 146-7, 168, 194
Pakistan Rural Propoganda Committee 181
Patel, Vallabhbhai 99, 184
pirs 34, 36, 56nn32 & 33, 75, 94, 133, 176, 177, 179, 187
Printing Press Control Bill 124
Provincial autonomy 157; introduction of 88, 112, 120, 121
Punjab Agricultural Marketing Bill 64
Punjab Agricultural Produce Market Act 116, 117
Punjab Alienation of Land Act 1901, 25, 26
Punjab Alienation of Land Amendment Bill 115-16
Punjab Borrowers Protection Bill 63
Punjab Hours of Work Bill 124
Punjab Khilafat Committee 80
Punjab Land Revenue Amendment Bill 64
Punjab Land Revenue Bill 64, 65, 69, 70
Punjab Legislative Assembly 88, 104, 109, 110, 113, 135, 145, 154, 158, 161, 175, 183, 189, 190, 194
Punjab Legislative Council 37, 46, 47, 52, 53, 64, 65, 68, 71, 74, 88, 95, 162
Punjab Moneylenders' Bill 62, 65, 161-2
Punjab Muslim Students' Federation 181
Punjab National Unionist Party, and big landowners 28; and the 'consociational system' 43-4; and education 61, 72-3; features of 50-1; and industrial development 74; and irrigation 63; and the issue of debt 23, 62, 70, 73-4; and land revenue 69; and municipal committees 62; origin of the 19, 26, 50, 52; and Panchayats 62, *see also* Punjab Unionist Party and 'Rural Block'
Punjab Primary Education Act 123
Punjab Provincial Congress 40, *see also* Congress Party
Punjab Regulation of Accounts Bill 63, 64, 66, 70
Punjab Relief of Indebtedness Act 117
Punjab Relief of Indebtedness Bill 73
Punjab Sikh United Party 158
Punjab State Aid to Industries (Amendment) Act 124
Punjab Unionist Party 91; demise of the 194; and the development of irrigational infrastructure 119-20; and education 123-4; and its election

manifesto 93, 106n14; and erosion of its support in rural Punjab 169-74; and industry 124; and the interference of the Muslim League 139; and landlord families 94, 130, 131; and 'limited liability socialism' 193; and local self-governing institutions 122; and political relations with the Indian National Congress 154-7; and public health 121-2; and relations with the Akalis and Khalsa National Party 158-60; and relations with the National Progressive Party 160-2, *see also* Punjab National Unionist Party
Punjab University Enquiry Committee 37
Punjab Village Panchayat Act 122-3
Punjab, agricultural indebtedness in 23-4, 82n11, 112; banking in 23; communal violence in 186-7; demographic distribution in 32-4, 38; domination of Hindus and Sikhs in economic and commercial activity in 37; education in 34-7; moneylenders in 24, 112; predominently rural character of 20; social system of 30-1
Puri, M.L. 73

Qizilbash, Nawab Muzaffar Ali Khan 185
Quit India Movement 150

Rai, Gulshan 77
Rai, Lala Lajpat 29, 39-40, 42, 62, 65, 69, 70, 78
Rashtriya Swayamsevak Sangh 187
Reforms Act of 1919, 26, 28, 29, 42, 49, 52, 53, 60, 61; and the introduction of communalism 29
Registration of Moneylenders Bill 112-13
Restitution of Mortgaged Land Bill 114
Revolt of 1857 19, 32
Roberts, William 109
'Rural Block' 26, 43-9 *passim*, 52, *see also* Punjab National Unionist Party

Sacchar, Bhim Sen 185
Sadat Ali Khan, Nawab 141
Sadiq Hasan, Sheikh 110, 141
Sahni, Ruchi Ram 77
sajjada nishins 34, 36, 56nn32 & 33, 75, 81, 94, 103, 133, 177, 179
Sattar, Abdul 181
Satyapal 78, 86n92, 102
Sehgal, K.N. 102
Shah, Syed Ahmad Alik 109
Shahab-ud-din, Chaudhary 90, 92, 126n3
Shahidganj Mosque dispute 81, 137, 142
Shano Devi 102
Sharma, Neki Ram 65
Shaukat Hayat Khan 147, 148, 149, 152, 153, 154, 187
Shiromani Gurudwara Prabandhak Committee (SGPC) 48, 80
Sikander Hayat Khan 69, 71, 72, 85n61, 89, 90, 98, 109, 110, 111, 112, 114, 118, 122, 126, 131-51 *passim*, 157, 159, 160, 161, 169, 195; and his family 131
Sikander-Baldev Pact 159
Sikander-Jinnah Pact 135, 136, 137, 140, 142, 151, 152, 160, 175
Sikh Akali Fauj 187
Sikh League 66
Simla Conference 175
Simon Commission 70
Singh Sabha, of Amritsar 38
Singh, Baldev 146, 158, 160, 185
Singh, Dasaundha 109, 111
Singh, Gopal 109
Singh, Kartar 124
Singh, Lehri 185
Singh, Ripudaman 109
Singh, Sardar Joginder 67, 71, 84n39, 98, 160
Singh, Tara 99, 160, 190
Singh, Ujjal 109
Smith, W.C. 180
Sufism 31
Swaraj Party 41, 42, 48, 49, 65

Tajewala Headworks 120
Tajuddin, Pir 141
Talbot, I. 19-20, 28, 29, 31, 32, 100, 103, 135, 151, 172, 175, 181, 188
Thal Project 63, 120
The All Punjab Non-Agriculturists Association 117
The Relief of Indebtedness (Amendment) Act 117
Thorburn, S.S. 25
Tika Ram 109
Tiwana, Malik Umar Hayat Khan 92, 109, 110, 114; and his family 132
Tiwana, Nawab Khizr Hayat Khan 137, 141, 147, 148, 151, 152, 153, 154, 178, 179, 184, 185, 186, 188, 189, 190, 191, 195
Trade Employees Act 125

Western Yamuna Canal System 120

Zafar Ali Khan, Maulana 141
Zafarulla Khan 92
Zaman Mehdi Khan, Malik 141
Zamindar Sahukar Act, *see* Punjab Alienation of Land Amendment Bill
Zamindara Conference 118, 119, 148